Kenneth McLeish is known as an author, translator and playwright. His published books (more than 80) include *The Good Reading Guide, Shakespeare's People, Companion to the Arts in the Twentieth Century, Listener's Guide to Classical Music* and *Crucial Classics* (both with Valerie McLeish), and *Bloomsbury Guide to Human Thought* (general editor). His translations, performed on stage, TV, film and radio, include plays by all the Greek and Roman dramatists, Ibsen, Feydeau, Molière and Strindberg, and his original plays and films include *Tony, I Will if You Will, Just Do It, Orpheus* and *Vice at the Vicarage* (written for Frankie Howerd). He died in November, 1997.

KENNETH MCLEISH

MYTH

MYTHS AND LEGENDS
OF THE WORLD
EXPLORED

BLOOMSBURY

First published in hardback in 1996
First published in paperback in 1998 by
Bloomsbury Publishing plc
38 Soho Square
London W1V 5DF

Copyright © 1996 by Kenneth McLeish

The moral right of the author has been asserted

A copy of the CIP entry for this book is available from the British Library

ISBN 0 7475 3019 X

10 9 8 7 6 5 4 3 2 1

Designed by AB3
Typeset by Andrew McLeish and Hewer Text Composition Services, Edinburgh
Printed in Great Britain by Clays Ltd, St Ives Plc

INTRODUCTION

The word 'myth' (*mythos*) originated in ancient Athens, as the antithesis of *logos*. *Logos* was an objective account of an event or phenomenon, following the rules of reason and logic. Myth was an account of the same subject-matter organized to give specific information or to make a particular effect. *Mythos* was associated with the spoken word (which Greek poets imagined as a bird fluttering from one person's lips to another's ears). *Logos* was connected with the worlds of law and accounting, and referred especially to evidence presented in court or to the balance-sheet state officials were compelled to submit for moral and ethical (as well as financial) audit at the end of each year in office.

As early as the fourth century BCE, the same distinction was being applied to accounts of grander matters: the origins of the universe, the hierarchy of creation, the nature and demands of supernatural powers, the causes of things, the reasons for certain social customs and popular beliefs and the self-image of this or that community. Philosophers discussed such matters in terms of *logos*, trying to reach the truth by a purely intellectual process of reduction and elimination of the inessential. Poets and historians used *mythos*, aiming to discover truth in flashes of insight triggered by a mass of evocation and anecdote. Neither method was considered more fallible than the other – though if anyone had asked, the Greeks might have claimed that the conclusions of philosophy were less 'true' than myth, since they were the results of an activity practised and understood by a select few only, whereas myths were universally accepted and governed the lives and attitudes of all who used them. They offered a focus for thought; they put people in touch not only with one another's minds but with those of their forebears and ancestors; they validated each present moment in terms of a wider picture, both in time and space; they were a net of ideas and attitudes which guaranteed identity.

In recent years, it is this last function of myth which has chiefly interested those who study them professionally. Bronislaw Malinowski and others used myth-stories as windows, so to speak, into the mind and soul of the communities which created them. Unlike law, politics and the other systems which 'validate' a society, myths are not substantially altered by influences from outside the community; they are primary evidence. Other researchers, led by Claude Lévi-Strauss, deconstructed the myths to discover the cultural, psychological, religious and other impulses which underlay the stories; they hoped that the process would reveal basic structures of human thought, universal ways of dealing with the world as we perceive it. Still other scholars treat a society's myths not as a 'primitive' stage in its historical evolution, but as the persistent and undeviating context itself, the continuum of identity which allows the community to make sense of everything it experiences or thinks.

The myths in this book come from every part of the world, and represent a score of such continuums. They reveal a wealth of individual, local feelings and attitudes: the mindset of (say) Melanesian myth is easily distinguishable from that of North American, Celtic or Japanese, and recognizing such differences is part of the pleasure the stories give outsiders. But immersion in the whole pool of myth also shows a far wider consistency, in which the stories reveal a single, overarching human attitude to our universe and its inhabitants. Jung talked of 'archetypes' (Hero, Magician, Orphan, Wanderer and so on) arising not as the inventions of individual communities or creators, but from the 'collective unconscious' of the whole human race. This is more than just phrase-making. Human beings every-where, at all periods of world history (at least until the scientific present) have had much the same attitudes to sex, birth, the supernatural, morality and mortality, and have also used remarkably similar images and fancies to embody those attitudes in stories. To put it grandly, myths give us for the whole of humanity what Malinowski claimed for individual communities: a window into mind and soul, into the condition of the species.

Such assertions directly challenge another attitude of the recent past: that myths have no validity outside the society which devises them, that once a culture or a religion is dead, its myths are no more than fairy-tales – interesting, colourful or both, but invested with only a fraction of their original importance. We live in an age, the argument goes, in which *logos* has made *mythos* obsolete. Stories are for children; grownups concern themselves with scientific exploration, religious or political 'truth' (that is, orthodoxy) and the serious concerns of everyday living. We deal with facts; we have no need of the poetic, the inspired, the evocative.

All this may be arguable, but it is also deplorable. In a world where 'truth' is regularly confused with 'fact', in which knowledge is measured in terms not of quality but of quantity – facts learned, examinations passed – our humanness itself can be easily dismissed, our reality reduced to figures in a computer or a checklist of attitudes on some pollster's or advertiser's clipboard. The mass of us become malleable clay in other people's hands, invited to use imagination less often than amazement, to 'look at this' rather than to 'think about this', to relate to the wider world not as participants but as spectators, tourists. The connection is not proven between this diminution of individual involvement and the collapse of moral and ethical values which many people, at least in 'advanced' society, currently and increasingly perceive – but it is undeniable that the two phenomena characterize our age more than any other in history.

Myth offers a completely different view of the human condition. It is concerned not with tidiness but with the gaps, chinks, hinges, holes, awkwardnesses, uncertainties and epiphanies of life. It deals, by definition, with what is unpredict-able, unquantifiable, uncontrollable, terrifying, inspiring. This gives the stories their simple narrative appeal – one of the main reasons for their survival outside the times and societies which created them. But it also lets them seduce us into walking the border between what exists and what we think *might* exist, reminds us that 'truth' is not an objective but a subjective phenomenon, that in terms of our humanity, what we imagine is just as important as what we know.

*

Robert Yeatman commissioned my first myth-retellings of Greek, Roman and British myth: a few extracts have survived into the present book. Hilary Rubinstein first encouraged me to tackle the entire subject in a single volume, and Kathy Rooney and Kate Bouverie guided the project from outline proposal to publication. Valerie McLeish did much research and compiled the index and cross-references; Cesare Marino read and commented on the American myths here included. David Grant and Andrew McLeish prepared the book for press. To them all, warm thanks. .

Kenneth McLeish, 1996

Note: The myths are told in alphabetical sequence. Embedded in this are general articles each of which mentions or lists all the stories retold in this book on its particular subject. They are: African Myth, American Myth, animal-gods, archers, Australian Myth, beauty, bulls and cows, Celtic Myth, childbirth and infant care, Chinese Myth, civilization, crafts, creation, death, demons, disease and healing, dragons, earthquakes, Egyptian Myth, farming, fate, fertility, Finnish Myth, fire, floods, food and drink of immortality, Germanic Myth, ghosts, giants, good luck, Great Goddess, Greek Myth, guardians, Heaven, heroes, household and family, human ancestors, hunting, immortality, Indian Myth, Japanese Myth, justice and universal order, light and dark, lightning, love, Mesopotamian Myth, messengers, monsters, Moon, Mother Earth, mountains, music and dance, mysteries, Nordic Myth, Oceanian Myth, prophecy, prosperity, rain, Rainbow Snake, Roman Myth, sea, sex, shape-changers, Sky, Slavic Myth, smiths, snakes, storms, Sun, supreme deity, thunder, time, tricksters, twins, Underworld, war, water, wind, wisdom and writing.

Throughout the book, BCE after a date means 'before Christian (or Common) Era'; CE means 'Christian (or Common) Era'.

All the myths retold and discussed in this book, grouped by traditions:

AfRICAN MYTH

AMERICAN MYTH

Adekagagwaa
Agwe
Ah Puch
Ahsonnutli
Aiomum Kondi
Amana
Amotken
Annency
Ariconte and Tamendonare
Asgaya Gigagei
Ataentsic
Atsehastin and Atseestan
Auchimalgen
Aulanerk
Aunyainá
Awonawilona
Bachue
Baxbakualanuchsiwae
Black God
Bochica
Bossu
Catequil
Chac
Chalchihuitlicue
Chantico
Chiminigagué
Chinigchinich
Chonchonyi
Cihuacóatl
Coatlicue
Coniraya
Copper Woman
Corn Woman
Coyolxauhqui
Coyote
Cupay
Dajoji
Damballah
Dayunsi
Disemb-oweller

Doquebuth
Dzoavits
Eeyeekalduk
Ehecatl
Ekkekko
El Dorado
Ellall
Enumclaw and Kapoonis
Erzulie
Esaugetuh Emissee
Estsanatlehi
First Made Man
Five Sisters
Flying Head
Ga-oh
Gendenwitha
Ghede
Gluskap
Gudratrigakwitl
Guecufu
Guinechen
Gukumatz
Gunnodayak
Hahgwehdiyu and Hahgwehdaetgah
Hinun
Huitzilopochtli
Humanmaker
Hunab
Hurukan
Ictinike
Igaluk
Ilamatecuhtli
Ilyap'a
Inti
Ioskeha
Itzamná
Itzpapalotl
Ixchel
Ixtab
Ixtlilton

Kadlu
Kananeski Amaiyehi
Kanassa
Kasogonaga
Kilya
Kitshi Manitu
Kloskurbeh
Kodoyanpe
Kokyangwuti
Komokwa
Kononatoo
Kuat
Kukulkan
Kumokum
Kumush
Kururumany
Kwatee
Legba
Macuilxóchitl
Maheo
Mait' Carrefour
Malsum
Mama Brigitte
Mama Quilla
Manco Capac
Mani
Mayauel
Michabo
Mictlan
Mictlantecuhtli
Mixcóatl
Na'pi
Nagaitcho
Nanabush
Nanook
Nayenezgani and Tobadzistsini
Nipinoukhe and Pipinoukhe
Nocoma
Nokomis
Ogoun
Ometecuhtli
Onatah
Oshadagea

Owiot
Pachacamac
Page Abe
Pah
Paraparawa
Payatamu
Pillan
Pinga
Poshaiyankayo
Qamaits
Quaayayp
Quetzalcóatl
Raven
Sedna
Sinaa
Snoqalm and Beaver
Star Country
Szeukha
Tamusi and Tamulu
Tawiskaron
Temazcalteci
Ten Corn Maidens
Tezcatlipoca
Thunderbirds
Tirawa
Tlaloc
Tlazoltéotl
Tochopa and Hokomata
Tonatiuh
Tonenili
Torngarsak
Tsohanoai
Tupan
Uaica
Umai-hulhlya-wit
Uncegila
Underwater Panthers
Unelanuki
Utset
Vaimatse
Valedjád
Viracocha
Wahari and Buoka Wakan Tanka

Wakonda
Wheememeowah
White She-Buffalo
Wishpoosh
Wonomi
Xipetotec

Xiutecuhtli
Xochipili
Xochiquetzal
Xólotl
Yacatecuhtli
Yanauluha

AUSTRALIAN MYTH

Bagadjimbiri
Bildjiwuaroju
Bobbi-Bobbi
Darana
Great Rainbow Snake
Julunggul
Jurawadbad
Jurumu
Kunapipi
Kurukadi and Mumba
Mangarkungerkunja
Marindi and Adnoartina
Mimi

Minawara and Multultu
Miralaldu and Djanggawul
Mudungkala
Namorodo
Ngurunderi
Purukapali
Tjinimin and Pilirin
Uluru
Waramurungundju and Wuraka
Widjingara
Wondjina
Yalungur

CELTIC MYTH

Albion
Annwn
Arawn
Arthur
Avalon
Aywell
Balor
Belenus
Beowulf
Bran
Bres
Brigid
Brit
Camelot
Cernunnos
Cormac MacAirt
Cuculain
Danaan
Deirdre
Dian Cecht
Excalibur
Finn MacCool
Fintan
Galahad
Gawain
Gogmagog
Grail

Guinevere
Lady of the Lake
Lleu Law Gyffes
Mabinogion
Manannan MacLir
Medb
Merlin
Mm
Modred
Morgan le Fay
Morrigan
Nimue
Oberon
Ogmios
Oisin
Pelles
Perceval
Pwyll
Rosmerta
Sucellus
Taliesin
Taranis
Teutatis
Tristram and Yseult
Uther Pendragon
Volund
Wyrd sisters

CHINESE MYTH

Ba Ja
Begdu San
Di
Di Jun
Di Kanh Wang
Eight Gods
Eight Immortals
Erh Jang
Erh Long
Fan Guei
Fei Lian
Five Buddhas
Five Elements
Five Emperors
Four Diamond Kings
Four Dragon Kings
Four Kings of Hell
Fu Xi
Gong Gong
Guan Di
Guan Yin
Hang Ha
Heng O
Huai Nan Zu
Huang Di
Huang Gun
Hun Dun
Jang Xien
Jou Wang
Jun Di
Kuafu
Kui
Lei Gong
Lei Jen Zu
Li No Zha

Li Papai
Long Wang
Lu Ban
Mi Hung Tang
Mi Lo
Nü Gua
Pan Gu
Penglai Shan
Qi Yu
Qian Nu and Zhi Nu
Shang Di
Shen Nong
Shi Zong Di
Shou Lao
Shun
Song Jiang
Sun Bin
Ten Yama Kings
Three Door Gods
Three Gods of Happiness
Three Lavatory Ladies
Three Sovereigns
Tian
Tsai Shen
Tsao Jun
Wen Jang
Xi He
Yao
Yen Lo
Yi
Yu
Yu Huang
Yu Zu
Zhuan Hu

EGYPTIAN MYTH

Aapep	Mahaf
Amaunet	Meskhent
Ammut	Min
Amun	Mut
Anubis	Naunet
Aset	Nebthet
Aten	Nefertem
Bastet	Nehebkau
Benu Bird	Neit
Bes	Nun
Duat	Nut
Ennead	Ogdoad
Geb	Osiris
Hap	Ptah
Hapi	Ra
Hapy	Sekhmet
Hathor	Serapis
Heqet	Serqet
Horus	Seshat
Imhotep	Set
Khepri	Taweret
Khnum	Thoth
Maat	

ꜰINNISH MYTH

Ahto
Akka
Antero Vipunen
Ilma
Ilmarinen
Joukahainen
Jumala
Kalevala
Kalma
Kipu-Tyttö
Kuu
Kylliki
Lemminkäinen
Louhi
Loviatar

Kullervo
Luonnotar
Otava
Ovda
Päivä
Pohjola
Sampo
Surma
Tapio
Tuonela
Tuonetar
Tuoni
Ukko
Väinämöinen

GENERAL

animal-gods
archers
beauty
bulls and cows
childbirth and infant care
civilization
crafts
creation
death
demons
disease and healing
dragons
earthquakes
farming
fate
fertility
fire
floods
food and drink of immortality
ghosts
giants
good luck
guardians
Heaven
heroes
household and family
human ancestors
hunting
immortality
justice and universal order
light and dark

lightning
love
messengers
monsters
Moon
Mother Earth
mountains
music and dance
mysteries
prophecy
prosperity
rain
Rainbow Snake
sea
sex
shape-changers
Sky
smiths
snakes
storms
Sun
supreme deity
thunder
time
tricksters
twins
Underworld
war
water
wind
wisdom and writing

GERMANIC MYTH

Andvari
Atli
Donar
Faust
Flying Dutchman
Mephistopheles
Nibelungs

Norns
Sigmund
Signy
Sinfiotl
Tiwaz
Woden

GREEK MYTH

Achates
Achelous
Acheron
Achilles
Adonis
Aegeus
Aegisthus
Aeneas
Aeolus
Aesculapius
Agamemnon
Agave
Ajax
Alcinous
Alcmaeon
Alcmena
Amazons
ambrosia
Amphion
Amphitrite
Amphitryon
Andromache
Antigone
Antiope
Aphrodite
Apollo
Arachne
Ares
Arethusa
Argonauts
Argus
Ariadne
Aristaeus
Arne
Artemis
Astyanax
Atalanta
Ate
Athamas
Athene
Atlas

Atreus
Atropus
Attis
Augeas
Aurora
Autolycus
Bellerophon
Boreas
Briareus
Cadmus
Caeneus
Calchas
Calypso
Campe
Cassandra
centaurs
Cerberus
Chaos
Charon
Chimaera
Chiron
Chrysothemis
Circe
Clashing Rocks
Clytemnestra
Cocytus
Creon
Cretan Bull
Cronus
Cyclopes
Dactyls
Daedalus
Danaë
Deiphobus
Demeter
Deucalion and Pyrrha
Diomedes
Dionysus
Dioscuri
Earthborn Giants
Electra

Elpenor
Elysium
Empusa
Endymion
Eos
Eriphyle
Eris
Eros
Erymanthian Boar
Erysichthon
Eteocles
Europa
Eurynome
Eurystheus
Fates
Five Ages of Mortals
Furies
Gaia
Ganymede
Geryon
Golden Fleece
Gorgons
Graces
Graeae
Hades
Harpies
Hebe
Hecate
Hecuba
Helen
Helenus
Helius
Helle
Hephaestus
Hera
Heracles
Hermes
Hermione
Hesperides
Hippolyta
Hippolytus
Hundred-handed Giants
Hyacinthus

Hydra
Hylas
Hymen
Hyperion
Hypnus
Hypsipyle
Icarus
Idomeneus
Ilythia
Io
Ion
Iphigenia
Iris
Ismene
Ixion
Jason
Jocasta
Keryneian Hind
Laertes
Laius
Lamia
Laomedon
Leda
Leo
Lethe
Lotus-eaters
Lycaon
Lycurgus
Medea
Medusa
Melampus
Menelaus
Metis
Midas
Minotaur
Mount
Muses
Narcissus
Nauplius
Nausicaä
nectar
Nemean Lion
Nemesis

Neoptolemus
Nephele
Nereus
Nike
Niobe
Nisus and Euryalus
Odysseus
Oenomaus
Olympian Gods
Olympus
Omphale
Orestes
Orpheus
Ouranos
Palamedes
Palladium
Pallas
Pan
Pandora
Paris
Pasiphaë
Patroclus
Pegasus
Peleus
Pelias
Pelops
Penelope
Pentheus
Persephone
Perseus
Phaedra
Phaethon
Philoctetes
Phineus
Phion
Phlegethon
Phrixus
Pirithous
Polydorus
Polynices
Polyphemus
Polyxena
Poseidon

Priam
Priapus
Procrustes
Prometheus
Proteus
Psyche
Pygmalion
Pylades
Pyrrha
Pyrrhus
Rhadamanthus
Rhea
Rhesus
Salmoneus
Satyrs
Scamander
Scylla and Charybdis
Selene
Semele
Seven Against Thebes
Sibyls
Silenus
Sirens
Sisyphus
Sown Men
Sphinx
Stymphalian Birds
Styx
Tantalus
Telchines
Telemachus
Tereus
Thanatos
Thebes
Tiresias
Titans
Trojan War
Trophonius
Tyndareus
Typhon
Wooden Horse
Zephyrus
Zeus

INDIAN MYTH

Aditi
Agastya
Ages of Brahma
Agni
Airavata
Ambalika
Ambika
Amitabha
amrita
Ananda
Anjana
apsaras
Ardhanarishvara
Arjuna
Ashvathaman
Ashvins
Asuras
Atri
Avalokiteshvara
Balarama
Bali
Balin
Bhagiratha
Bharata
Bhima
Bhisma
Bhutas
boddhisattvas
Brahma
Brighu
Brighus
Brihaspati
Buddha
Candramus
Chandra
Chyavana
Daityas
Daksha
Dasaratha
Deva

Devadatta
Devaki
devas and *devis*
Devi
Dhanvantari
Dharma
Dhatar
Dhritarashtra
Diti
Draupadi
Drona
Drumalika
Durga
Dyaus
Dyavaprivithi
Gandharvas
Ganesh
Ganga
Garuda
Gommateshvara
Hanuman
Harihara
Hayagriva
Hiranyakishipu
Hiranyaksha
Ida
Indra
Jaganath
Jalandhara
Jambavan
Janaka
Jara
Jarasandha
Jatayu
Kadru
Kaikeyi
Kalanemi
Kali
Kaliya
Kalki

Kama

Kamadhenu

Kansa

Karttikeya

Kasyapa

Kauravas

Kausalya

Krishna

Kubera

Kumbhaka

Kunti

Kurma

Lakshma

Lakshmi

Madri

Mahabharata

Mahavira

Maitreya

Manasa

Manu

Mara

Maruts

Matsya

Maya

Meru

Mithra

Mount

Muchalinda

nagas and *naginis*

Nakula

Nanda

Nandi

Narasimha

Pandavas

Pandu

Parashurama

Parjanya

Parshva

Parsu

Parvati

Pavanareka

Pisakas

Prahlada

Prajapati

Prisni

Privithi

Purusha

Pushan

Putana

Radha

Rahu

Rakshasas

Rama

Rashnu

Rati

Ratri

Ravana

Ribhus

Rig Veda

Rishabha

Rishis

Rohini

Rudra

Rudrani

Rukmini

Sagara

Sahadeva

Saktasura

Sandhya

Saranyu

Sarasvati

Sati

Savitri

Seven Seers

Shashti

Shatrughna

Shesha

Shitala

Shiva

Siddhartha Gautama

Sisupala

Sita

Skanda

soma

Sugriva

Surya

Tara
Taraka
tirkanthara
Trinavarta
Tripitaka
Tvashtri
Ugrasena
Ugrasura
Uma
Urvashi
Ushas
Vamana
Varaha
Varuna
Varuni
Vashishtra

Vasudeva
Vasuki
Vasus
Vibishana
Vinata
Viraj
Vishnu
Vishvakarman
Vivasvat
Vritra
Vyasa
Yama
Yashodhara
Yasoda
Yudhishthira

JAPANESE MYTH

Ajisukitakahikone
Amaterasu
Bimbogami
Chimatano
Daikoku
Fujiyama
Futen
Gaki
Hachiman
In and Yo
Inari
Izanami and Izanagi
Jizo
Kagutsuchi
Kappa
Kojin

Kotoamatsukami
Moshirikkwechep
Musubi
Ninigi
Okuninushi
Oni
Raiden and Raiju
Seven Gods of Good Luck
Susano
Tide Jewels
Tsukuyomi
Ukemochi
Umashiashikabihikoji
Yamasachi
Yomi
Yuriwaka

MESOPOTAMIAN MYTH

Adam and Eve	Leviathan
Adad	Lilith
Adapa	Mammitu
Ahriman	Marduk
Ahura Mazda	Mary
An	Nabu
Anat	Nabu
Ashur	Nanna
Astarte	Nergal
Atrahis	Ninhursaga
Baal	Ninurta
Beelzebub	Noah
Borak	Og
Cain	Samson
Dagon	Satan
Ea	Shamash
El	Sheol
Enki	Sin
Enlil	Telepinu
Ereshkigal	Tengri
Gabriel	Teshub
Gilgamesh	Tiamat
houris	Utnapishtim
Illuyankas	Utu
Imdugud	Yahweh
Kusor	

NORDIC MYTH

Aegir
Aesir
Agnar
Alvis
Andvari
Asegeir
Asgard
Ask and Embla
Audumla
Baldur
Bergelmir
Berserkers
Bestla
Bifröst
Bor
Bragi
Brisingamen
Brynhild
Buri
Donar
Elli
Fafnir
Forseti
Frey
Freyja
Freyja
Frigg
Gefion
Geirröd (giant)
Geirröd (mortal)
Gilling
Ginungagap
Grid
Gunnlod
Heimdall
Hel
Hlin
Höd
Honir
Hraesvelg

Hrungnir
Hrym
Hymir
Idun
Jormungand
Kvasir
Lif
Loki
Midgard
Mimir
Muspell
Nerthus
Nidhogg
Niflheim
Nine Wave-maidens
Nine
orlds
Njörd
Norns
Od
Odin
Odin
Otr
Ragnarök
Ran
Regin
Sif
Sigmund
Sigurd
Skadi
Skrymsli
Sleipnir
Surt
Suttung
Thiazi
Thor
Thor
Tiwaz
Tyr
Ull

Utgard
Valhalla
Valkyries
Vanir
Ve
Vidar

Vili
Wyrd
Yambe-Akka
Yggdrasil
Ymir

OCEANIAN MYTH

Areop-Enap	Papa
Atea	Pele
Dudugera	Rangi
Ha'iaka	Rangi's and Papa's Immortal Children
Hina	Ruaumoko
Honoyeta	Haumea
Jari and Kamarong	Sido
Jugumishanta and Morufonu	Soido
Kamapua'a	Sosom
Kava	Ta'aroa
Loa	Tagaro
Maui	Tane
Na Kaa	Tangaloa
Nareau	Tangaroa
Nu'u	To Kabinana and To Karvuvu
Olifat	Totoima

ROMAN MYTH

Achates
Aeneid
Anchises
Angerona
Baucis and Philemon
Bellona
Cacus
Dido
Epona
Faunus
Flora
Fortuna
Hersilia
Horatius Cocles
Janus
Jupiter
Lar
Latinus
Lavinia

Lucretia
manes
Mania
Mars
Metamorphoses
Mors
Nisus and Euryalus
Penates
Picus and Canens
Pomona and Vertumnus
Psyche
Pylades
Pyrrhus
Romulus and Remus
Saturnus
Tiber
Troilus and Cressida
Turnus

SLAVIC MYTH

Baba Yaga
bogatiri
Byelobog
Dazhbog
Domovoi
Dugnai
Ilya Muromets
Leshy
Mati-Syra-Zemlya
Meness
Miktula
Polevik
Potok-Mikhailo Ivanovich
Priparchis
Pyerun

Rod
Rugievit
Russalki
Sadko
Saule
Simorg
Stribog
Svarozich
Svyatogor
Varpulis
Vodyanoi
Yarilo
Zoryas
Zosim

AAPEP
Africa (North)

Aapep ('**moon**-snake', also known as Apep and, in Greek, Apophis, 'Aa-**snake**'), in Egyptian myth, was Nothingness, the gulf that swallows Light. He took the form of a huge snake, not coiling but forming a concertina of S-bends, and instead of hissing he uttered a silent roar – the opening of the abyss – which filled the entire world and terrified all who heard it. This roar was also his own nourishment, and he needed no other food. His main task was to snatch the souls of the Dead in their precarious journey between one life and the next; those he swallowed entered non-existence, and stayed there until one of the gods rescued them. Aapep lay in wait for **Ra** the **Sun** each day, opening his mouth to engulf him as he sailed towards evening on the Sun-ship. It took the concerted efforts of gods and mortals to kill Aapep and help Ra to escape each day: in one typical story, everyone else was eaten and it was only when **Set** speared Aapep in the gullet that he disgorged his prey again. Each time Aapep was destroyed, all the souls he had eaten were regurgitated and could travel on to judgement in the **Underworld**. But Aapep himself regenerated, ready to lie in wait on the Western Mountains at the edge of the universe for the next day's Sun.

ABASSI AND ATAI
Africa

Abassi ('god') and Atai ('fate'), in the myths of the Efik people of Nigeria, had two children. When the children were grown, they wanted to leave **Heaven** and settle on Earth. Abassi hesitated,

Amitabha Buddha, with a canopy of *apsaras* (*5th-century print*)

in case they bred a warrior-people and attacked him. But Atai persuaded him to let the children live on Earth providing that they never mated or worked and that they came to Heaven to eat whenever he rang the dinner-bell. For a time this arrangement worked, but then the children began experimenting with ploughing, sowing, harvesting and **sex** – and soon Earth was swarming with their descendants. Atai solved this by giving them two gifts of her own: argument and death. The primordial parents died immediately, and their offspring have been brawling and death-haunted ever since. As for Abassi and Atai, they were so disenchanted with their descendants that they lived utterly aloof in Heaven, taking no heed whatever of the human race.

ACHATES
Europe (South)

Achates ('agate'), in Greek and Roman myth, was a Trojan warrior. In some accounts he was the man who killed Protesilaus, the first Greek to leap ashore when the expedition reached Troy to fetch **Helen** back. Achates became **Aeneas'** close friend (and some say, squire), accompanying him on all his subsequent adventures except the journey to the **Underworld**.

*Achates would be a shadowy figure if it were not for his featured role in Virgil's **Aeneid**. Even there he does little but act as Aeneas' squire and confidant, so much so that the phrase fidus Achates ('faithful Achates') became proverbial for someone whose devotion is unthinking, unquestioning, doglike. The phrase is, in fact, the*

origin of the name 'Fido' sometimes given to dogs in English-speaking nations.

ACHELOUS
Europe (South)

Achelous (Acheloös, 'who drives out grief'), in Greek and Roman myth, the son of Ocean and **Gaia** (**Mother Earth**) – or, some say, of the **Sun** and Tethys – was a river-god, a **giant** with a serpent's tail, a man's body and a bull's head from whose beard and mane streams of river-water unceasingly flowed. He wanted to take Deianira for wife, and wrestled **Heracles** for her. Achelous wriggled like a serpent, wrestled like a man, and finally lowered his head like a bull and charged. This was the end of the fight: for Heracles remembered how he had tamed the fire-breathing **Cretan bull**, took hold of one of Achelous' horns and vaulted on to his back. The horn snapped off in his hand, and Achelous, disfigured and ashamed, withdrew from the contest and left Deianira to Heracles. Heracles gave the broken horn to the **nymphs** of fields and woods, who filled it with an unceasing supply of fruits, nuts and berries of all kinds and presented it to Plutus god of wealth: the Horn of Plenty.
⋙ **water**

ACHERON
Europe (South)

Acheron ('distress'), in Greek and Roman myth, was the son of **Demeter**, goddess of harvest, who conceived him without a father. In some accounts, he supported the gods against

3

the **Titans**, and was so terrified of retribution that he hid in the **Underworld**. In others, he helped the Titans, taking them **water** during their fight with the gods, and **Zeus** punished him by hurling him into the Underworld. Once there, he turned into a river of bitter water, became a tributary of the river **Styx**, and took charge of mortal bodies as soon as their souls left them, beginning the process of decay.

ACHILLES
Europe (South)

Achilles (Achilleus, 'child of sorrow'), in Greek myth, was the son of a mortal, **Peleus**, and the sea-**nymph Thetis**. He was thus a **hero**: immortal and mortal striving to coexist in the same mind and body. His mother tried to make him fully immortal, either by charring his bones clean of flesh or by dipping him in the river **Styx**. The treatment failed, but made Achilles invulnerable to weapons – except for one heel, by which Peleus grabbed him to save him from the fire, or Thetis held him while dipping him in the Styx.

Achilles before the Trojan War. Like all Greek heroes, Achilles was fated to fight at Troy. Thetis, knowing that he was also doomed to die there, tried to prevent him hearing the call to arms by dressing him as a woman and hiding him in the harem of King Lycomedes of Scyros. But when the recruiting-party blew an alarm-call, Achilles ran out in dress and veil, brandishing a sword. His arrival among the Greeks was opportune. To appease **Artemis** (who was holding back the winds and keeping the fleet from sailing), the Greek leader

Agamemnon had been ordered to sacrifice his daughter **Iphigenia**. He sent word to **Clytemnestra**, his wife, that Achilles had demanded Iphigenia's hand in marriage, and Clytemnestra sent the child to Aulis, the harbour from which the Greeks sailed.

Achilles at Troy. For much of the ten years of the **Trojan War**, Achilles' unpredictable blend of bravery and bravado terrified all who faced him. In the end the gods used it to engineer the end of the fighting. The underlying reason was rivalry between Achilles and Agamemnon, and the immediate causes were Briseis and Chryseis, beautiful Trojan prisoners-of-war allocated to each of them respectively. Chryseis' father, the priest Chryses, demanded his daughter back, and when Agamemnon refused, he cursed the Greeks with plague. Hastily, Agamemnon returned Chryseis, and compensated himself by taking Briseis from Achilles. At once Achilles withdrew himself and his Myrmidons from the fighting and refused to play any further part in the war.

The Trojans massed for a final attack. Agamemnon proposed that the war be settled by single combat between the two rivals for **Helen**, Greek **Menelaus** and Trojan **Paris**. But before this could happen, the gods acted. They sent Chryseis back from Troy to Agamemnon, and the Trojans claimed treachery and rallied to destroy the Greeks. Agamemnon sent a deputation to Achilles, led by the silver-tongued **Odysseus**, offering him Briseis again and begging him to change his mind. Achilles sulkily refused.

Hector and Patroclus. Next morning, Prince **Hector** of Troy and his soldiers sliced through the Greek lines and attacked the Greek ships. Achilles still refused to fight in person. But he told his friend and lover **Patroclus** to put on his (Achilles') armour and ride out to protect the ships. Thinking that Patroclus was Achilles, the Greeks rallied and the Trojans fled. Patroclus climbed a siege-ladder to lead his men into the city, but **Apollo** heard Hector's prayer for aid and knocked Patroclus to the ground. His helmet flew off, the Greeks saw that he was not Achilles and fell back, and the Trojans swarmed out of the city. Hector stabbed Patroclus dead and carried Achilles' armour back in triumph.

Achilles and Hector. Achilles swore not to rest until Patroclus was avenged. His mother Thetis gave him magnificent new armour, crafted by **Hephaestus** himself, and he challenged Hector to single combat. Trying to tire Achilles, Hector ran away round the city, taunting him: he hoped that the divine armour would slow him down. But Achilles caught him, killed him, and dragged his body behind a chariot three times round the city walls.

Achilles' death. Hector's father **Priam** offered Achilles Hector's weight in gold in return for the body – and when the amount fell short, Priam's daughter **Polyxena** offered her earrings to make up the total. Overwhelmed by her beauty, Achilles rejected the gold and asked for her instead. The Greeks accused him of taking her as a bribe to desert them, and once more he went back to his tent and sulked.

This time the gods sent the Egyptian warlord Memnon to stir Achilles' fury. Memnon killed Antiochus, who had replaced Patroclus as Achilles' catamite, and Achilles ran out in rage, chasing Memnon and his followers right into Troy. The gods now took final action. Apollo guided Paris' hand and he killed Achilles by shooting him in the (vulnerable) ankle with a poisoned arrow. There was a fierce battle over his body, ended only by a thunderstorm from Zeus. The Greeks cremated the body and buried Achilles' ashes with those of Patroclus, in a golden urn made by Hephaestus. He travelled to the **Underworld**, where he married **Medea** and spent his afterlife in the Fields of the Blessed.

Another version of Achilles' death says that Polyxena cajoled from him the secret of his invulnerability and passed it to Paris, who lay in hiding at Achilles' and Polyxena's marriage, then leapt out and stabbed his heel. After the war, Polyxena was given to Achilles' son **Neoptolemus**, who sacrificed her on his father's grave.

Achilles is a central character in Homer's Iliad, from the tenth or ninth century BCE. This took a powerful hold on later Greek imagination: it was, for example, read aloud at a huge annual festival in Athens, and vase-painters made exquisite drawings of practically every scene described above. The events of the Iliad were revisited and reinvented by the great fifth-century Greek dramatists, notably Aeschylus and Euripides, and figured in rhetoric and poetry. In the fourth century BCE, the Iliad dominated the thinking of no less a person than Alexander the Great. He is reputed to have regarded himself as Achilles reborn, to have carried an Iliad everywhere, and to have consciously set out to repeat Achilles' more spectacular exploits.

In later times, however, the Iliad lost favour, yielding its place to the Odyssey and to Virgil's Aeneid. Curiously, it hardly influenced later European epics, such as those telling of King **Arthur**'s knights or Charlemagne's paladins. In modern times it has inspired a few creative artists (for example the British writers John Cowper Powys and Christopher Logue), but it has never recaptured the pre-eminence it had in ancient Greece. This, in turn, has led to Achilles becoming sidelined as a 'favourite' Graeco-Roman hero. Agamemnon, **Heracles**, **Odysseus** or **Aeneas** easily outrank him in modern eyes.

ACHIMI: *see* Itherther and Achimi

ADAD
Asia (West)

Adad ('crasher'; also spelled Addad, Addu and Haddad), in Sumerian myth, was the **thunder**-god, storm-bringer and giver of **rain**. He was one of the seventy children of the **sea**-goddess Asherat, but moved inland to control fresh water, supervising in particular the annual **floods** of the rivers Tigris and Euphrates. In some accounts he was reborn each year, manifesting himself to mortals in the vegetation which grew in the fields when the floods subsided and died when it was harvested: to eat the crop was to take in the god. In art he was shown as a warrior, brandishing a thunderbolt and striding into battle, or riding a cloud-chariot or a white bull whose horns he wore on his helmet, not erect but flat like folded wings. Bulls were sacrificed to him each winter, to ensure the flood and successful planting. His sacred fruit, the pomegranate, was thought to contain the **Sun**'s blood: life.

Adad, Prince Sea and Mot. In some Syrian and Canaanite accounts, Adad created the world from chaos. In the beginning, Prince Sea, the primordial ocean, ruled, but then his son Adad dethroned him by the power of **lightning**. Adad sliced Prince Sea into pieces, and put ramparts of land between them to prevent them ever reassembling again. Prince Sea still flails and roars against the land, and Adad is the only god able to stop him, channelling his energy into rivers and irrigation-channels.

In some accounts, Adad was so proud of defeating Prince Sea that he called himself Baal-Hadad ('Thunder-prince'), built himself a palace on the slopes of Mount Saphon, and announced that he had power even over Mot, god of **death**. Mot challenged him to prove it by visiting the **Underworld**, eating the food of the Dead (mud) and surviving. Adad did so, and as soon as the mud passed his lips he died. His wife **Anat** dragged his body to the Upper World and tried to revive him. But he lay inert on the mountain-side, and Anat hauled Mot out of the Underworld, chopped him to pieces and soaked the mountain with his blood. This sacrifice brought Adad back to life, and he grew to full strength as a seed becomes a tree. This event, the myth ends, has been endlessly repeated in the cycle of the seasons, and unless Adad dies and is reborn through sacrifice each year, the world's **fertility** will end.

The story of Adad and Mot is sometimes told of another Syrian god, Rimmon. But most scholars think that the two names, Rimmon ('roarer') and Adad ('crasher') are simply alternative honorific names for the same god, whose main identity is lost.
⇛ creation, supreme deity

ADAM AND EVE
Asia (West)

Adam ('clay-red'), in Hebrew myth, was the first human being, moulded by **Yahweh** and given the breath of life on the sixth day of **creation**. Eve (Hawwah, 'life') was made soon afterwards (in some accounts, from one of Adam's ribs). Adam invented language, naming everything in creation – and in some accounts, this gave him and his descendants authority over all other creatures.

Adam and Eve lived in Eden, the earthly paradise where grew the Tree of All-knowledge and the Tree of **Immortality**. Yahweh allowed them to eat the fruits of every plant on Earth, except for these trees, the divine prerogative. But Eve (in some accounts tempted by **Satan** in the form of a **snake**) picked the fruit of the Tree of All-knowledge and shared it with Adam. At once they acquired the knowledge of **sex**, the ability to create life – and Yahweh, fearing that they might go on to eat the fruit of the Tree of Immortality and become gods, sent **Gabriel** to banish them from Eden and punished them further, forcing Adam to till the ground and grow food instead of picking it at random, and giving Eve and her female descendants the pains of **childbirth**.

The Bible account of this myth adds the element of shame. As soon as Adam and Eve ate the fruit of Knowledge, they realized that they were naked, and made clothes to cover themselves, first from fig-leaves and then from animal-skins.
⇛ farming

ADAPA
Asia (West)

Adapa, creation of the **water**-god **Ea** in Mesopotamian myth, was the first human being. The mud from which he was moulded made him half mortal, but the god's creating hand made him half divine; he had immortal strength and Ea taught him everything he knew, one third of all the knowledge in the universe. Adapa lived with the rest of humanity (made later from the same mould which had formed him), and taught them language. He spent his days glorifying his maker and the other gods. But one day, when he was sailing in the estuary of the river Euphrates, Shutu the South Wind bore down on the ship and all but sank it – and Adapa lost his temper, snatched Shutu's bird-like wings and tore them off. The god's wings were immortal and grew back, but in the time that took, the sky-lord **An** noticed the calm which had fallen on the world and summoned Adapa to **Heaven** to explain it. Adapa asked his father Ea what to do, and Ea told him to dress in mourning, speak humbly and refuse any food and drink he was offered. The first two pieces of advice got Adapa safely through his trial before the Heavenly court. But the third was a trap, for An offered Adapa the gods' food and drink of **immortality**, and when Adapa refused he condemned the entire human race, Ea's creation, to be bound by **death**.

Adapa was the first of the seven Apkallu, sages created by Ea to be intermediaries between gods and mortals, to teach human beings as much as they could understand of the knowledge of the gods. (Ea himself was the Apkallu of the gods.) All human wisdom was later attributed to these Seven Sages: among other things, one of them was said to have composed the Epic of **Gilgamesh**.

ADEKAGAGWAA
Americas (North)

Adekagagwaa, in the myths of the Iroquois people of the Northeastern US woodlands, was the spirit of Summer. For half the year he ruled the Northern forests and fields, blessing them with **fertility**, but then he went South for six months' holiday, leaving his 'sleep spirit' to watch over the people. The sleep spirit was watchful but powerless, unable to stand up to **Ga-oh** the wind-lord, Gohone the frost-spirit or **Hinu** the thunder-god, who did as they pleased until Adekagagwaa returned and brought back Spring.

ADITI
India

Aditi ('boundless') came to India from ancient Iran with the Aryan invasions of the seventeenth century BCE. She was the vault of **Heaven** and the mother of the gods. In Aryan myth, her children, each of whom was called Aditya ('Aditi's child' or 'heavenly light') after her, included **Dhatar**, **Indra**, **Mithra**, **Savitri**, **Surya**, **Varuna** and **Vivasvat**. In some later myths the number was increased to twelve, and each took charge of the **Sun** and the revolution of night and day for one month of the year; by the fifth century BCE Aditi was often honoured as the mother of all the gods. But there is no consistency: in some accounts, for example, **Vishnu** was her only son, in others just one of them.
➤ **sky**

ADNOARTINA: *see* Marindi and Adnoartina

ADONIS
Europe (South)

Adonis ('prince'), in Greek myth, was one of the few mortals favoured with the amorous attentions of **Aphrodite**, goddess of love. His birth was unusual. King Cinyras of Assyria boasted that his daughter, Smyrna, was more beautiful than Aphrodite herself. As punishment, Aphrodite filled him with lust for Smyrna, and he raped her and made her pregnant. Realizing this, he tried to kill her, but Aphrodite rescued her and turned her into a myrrh tree. This particular tree splits its trunk in the spring to allow new growth – and Adonis was discovered inside.

As soon as Aphrodite saw Adonis, she fell in love with him and planned to make him her lover when he was old enough. She hid him in a box and gave it to **Persephone** to guard. However, Persephone too fell in love with Adonis and refused to give him up. The goddess asked Calliope, **Muse** of eloquence, to settle the dispute, and she ordered Adonis to spend four months with

Aphrodite, four with Persephone and the rest of the year with whichever he chose.

At the end of Aphrodite's four months, she charmed Adonis with her girdle of desire and he swore to stay with her always. Persephone went to the war-god **Ares** (who was himself in love with Aphrodite), and told him he had a mortal rival. The next time Adonis went hunting, Ares disguised himself as a boar and killed him. Wherever drops of Adonis' blood fell, wood anemones sprang up.

Now **Zeus** took a hand, decreeing that half of Adonis' year should be spent with Aphrodite, and the other half with Persephone (the six months she spent as queen of the **Underworld**). Adonis and Aphrodite had three children. Two of these, Golgus and Beroe, were mortal and beautiful; the third, **Priapus**, was immortal, ugly, and so shamelessly lustful that the other gods refused to have him in Olympus.

⟫➤ **beauty, Endymion, Ganymede, Hylas, Narcissus**

ADROA
Africa

Adroa ('up there'), in the myths of the Lugbara people of Zaïre and Uganda, created the universe and everything in it, including himself. He was thought alone, shapeless, all-good, remote. But to make his second creation, Adro (Earth), he had to divide himself in two and give the new half form. Adro the Earth-spirit was like half of a human body divided from crown of head to toes: one eye, half a mouth, one arm, one leg and no generative organs.

Deprived of union with its heavenly half, it swam eternally in the rivers of the world, and was the spirit of evil. It and its children, the water-snakes known as Adroanzi (produced from a slit in their parent's single side), were permanently on watch for humans to drown and eat.

⟫➤ **creation, Haiuri**

AEGEUS
Europe (South)

Aegeus (Aigeus, 'goaty'), son of King Pandion of Athens in Greek myth, inherited his father's throne. But he had no children, and was afraid that after his death his kingdom would be snatched by one or another of his quarrelsome brothers Lycus, Nisus and Pallas, or by one of Pallas' fifty warrior-sons. He asked advice from the Delphic oracle, and the priests told him 'not to unfasten the wineskin's foot' until he reached the Acropolis, or he would cause his own death. Finding this advice incomprehensible, Aegeus went to ask his old friend Pittheus, prophet-king of Troezen, if he could explain it. On the way he visited **Medea** in Corinth. Tormented with rage because **Jason** had just taken a new wife, she told Aegeus that if he promised her shelter in Athens she would end his childlessness.

In Troezen, King Pittheus gave a banquet in Aegeus' honour, and Aegeus enjoyed himself so much that he forgot the oracle's advice. Wineskin after wineskin was unfastened and drained, and he staggered drunk to bed without telling Pittheus why he'd come. Not only that, but the bed he staggered to belonged to Pittheus' daughter Aethra. He made love with her – and then in the sober dawn, rather than face her father, slipped out of Troezen and hurried back to Athens. Before he went, he buried a golden sword and a pair of sandals under a rock, and told Aethra, if she proved to be pregnant and bore a son, to wait until the boy grew up and then tell him about the sword. If the gods gave him strength to lift the rock and find the sword he should go to Athens, where he would be welcomed as Aegeus' heir.

Back in Athens, Aegeus found that Medea had reached the city before him, having killed her children by Jason and fled from Corinth. She used her magic powers to protect the city against Aegeus' quarrelsome family, and she also fed Aegeus herbs to increase his potency, so that he and she had a son, Medus. Aegeus lived happily with her for twenty years. Then a young stranger arrived from Troezen: **Theseus**. Medea at once realized that he was a threat to her power. She tried to poison him – and Aegeus, just in time, recognized the golden sword he'd left under the rock, dashed the poison-cup from Theseus' hand and welcomed him as the son he never knew he'd fathered. (Medea stormed off to the **Underworld**, and Medus fled to Asia Minor, where he became the ancestor of the Median people.)

As soon as Medea was gone, Aegeus' brothers and nephews ran to attack Athens. But Theseus killed all of them, and Aegeus made him heir-apparent. He would have abdicated in Theseus' favour, but Theseus left almost immediately for Crete to put an end to the **Minotaur**, and Aegeus agreed to rule in Athens until he returned. He told Theseus that he would watch for a signal each day from the heights of the Acropolis (or some say, from Cape Sunium overlooking the sea). If Theseus succeeded, he should hang purple-red (or some say white) sails on the ship that brought him back to Athens; if he failed, his crew should hang a black sail. Each day, as agreed, Aegeus climbed to the top of Acropolis hill (or rode to Sunium) and gazed out to sea. At last he saw a ship – and it had black sails. In fact, Theseus *had* killed the Minotaur and was coming back alive, but **Dionysus** had blurred his memory, making him forget the arrangement about the sail. As soon as Aegeus saw the black sail he hurled himself to his death, either dashing his brains out on the rocks below the Acropolis, or throwing himself from Sunium into the sea which was later called the Aegean after him.

Aegeus' best-known appearance in literature is as the doddering old fool charmed by Medea in Euripides' play. Euripides started his characterization from one myth-account that Aegeus had ruled in Athens for four mortal generations, and the reason he was childless was that he was over a hundred years old. To the Athenian spectators, who regarded Aegeus as one of the founders of their city, this characterization must have come as a surprise, but it has affected Aegeus' depiction in all subsequent literature and art.

AEGIR
Europe (North)

Aegir, personification of the primordial ocean in Nordic myth, held himself aloof from such newer families of gods as the **Vanir** and **Aesir**, living with his wife **Ran** in a golden underwater palace. He contented himself with rule over the **sea** and all its creatures, and sent his rage to the surface in storms and tidal waves to frighten off any gods, **giants** or mortals rash enough to stray into his domain. Occasionally he held underwater parties, feasting the gods on seafood and ale brewed in an enormous pot which **Thor** and **Tyr** stole for him from Tyr's father, the giant **Hymir**.

Aegir's aloofness led him to ignore the presence in his realm of **Jormungand**, the world-**snake** which bound the waters together. Unknown to him, Jormungand is continually growing, and when **Ragnarök** comes and the sea-serpent surges to the surface to overwhelm **creation**, Aegir will be so feeble in comparison that he will be unable to stop it.

AEGISTHUS
Europe (South)

Aegisthus (Aegisthos, 'strength of goats'), in Greek myth, was born of the incest between his father **Thyestes** and Thyestes' daughter Pelopia. As soon as he was born he was sent to be brought up by goatherds, but was later rescued and taken to the court of King **Atreus** of Mycenae, who brought him up as a royal prince together with Atreus' own sons **Agamemnon** and **Menelaus**.

What no one knew was that Aegisthus' birth had been ordered by the gods. He was to take revenge for an atrocity committed years before by Atreus, who had butchered Thyestes'

other children and served them in a stew to their father. Atreus had no idea that Aegisthus was related to Thyestes. Thinking him a foundling, he gave him the name Aegisthus because of the goatherds. But when Aegisthus grew up his true birth was revealed, and he avenged his dead brothers and sisters by murdering Atreus, exactly as the gods had planned.

For a few weeks after the murder, Aegisthus ruled Mycenae. But Atreus' son Agamemnon raised an army in Sparta, deposed him and took the throne, ruling with his queen **Clytemnestra**. Agamemnon thought that there was nothing to fear from Aegisthus. He had no idea that Aegisthus was conducting a long-standing affair with Clytemnestra, and planning revenge on him. When Agamemnon was chosen as commander of the Greeks who went to fight the **Trojan War**, he rashly left Mycenae in Clytemnestra's and Aegisthus' joint charge – and by the time he came home, after ten years away, they had become tyrants, and murdered him. They continued their reign of terror until Agamemnon's son **Orestes** (who had been exiled soon after Agamemnon sailed for Troy) returned in secret and killed them both.

AENEAS
Europe (South)

Aeneas' youth. Aeneas (Aineias, 'praiseworthy'), in Greek and Roman myth, was the son of Prince **Anchises** of Troy and the goddess **Aphrodite**. Even as a child he was admired for his attention to duty, his respect for gods and family and his qualities of leadership. As a youth he fought in the **Trojan War**, and though he was too young to play a large part in either fighting or counsels – both of which were dominated by **Priam**'s fifty sons, the senior branch of the royal family – he made his mark for diligence and bravery. **Poseidon** prophesied that when Troy fell Aeneas would lead his people to a new kingdom and new greatness, and the gods protected him during the fighting, rescuing him from such powerful adversaries as **Achilles** and **Diomedes**.

Aeneas after the fall of Troy. As soon as the Greeks breached the walls of Troy and began pillaging and burning the city, the gods told Aeneas to gather several shiploads of survivors, including his aged father Anchises, and sail with them to a new destiny far to the South. Aeneas took with him the ancestral gods of Troy, intending to make them the hub of whatever new city the gods found for him. He sailed past the **Clashing Rocks** into the Aegean, South along the coastline, and then through dangerous open water to landfall in Sicily, where his crew narrowly avoided being eaten by the **Cyclopes**, whose leader **Polyphemus** had already tried to kill **Odysseus** and his men.

Aeneas and Rome. From Sicily Aeneas went to Africa, where he visited Queen **Dido** of Carthage. He would have stayed there with her forever, allowing his people to intermarry with the Carthaginians and building Carthage into the second Troy promised by the gods. But **Zeus** intervened, sending **Hermes** to tell Aeneas that his destiny lay in Italy, not Africa. The Trojans sailed, leaving Dido heartbroken, and landed in Cumae, whose **Sibyl** took

Aeneas into the **Underworld** where Anchises' ghost showed him the whole future of his people: the city of Rome and the generations of **heroes** still unborn. Fortified by this vision, he sailed up the coast to Latium, at the mouth of the river Tiber, where he made an alliance with King **Latinus** and agreed to marry Latinus' daughter **Lavinia**. At this **Turnus**, king of the Rutulians (the most powerful of the local peoples), to whom Lavinia had previously been promised, declared war against the Trojans and Latins, and it was not until after months of fierce fighting that the gods helped Aeneas to kill Turnus in single combat, to unite the warring peoples and declare himself king of the whole area.

The end of Aeneas' life. Not long after killing Turnus, Aeneas vanished. In some accounts he was either killed in a skirmish or dived for safety into the river Numicus, and the current swept his body away so that it was never found. His people claimed that he had been taken into **Heaven**, and worshipped him as a god. In other accounts, he handed his throne to his son **Ascanius** (Iulus), and went alone on a second journey, either back to Carthage (whose people murdered him for betraying Dido years before) or North to the ruins of Troy, where his mother Aphrodite took him into Heaven.

In Greek myth, Aeneas is a minor figure, a lordling who fights bravely for Troy but disappears from the action as soon as the city falls. In Roman myth, however, he is central: he is the link between the gods (his mother Venus/Aphrodite) and the Roman

*people (descended from his son lulus/As-
canius), and an important intercessor between mortals and immortals. The story of
his wanderings was sketched by a number
of writers, from Hyginus to Ovid, but was
given definitive form in Virgil's* **Aeneid** *in
the early first century* CE. *Virgil modelled the
Aeneid on the grandest epics he knew,
Homer's Iliad and Odyssey – and he built
into it sustained, if dignified, propaganda
about Rome's divine destiny and the nobility and honour of the Roman character.
These last qualities are embodied by Aeneas himself, and some scholars think that
Virgil invented several episodes of the Aeneid to highlight them, not least the story of
Aeneas' love-affair with Dido.*

*In the Middle Ages, the Aeneid was
known throughout Europe, and its vision
of heroic obedience to the will of Heaven,
of self-denying heroism and unfaltering
nobility – Aeneas' character, in short –
became a model for the knights of Charlemagne's court, and from there the foundation of the chivalric code of social morality
and Christian ethics.*

AENEID

The *Aeneid* ('story of Aeneas') is a Latin
epic poem by Virgil, brought out after
his death in 19BCE. Its twelve sections
tell of the fall of Troy, the wanderings of
Aeneas and his companions in search
of a new homeland, and their battles to
win the area of Italy which became the
site of the future Rome. Virgil modelled
his style and form on Homer's *Iliad* and
Odyssey, and reworked several episodes
from those books, for example the
funeral games held for Aeneas' father
Anchises, Aeneas' hand-to-hand duels
with various Italian leaders, and – most

memorably of all – Aeneas' descent into
the **Underworld**, to hear from his
father's ghost the future destiny of
Rome. The *Aeneid*'s purposes were pa-
triotic, even propagandist: to trace the
descent of the ruling Julian dynasty
from Aeneas' son Ascanius (Iulus),
and therefore from his ancestors the
gods, and to hymn the virtues of obedience, moral uprightness and disci-
pline which were highly regarded in
aristocratic Roman circles of the time.
The *Aeneid* was popular not only in
ancient Rome, but throughout medieval Europe, where it was the second
most copied book after the Bible.

Because of its popularity, the *Aeneid* is
one of the most frequently illustrated
books of Western literature. Artists,
from medieval monks decorating
manuscripts to nineteenth-century
painters of vast panoramic scenes, concentrated on such sequences as Virgil's
account of the Fall of Troy, the funeral
games for Anchises, the suffering souls
in the Underworld, Aeneas' battle with
Turnus and – on a more domestic if
hardly less stiff-upper-lip scale – the
parting of **Dido** and Aeneas and Dido's
subsequent madness and suicide.

AEOLUS
Europe (South)

Aeolus (Aiolos, 'Destroyer'), in Greek
myth, was the son of **Poseidon** and the
mortal Arne, wife of King Desmontes.
His twin brother was Boeotus. Desmontes realized that he was not the
children's father, and was so furious
that he blinded Arne, imprisoned her
in an underground pit and left the
children on a mountainside to die.

Here, however, a shepherd found them and took them to his employer, Queen Theaeno. She brought them up as princes in the palace until they were adolescents, when she began to fear that they would steal the throne from her own two sons. She and her sons tried to kill them in a hunting accident, but Aeolus and Boeotus, equipped with supernatural strength by their father Poseidon, easily killed the two mortal princes, and Theaeno stabbed herself dead from grief.

The gods now told Aeolus and Boeotus the true story of their parentage, and they hurried home, killed Desmontes and rescued their mother Arne from her pit. Boeotus settled to farm the part of Greece later called Boeotia after him. The gods gave Aeolus a kingdom on the floating island of Lipara. **Zeus** and Poseidon honeycombed it with caves and tunnels, and Zeus forced the winds into them, sealing the entrances. Whenever the gods wanted help from a wind, Aeolus used his trident (a replica of the **earthquake**-causing trident of Poseidon, his father) to prise open a vent-hole, allowed the chosen wind to escape, and then resealed the hole.

Aeolus and Odysseus. **Odysseus** visited Lipara on his journey home from the **Trojan War**. Aeolus gave him a bagful of winds, and showed him how to untie the magic knot which fastened it if he ever needed to fill his sails. Odysseus' crew, however, jealous that he was the only one to be given a present, waited until he dozed – it was just after he'd caught the first glimpse of Ithaca on the horizon – and slashed open the bag with knives. The winds rushed out and blew them all the way back to Lipara. This time Aeolus refused to help them, and they were left to limp to Ithaca under their own oar-power.

Some later writers claimed that Aeolus was not a supernatural figure at all but a real person, Aeolus King of Aeolia. Whether myth or legend came first is a moot point – and by Homer's time (c10th century BCE) the two were inextricably intertwined.

⫸ **twins**

AESCULAPIUS
Europe (South)

Aesculapius (or Asclepius, Greek Asklepeios, 'always gentle'), in Greek myth, was the son of **Apollo** and the mortal princess Koronis. While Koronis was pregnant, she had an affair with a mortal, Ischys, and for this Apollo and **Artemis** shot her dead. However, even as the flames burned Koronis' body on the funeral pyre, Apollo remembered his child and cut Aesculapius free.

Aesculapius was educated by the centaur **Chiron**, who taught him medicine. **Athene** gave him two bottles of **Gorgon**'s blood: one held poison and the other a potion which could raise mortals from death. At Artemis' request, he used the latter to save **Hippolytus**, and for this **Zeus** struck him dead with a thunderbolt. At once, Apollo began killing the **Cyclopes** who made Zeus' thunderbolts, and Zeus, afraid that he would lose the weapons which guaranteed his power, released Aesculapius from the **Underworld** and gave him all the rights and honours of an immortal.

Aesculapius was worshipped as a healing god and the founder of medicine for 2000 years, and people throughout the Greek and Roman world visited his shrines to be cured of illness. (One such shrine was at Epidaurus, where the theatre was part of a huge complex used for sacred rituals and for entertaining visitors.) The sick spent a night in the temple, and Aesculapius and his daughters Iaso ('healer') and Panacea ('cure-all') were supposed to move amongst them, telling them how they might be healed or even curing them on the spot. After this ceremony, Aesculapius' priests prescribed herbal medicines, or performed operations (though not surgery, which was anathema) to guarantee the cure.
≫→ disease and healing

AESIR
Europe (North)

The Aesir, in Nordic myth, were a vast family of war-gods and creator-gods. The first three, **Odin**, **Vili** and **Ve**, created the universe and everything in it from the corpse of the giant **Ymir**. Other gods joined them – later offspring of their parents **Bor** and **Bestla**, the first beings – and the family mated incestuously to produce still more gods. The chief Aesir were **Baldur**, **Bragi**, **Frigg**, **Heimdall**, **Höd**, **Honir**, **Idun**, **Loki**, **Mimir**, **Sif**, **Thor**, **Tyr** and Vali. They built a citadel, **Asgard**, and defended it against all-comers, particularly the **giants**, who were determined to steal the apples of **immortality** which Idun guarded and which gave the gods supremacy in the universe.

For the war between the Aesir and another group of gods, the Vanir, see **Vanir**.

No one knows the meaning or origin of the word 'Aesir'. In the thirteenth century CE, Snorri Sturluson drew a fanciful derivation from 'Asia', and this led him and others to make genealogical trees relating the Aesir to the gods of ancient Greece – or even to such figures as King **Priam** of Troy: they were the 'lost' Trojans who sailed North after the **Trojan War**, as **Aeneas** sailed South. A more plausible connection is with the root-word for 'ancient', and suggests that Aesir simply means 'Old Ones'.
≫→ creation

AFRICAN MYTH

If, as is currently believed, the earliest human beings came from East Africa, then one might logically expect African myth to include some of the primal ideas borrowed and elaborated by many other systems throughout the world. This may have been the case – a typical example is the idea, widespread in African myth, that the world was made by a single, beneficent deity – but evidence is scanty. In a way which at first seems incredible for a continent with so many thousands of peoples, languages and traditions, African myth is sparse and stark. Taken as a whole, and with a few areas of exception (such as ancient Egypt), the continent is richer in folk-tale than in true myth, more fertile in ritual practice than in the stories and ideas on which it is based.

The reasons are geographical and historical. The size of the continent, and the difficulties of travel in ancient times, tended to isolate communities. Except in huge empires like those along the Congo or Zambezi rivers, or the later Zulu kingdoms in the South, people lived in small groups. A few dozen might speak an entirely different language from their immediate neighbours, and have no contact with them whatever. Myths served single villages or small clusters of communities, and were not codified or systematized, remaining a kind of joint property like gossip or family history. When conquerors came – and the history of Africa for the last 2000 years has been one of continuous imperialism, both internal (as when the Bantu peoples swept into Southern Africa) and external (for example from Rome, Muslim Arabia, Viking and then Christian Europe, China and India) – they either assimilated local peoples into their empires or marginalized them: examples are the Pygmy peoples on the fringes of the equatorial forests or Bush people in the Kalahari desert.

Each of these procedures was damaging to myth. Marginalized communities tended to turn inwards, fighting for survival – as many still do today – and making their rituals and sustaining myths matters of pride-in-identity and above all secret, with the result that when the people disappeared, their myths vanished with them. The imperialists, almost without exception, treated the peoples they assimilated as second-class citizens, and dismissed their myths and practices as primitive. It was no part of the agenda to admit that myths might have serious ethical, philosophical and social point, particularly if the ideas they contained were different from those of the dominant culture. This attitude, which was eagerly shared by many of those assimilated, pushed ancient myths to the side

of the plate (so that former gods turned into the **demons** of the new religions) or off the table altogether (in which case the gods now survive only dimly, in folktale, or are entirely lost).

Surviving African myth – as opposed to a myriad folktales explaining local customs – is concerned largely with two questions: 'Who is God?' and 'Why do mortals die?' In almost all areas, God the creator is a single figure, a father, mother or grandfather (or in one case, **Itherther**, a buffalo). The deity – **Adroa**, **Amma**, **Akongo**, **Juok**, **Libanza**, **Mawu-Lisa**, **Modimo**, **Ngewo**, **Njinji**, **Ruwa**, **Unkulunkulu**, **Wak**, **Woyengi**, **Zanahary** – is a mysterious, amorphous being, creativity itself given energetic purpose. He, she or it makes the world sometimes as an expression of selfness, sometimes out of loneliness. The methods of **creation** are sometimes left unexplained, sometimes given in remarkable detail – **Bumba** vomits everything into existence, **Dxui** becomes each new thing in turn, **Nyambe** gathers created objects like fruit from the Tree of Life, **Ruhanga** dances the universe into being. God sometimes rejoices in the world, but more often comes to regret the way it turns out: **Deng** and **Onyankopon** are pounded, to the point of irritation, by the pole of a woman grinding corn, **Huveane** scrambles away from the world's noise up a series of sky-pegs, **Nyambi** is plagued by a neighbour who copies everything he does.

When it comes to human beings, the stories show a similar kind of unity-through-diversity. We are usually made from mud, and often descended from an original pair of parents such as

Andriambahomanana and **Andriama-hilala**, **Kintu** and **Nambi**, **Mwambu** and **Sela** or **Mwuetsi** and **Morongo**. Our first gift from God is **sex**, and our second is mortality. Sometimes **death** comes as a result of a war in **Heaven** – we are the prey of such demons as **Gauna**, **Ogo** and **Oduduwa** – but more usually it is because God sends fallible **messengers**, and the one which promises us **immortality** arrives later than the one guaranteeing death. **Leza** sends three sealed calabashes, with instructions to the Messenger (Honeybird) not to open the last one – and the results are predictable. In fact, messengers are invariably untrustworthy. **Anansi** and **Legba** are **tricksters** who delight in the confusion they cause by lying; the **Imilozi** give messages by whistling in a language no mortal can understand; **Mulungu** sends his instructions by a messenger-chain so long that they are completely garbled by the time they reach us, as are our prayers to him.

These core-myths are surrounded by others, more mundane. Some explain **thunder** and **lightning** as gods (for example **Sudika-Mbambi** and **Kabundungulu**). Others – **Aigamuxa**, **Haiuri** – tell of spectacular **monsters**, or of **heroes** such as **Ditaolane** and **Dubiaku** who deal with them. What may be one of the oldest of all African myths, the story of **Ataokoloinona**, tells why the human race spends most of its time searching for water. Above all, African myths have a slyness, a wit in the telling which is rivalled in few other systems. **Gu** the blacksmith-god is a lump of stone with a blade for a face. **Heitsi-Eibib**, god of difference, keeps falling over his own feet. Juok quickly tires of making human beings from mud, so he gives them sexual organs and leaves them to get on with it. **Muluku** offers civilized ways first to humans, and then to monkeys because their manners are better. **Imana** builds a universe like a tottering house of cards, and has to spend eternity shoring it up and repairing it to avoid catastrophe. The world of African myth is immense, unpredictable, dangerous – and, in all senses of the word, absurd.

»→ *Abassi and Atai, Ajok, Chuku, Da, Eshu, Holawaka, Kaang, Kalumba, Katonda, Khonvum, Ogun, Olorun, Shango, Wele, Zamba*

AGAMEMNON
Europe (South)

Agamemnon ('very warlike'), in Greek myth, was the son of King **Atreus** of Argos and his queen Aerope, and the brother of **Menelaus**. When their uncle **Thyestes** killed Atreus and took his throne, Agamemnon and Menelaus fled, first to Aetolia and then to Sparta. In Sparta, they married twin princesses: Menelaus married **Helen** (and in due course succeeded to her father's throne in Sparta), Agamemnon married **Clytemnestra**. The Spartans gave Agamemnon an army, and he went back to Argos, killed Thyestes and took his rightful place on his father's throne, ruling from an impregnable citadel built at Mycenae, on a hill from which all Argos could be easily surveyed.

Agamemnon and Iphigenia. Agamemnon and Clytemnestra had four children: **Iphigenia**, **Electra**, **Chrysothemis** and **Orestes**. In a dozen years, they built Argos, and Mycenae its citadel, into two of the most powerful places in Greece. It was natural, therefore, that when **Paris** of Troy stole Helen from Menelaus, the Greeks should ask Agamemnon to lead the huge expedition which was to sack Troy and bring Helen home to Greece. While their fleet assembled at Aulis and prepared to sail, Agamemnon passed his time **hunting**. One day, he shot and killed a magnificent stag, not realizing that it was sacred to the goddess **Artemis**. She retaliated by holding back the winds, becalming the fleet – and when Agamemnon asked the gods what to do (using the prophet **Calchas** as go-between), she said that he could buy back the winds only by sacrificing his daughter Iphigenia. Agamemnon cut the child's throat over Artemis' altar, the winds returned and the Greeks sailed for Troy.

Agamemnon at Troy. During most of the **Trojan War**, Agamemnon showed true qualities of leadership, fighting bravely and guiding his unruly army of **heroes** with a firm hand. But as the siege dragged into its tenth year, his sureness of touch deserted him. He and **Achilles**, the greatest and touchiest of the Greek heroes, were allotted twin sisters as prisoners-of-war, Briseis and Chryseis, and when their father, the priest Chryses, demanded her back, Agamemnon commandeered Briseis from Achilles. In the flurry of sulking and recrimination which followed, he lost so much face that he surrendered control to his fellow-warlords (notably Menelaus and **Odysseus**). After the sack of Troy, his share of the spoils included **Cassandra**, the prophetess daughter of King **Priam** – and he shipped her home to Mycenae despite warnings that both she and he would die there.

Agamemnon's death. In Mycenae, Clytemnestra had spent the ten years of the war planning revenge for Agamemnon's murder of Iphigenia. She had taken as lover Agamemnon's cousin **Aegisthus**, and when Agamemnon's ships arrived she went to meet him at the Lion Gate of Mycenae, unrolling a red carpet in pretended welcome. She took him to the bath-house, tangled him in the blood-red cloth, and beckoned Aegisthus from the shadows to butcher him with a double-headed axe.

In the myth-cycle of Argos, Agamemnon is actually one of the least important or active figures: a figurehead king whose rank and position are more significant than anything he does. Importance attaches more to his father Atreus, to his uncle Thyestes, to his wife Clytemnestra, and to his children Electra and Orestes. But successive generations of Greek writers, from Homer to Aeschylus, Sophocles and Euripides, made him a focal point of both the Trojan War and the tangled account of what happened after he went home to Argos. In the Iliad, the Oresteia and Euripides' Trojan-War-set plays – not to mention such later accounts as Shakespeare's Troilus and Cressida – he is memorable chiefly for pomp and circumstance, shading into pomposity, and in Sophocles' Electra and Euripides' Argos-set plays he is a kind of totem of kingliness, used by Electra and Orestes as the model of all fine fathers unjustly slain, and as the trigger for nobility in others. Only Euripides' Iphigenia in Aulis, which deals with the events leading up to the sacrifice of Iphigenia, gives him.

anything like a truly tragic dilemma or depth of personality. Similarly, in art, he is often the gaudiest and grandest person in a painting, but seldom the most significant.

AGASTYA
India

Agastya (or Agasti), in the Vedic myths of the Aryan people who invaded India in the seventeenth century BCE, was the son of not one but two fathers, **Varuna** and **Mithra** (or some say **Surya**). One day they were so enraptured by the dancing of beautiful **Urvashi** that they had orgasms on the spot. Their semen was gathered and stored in a jar, and Agastya grew from it. He was not a god but a sage, and he became a kind of heavenly historian, writing the gods' stories down and passing them to mortals in the form of the **Rig Veda**.

Agastya was the implacable enemy of **demons**. Once, realizing that demons were hiding from him in the primordial ocean, he drank it, and they crept out of their muddy holes, cowering and blinking in the sunlight. He penned a horde of demons in Southern India, erecting a **mountain**-chain round them as a mortal might make a mud-fence to keep in cattle. He sheltered **Rama**, **Sita** and **Lakshmana** when they were exiled in the Dandaka Forest, and he lent Rama the fearsome weapon, the 'arrow of Brahma', which killed the demon-king **Ravana**.

AGAVE
Europe (South)

Agave (Agaue, 'princess'), in Greek myth, was the daughter of **Cadmus** and Harmony. She helped to bring up the infant **Dionysus** (son of **Zeus** and her sister **Semele**), and later married Echion (one of the **Sown Men**) and became queen of Thebes. After Echion's death their son **Pentheus** inherited the Theban throne, and Agave ruled with him as queen mother. Some years later, Dionysus returned to the city, bringing his ecstatic religion, and Agave became one of his first followers, leading the women of Thebes in dancing and ritual worship on Mount Cithaeron. Pentheus resisted the god, who took him to the mountain and told the women that he was a wild animal and a spy. Agave led the women in tearing Pentheus to pieces; she spiked his head on a pole and danced with it all the way back to Thebes – and it was only when she entered the city gates that the trance left her and she realized what she'd done. She fled to Illyria, where she married King Lycotherses. Many years later, when the aged Cadmus and Harmony left Thebes and wandered the world looking for a place to end their lives on earth, she took them in, and it was here that they, and she, shed their mortality and ascended to **Olympus**.

AGES OF BRAHMA
India

Numerologists of the Brahmanic religion, working in the 600s BCE, held that eternity is measured in years of **Brahma**'s life, which is eternal but is itself part of the cycle. Each turn of the wheel of eternity takes 100 years of Brahma's life (157,680 million mortal years). Each turn is followed by another

100 Brahmanic years of chaos (absence of *brahman*, the 'power which is in everything'), after which Brahma is reborn and the cycle begins again.

So far as the universe is concerned, each cycle of its existence, from **creation** to dissolution, is equal to a single day of Brahma's life, the time between him waking and sleeping: 4,320 million mortal years. This period is divided into four ages, each of them only three-quarters as long as the one before. The first age (1,728 million mortal years) is a time of virtue and contentment, during which **Dharma** god of justice walks on all four legs, created beings live in harmony and God is the colour of snow. The second age (1,296 million mortal years) is one quarter less virtuous and contented. Dharma walks on three legs, created beings are occasionally quarrelsome and God is the colour of fire. The third age (972,000 mortal years) is one quarter less contented. Dharma hobbles on two legs, created beings are discontented, God is the yellow of snake's venom and only the spiritual exercises of the devout maintain the world in harmony. The fourth age (432,000 mortal years), the one in which we currently live, is one of violence, quarrels and injustice. Dharma hops on a single leg, created beings have lost all integrity and God is the colour of tar. At the end of the fourth age, the world will be destroyed, all creation will be absorbed into *brahman* and there will be 4,320 million years of nothing (during which Brahma sleeps) before creation recurs and the cycle begins again.

AGNAR
Europe (North)

Agnar, in Nordic myth, was deprived of his father's throne by his younger brother **Geirröd**, who thought he had killed him by pushing him out to sea in a storm. But Agnar survived, returned to Geirröd's court disguised as a servant, and helped Grimnir (the god **Odin** in disguise) when Geirröd tortured him. For this Odin rewarded him by bringing about Geirröd's death and giving Agnar his rightful throne.

AGNI
India

Agni ('Fire') came to India in the Vedic period (seventeenth century BCE), perhaps from ancient Iran. His power equalled that of **Indra** and **Varuna**, and he had a thousand names, including Abhimani ('proud'), Grihaspati ('master of the house'), Pramati ('forethought'), Tanunapat ('ever-young') and Vaicnavara ('belongs to all'). He was the god of all **fire**, from **lightning** to the heat of inspiration, from the hearth-fire to the blaze of anger and the warmth which creates good digestion.

Agni's nature and powers. Above all else, Agni was the guardian of sacrifice and a mediator between gods and mortals. He sent columns of smoke to guide the gods to the place of sacrifice (and was the mouth which ate the offerings for them); he gathered the souls of mortals from funeral pyres, and carried them to **Heaven**. Because he himself was reborn each time he was kindled, he was the god of **immortality**. He created the **Sun** and stars, and hung them in the sky; he made smoke-pillars to support the firmament. He cleansed impurities, eradicated sin – and, on a more practical level, made implacable war on **demons**, creatures of dark and water: as soon as his piercing eyes saw them, he chased them, licked them up and swallowed them alive. He was hot-tempered: if you poked a **fire**, you disturbed him, making him grumble or flare into sudden rage.

Agni's birth. Agni was thrice-born: first from **water**, as the Sun is born from the **sea**; second in Air, as **lightning**; third on Earth, as humans kindled him everywhere. Some accounts are more specific: **Brahma** created him by rubbing a lotus-blossom, or Indra made him by striking a stone against the Thunderstone to make a spark, or he was made when two dry sticks were rubbed together (and was thus life created out of death). The commonest account says that he was made from the mating of **Privithi** (**Mother Earth**) and **Dyaus** (Father Sky), and was Indra's brother. Like Indra, he was born full-grown, and he was insatiably hungry. He ate his parents, and then, unsatisfied, grew seven tongues and began lapping purified butter from the sacrificial altar – a practice he continued ever afterwards, wherever sacrifice was made. In one story, he ate so much – or drank so much **soma** – that he exhausted himself, and was able to recover only by eating the huge Khandava Forest and everything in it – a feat which he still regularly equals, in forest-fires throughout the world.

Agni and Brighu. In one story, Agni was not born insatiable but was cursed with all-hunger by the sage Brighu. Brighu stole Puloma, a beautiful woman betrothed to a demon – and Agni, who sees and knows everything, told the demon where she was hidden. Brighu cursed Agni, saying that he would eat everything in the universe, pure or impure, and would never be satisfied. Agni objected that all he'd done was answer the demon's questions, and asked Brighu if he'd rather the mouth of the gods told lies. Brighu relented and changed the curse. Agni was still condemned insatiably to bite, and consume, everything put before him; but since the mouth of the god was all-pure, everything he ate would be purified as soon as it touched his jaws. Agni and impurity could never coexist. At the end of the world, the myth ends, Agni will surge from the **Underworld** and lick up all **creation**. There will be no more darkness, no more secrets; truth will prevail.

*Agni is a favourite subject for poets, and some of the more fanciful descriptions above come from the **Rig Veda**, and from flights of metaphor in the **Mahabharata** and **Ramayana**. In art he is shown as a red-fleshed, smoke-robed prince who rides a sacred ram or a wind-wheeled chariot drawn by flame-red horses. His back and face glisten gold with butter; his hair is flames; his two faces each have seven tongues, knife-jaws, gold teeth and flames arrowing from his mouths. Sometimes he has three arms, sometimes four; he carries a bundle of fruit, an axe, fan, torch and ladle. He has seven legs, and his body sends out seven rays of light. One myth tells how he* changed his appearance to fight the flesh-eating demons the Kravyads. For this exploit he became a Kravyad himself, a bull with a boar's head armed with iron tusks – and some art-works show him in this uncompromising aspect.

≫→ light and dark

AGWE
Americas (Caribbean)

Agwe ('water'), in Voodoo myth, is the god of salt and fresh **water**. He and his mermaid-consort La Sirene live in a palace on the underwater island of Z'ile Minfort. They are propitiated by an annual ceremony of feasting, dancing, and the sacrifice of a blue-dyed ram and a banquet, laid on a bed-shaped altar and slid into the water for Agwe and La Sirene to sleep on and guarantee prosperity for the coming year.

AH PUCH
Americas (South)

Ah Puch, in Mayan myth, was the god of **death**, a **demon** who ruled the deepest and darkest of the nine Underworlds. In the **Underworld** he had no shape, but every night, when darkness made it possible for him to visit the Upper World, he took the form of a putrefying, walking corpse and padded round the houses of mortals, knife at the ready, looking for victims. For this reason, relatives of sick and dying people used to leave food outside the sickroom door to distract Ah Puch's attention, and shrieked and howled to make him think that other demons had fallen on his prey before him.

AHRIMAN
Asia (West)

Ahriman (a contraction of Angra Mainya, 'destructive force'), in Iranian myth, was the power of darkness, leader of **demons**, **twin** and implacable opponent of **Ahura Mazda**, lord of light. He had no good qualities whatever. When he was still in the womb of the primeval being **Zurvan Akarana**, sharing it with Ahura Mazda, he overheard Zurvan Akarana saying 'the firstborn will be greatest' – and at once ripped the womb apart and jostled into the world ahead of Ahura Mazda. He created and ruled all the destructive forces in the universe, and used storms, disease and **death** to try to force Ahura Mazda's human worshippers to abandon light and worship him instead.

For all this, Zoroaster taught, Ahriman was essential for the continued existence and harmony of the universe. For if darkness did not exist, how we would understand the true nature of light, or how to value it?

≫→ light and dark, twins

AHSONNUTLI
Americas (North)

Ahsonnutli, in the myths of the Navajo people of the US Southwestern desert, created Earth and **Sky**, and kept them apart by propping Sky on four **giants**, one at each main compass point. (The giants' panting as they bore Sky's weight caused winds and storms.) Ahsonnutli was originally mortal, but mated with the shape-changing Turquoise Woman (a being who could throw off mortality like a dress, as often as she wanted, and assume a new life and identity). **Sex with her gave him a share of her immortality**, and to enjoy it in peace he withdrew to a remote palace far above Sky, where he still lives in solitude, keeping apart from all other gods and humans.

➤➤ **creation**

AHTO
Europe (North)

Ahto ('**water**') or Ahti, in Finnish myth, was the god of seas, lakes and rivers. His palace was the hollow heart of a black cliff curtained by clouds and protected by waves. Forever jealous of the gods of the **sky**, he spent his time brooding, and because human beings prayed to the sky-gods and not to him, he sent his servants, whirlpools, genies and water-sprites, to harry them.

➤➤ **sea**

AHURA MAZDA
Asia (West)

Ahura Mazda ('creative light'), in Iranian myth, was the ruler of the universe. He was the **twin** of **Ahriman**, and was his opposite in every way: light instead of dark, calmness instead of fury, giving instead of taking, forgiveness instead of implacability. He created human beings, whereas Ahriman sought to destroy them. When Ahriman sent his three-headed dragon **Azhi Dahaka** to eat the universe, Ahura Mazda created his own son, **Atar**, **fire**, and sent him to fight for the powers of light.

In the Zoroastrian religion, Ahura Mazda's name is contracted to Ormahzd.

➤➤ **creation, light and dark, twins**

AIGAMUXA
Africa

Aigamuxa, in the myths of the Khoisan (Hottentot) peoples of the Southern African deserts, were man-eating **monsters**. They were hampered in chasing their victims because their eyes were not in their heads but in their insteps, so that they had to run blind, and when they wanted to see where they were going they had to lie on the sand and lift up their feet, during which time their prey could easily escape.

AIOMUM KONDI
Americas (South)

Aiomum Kondi, in the myths of the Arawak people of the Guianas, was king of the gods and ruler of the **sky**. He created mortals in the image of the gods, but was so disgusted by their debauchery that he destroyed them in a fire from **Heaven**. He remade them, and once again they disappointed him and he sent a flood to wash them from Earth. However, this time there was one good man, Marerewana, and he and his wife were allowed to survive the flood and regenerate the human race. This is why good and evil are permanent characteristics of human beings, alone of all earthly creatures – and the presence of evil in the world is why Aiomum Kondi, and the rest of the gods, nowadays take so little interest in it.

➤➤ **supreme deity**

AIRAVATA
India

Airavata (or Airavana), in the Vedic myths of the Aryan people who invaded India in the seventeenth century BCE, was a four-tusked, white elephant as big as snow-capped Mount Kailasa (site of **Shiva**'s palace on Earth). Two different accounts are given of its birth and functions. In one, it was created from the churning of the Sea of Milk (see **amrita**), and was immediately appropriated by **Indra** as his war-steed. It was a cloud-creature, and when Indra rode it, it sucked trunksful of water from the **Underworld** and sprayed them on Earth as rain. In the other account, Airavata was created by **Brahma**. He broke an egg, holding half the shell in each hand. From the right-hand half he made eight male elephants, led by Airavata: they had four tusks each, and their hides were as milky as egg-white. From the left-hand half he made eight female elephants, their mates. Brahma set the sixteen elephants to support the Earth: one pair at each of the eight main compass-points.

AJAX, 'GREAT'
Europe (South)

'Great' or 'Telamonian' Ajax (Aias, 'earthman') – so-called, in Greek myth, to distinguish him from 'Little' Ajax – was the son of King Telamon of Salamis. **Heracles**, a friend of his father, visited Salamis for Ajax's naming feast, and gave him the gift of heroic strength, by wrapping him in his cloak made from the skin of the **Nemean Lion**. Wherever the cloak touched Ajax's skin, he could not be hurt by mortal weapons; only one armpit (where Heracles' quiver got in the way) was vulnerable.

Ajax in the Trojan War. Ajax grew up to be one of the strongest and ablest warrior-princes in Greece. At Troy, his feats of arms were surpassed only by **Achilles**, and the Greeks nicknamed him 'Wall'. On one occasion, he fought **Hector** single-handed. The duel lasted all day, and the pair were so evenly matched that neither disturbed even a hair on the other's body. At last, as dusk fell, they agreed to part, and gave each other presents: Hector gave Ajax a sword, and Ajax gave Hector a baldrick of purple leather. The **Fates** were watching, and later involved each gift in its new owner's death. When Achilles killed Hector and dragged him after his chariot round the walls of Troy, he used Ajax's baldrick to fasten his corpse to the chariot. When Ajax killed himself (see below) it was with Hector's sword.

Ajax's death. After the distribution of spoils which followed the fall of Troy, the goddess **Thetis** (Achilles' mother) added another treasure: the armour **Hephaestus** had made in **Heaven** for her son. Because Achilles' son **Neoptolemus** was too young to wear it, she offered it to the bravest Greek hero still left alive. Everyone agreed that the choice was between Ajax (who had carried Achilles' body back from the walls of Troy) and **Odysseus** (who had protected him while he did so). **Agamemnon** asked each hero to make his case before the assembled leaders, and Ajax (who was as slow with words as he was quick with weapons) was no match for the plausible Odysseus.

Odysseus was awarded the armour, and the humiliation of being rejected sent Ajax mad. He buckled on his own armour, snatched up the sword Hector had given him, and went to butcher all the Greek leaders in their beds. But all he attacked, in his madness, was a flock of sheep, and when his wits came back and he found himself surrounded by their carcasses, he stuck Hector's sword point-upwards in the ground and fell on it, trying to commit suicide. At first the point would not pierce his invulnerable skin. But his repeated efforts bent the sword into a bow-shape, and its point slipped upwards into his one vulnerable part (his armpit) and pierced his heart. Years later, when Odysseus visited the **Underworld** and met all his dead companions from the **Trojan War**, Ajax's ghost was still blazing with rage because of Achilles' armour, and refused to speak to him.

AJAX, 'LITTLE'
Europe (South)

'Little' Ajax (Aias, 'earthman') – so-called, in Greek myth, to distinguish him from 'Great' Ajax – was the son of King Oileus of Locris. He was one of the unsuccessful suitors of **Helen** of Sparta, and later took forty ships and an army of soldiers to Troy to help win her back from **Paris**. During the sack of Troy, he found **Cassandra** in **Athene**'s temple, clinging for safety to the holy statue. He dragged her out to rape her, and in the struggle pulled the statue from its pedestal. Athene, furious, borrowed one of **Zeus**' thunderbolts and blasted him dead. His soldiers took his ashes home and buried them on the island of Mykonos.

Not surprisingly, many accounts confuse the two Ajaxes, saying that it was 'Great' Ajax who raped Cassandra and that it was to punish him for this that Athene drove him mad after he failed to win Achilles' armour. Some scholars think that the story of 'Little' Ajax was invented in Locris, to explain a curious custom there. Even though Athene killed Ajax with a thunderbolt, she was still not satisfied. She sent plague on Locris, and lifted it only when the people agreed to send two girls to her temple in Troy – the new Troy, built from the ruins of the city sacked by the Greeks – each year for a thousand years. The girls had to climb secretly into Troy, make offerings in Athene's temple and then become temple slaves. If they were caught before they reached the temple, they were stoned to death.

AJISUKITAKAHIKONE
Asia (East)

Ajisukitakahikone, in Japanese myth, was the chief of many **thunder**-spirits, and the father of Takitsuhiko, Lord of Pouring **Rain**. When he was a baby he was so noisy that his nurses carried him up and down a flight of steps to soothe him, and then put him in a boat to sail endlessly round and round Japan – which is why thunder seems to approach and recede.
≫→ **Raiden and Raiju**

AJOK
Africa

Ajok (or Adyok or Naijok), creator-god in the myths of the Sudanese Lotuko people, made human beings in his own image. When the child of the first human pair died, the woman begged him to bring it back to life. Ajok did so, and was preparing to grant it and all its descendants **immortality** when the child's father burst in. Furious that he had not been consulted, he killed his wife and baby – and Ajok was so annoyed that he left **death** to prey forever on human beings and never visited Earth again.

»→ creation

AJYSYT
Arctic

Ajysyt ('birthgiver'), in the myths of the Yakuts people of Siberia, owned the Golden Book of **Fate**, containing the names and destinies of every human being ever born. At the instant of each new birth, she gave the baby a soul and entered its name in the book – and the child was from then on a fully-fledged member of the human race, equipped with all our potential, both for good and ill.

AKKA
Europe (North)

Akka ('old woman'), in Finnish myth, was queen of the gods, consort of **Ukko**. Like Ukko, she did nothing active in the world, and stayed aloof from it. But her existence was essential to its continuation, guaranteeing the stability of marriage, family and society among human beings. Her sacred tree was the mountain-ash (after which she was also called Rauni, 'rowan'), and people planted single trees beside their houses to honour her and ask her blessing.

»→ justice and universal order

AKONGO
Africa

Akongo, supreme Sky-spirit in the myths of the Ngombe people of the river Congo, created human beings and regretted it. In some accounts, he lived with them on Earth until he could no longer stand their quarrelling, then moved away, either deep into the forest or up into the sky. In others, there were just two human beings and he shared his hut in **Heaven** with them; when they started arguing he lowered them on a rope to the as yet uninhabited Earth, giving them maize and sugarcane to plant and pulling up the rope as soon as they were safely down. In this version the two humans mated and had a daughter, who ran into the forest and had sex with the first wild animal that came along – the origin of every witch and demon on Earth, and yet another reason for Akongo to disdain his offspring.

»→ creation, supreme deity

ALBERICH: *see* Andvari

ALBION
Europe (North)

Albion ('white'), in Celtic myth, was a **giant** who took part in the epic battle against the **Olympian** gods, escaped being killed by **Heracles** and fled to the remote islands later known as Britain. He took with him one of the golden apples of **immortality**, and planted an apple-tree in his new kingdom. But he quickly tired of life in a backwater, went on a recruiting-drive South to gather a second giant-army to attack the gods, met Heracles and was killed by him.

This story survives principally in Geoffrey of Monmouth's twelfth-century History of the Kings of Britain, *and is a characteristic medieval attempt to marry the shreds of surviving indigenous myth (in this case Celtic) with lore distantly and imperfectly remembered from monkish classical education (in this case the story of the Greek giants' revolt against the gods). Albion was the original name for the islands; the name 'Britain' came later, and the myth of* **Brit** *– a similar farrago of half-digested pagan lore – was invented to explain it.*

ALCINOUS
Europe (South)

Alcinous (Alkinoös, 'strong-mind'), in Greek myth, was the King of Phaeacia and father of **Nausicaä**. When **Odysseus** was washed up on the shores of his kingdom, he welcomed him, listened to the story of his wanderings, and then gave a ship and a crew to carry him home to Ithaca.

ALCMAEON
Europe (South)

Alcmaeon and Eriphyle. Alcmaeon (Alkmaion, 'mighty endeavour'), in Greek myth, was the son of Princess **Eriphyle** of Argos and the prophet Amphiaraus who was one of the **Seven Against Thebes**. When **Polynices**' son Thesander was collecting a second group of heroes, the Epigoni, the gods told him that the expedition would fail unless Alcmaeon led it. Alcmaeon was reluctant to fight, just as his father had been before him – and, just as his father had done, agreed to leave the decision to Eriphyle. Thesander bribed her with the golden wedding-dress made by the gods for Harmony when she married

Cadmus years before, and Eriphyle sent Alcmaeon to war.

Alcmaeon knew nothing of the bribery until Thesander boasted about it after the fall of Thebes. He asked the Delphic oracle what the punishment was for a woman who took gold to send her husband and son to war, and the oracle answered '**Death**'. Alcmaeon murdered his mother, and the **Furies** drove him mad for it. He wandered all over Greece in search of purification. King Phegeus of Psophis helped him, and in gratitude he married Phegeus' daughter Arsinoe and gave her Harmony's golden dress and necklace. But then the Furies returned, and Alcmaeon forgot Arsinoe and began his wanderings again. Before she died Eriphyle had cursed him, saying that he would never find purification on any land then existing. The gods guided him to a patch of new land, sand washed down since Eriphyle's death by the river **Achelous**; there Alcmaeon was purified at last from madness, and married the river-god's daughter Callirrhoe.

Alcmaeon and Callirrhoe. Alcmaeon and Callirrhoe had two sons. But then, like Eriphyle before her, Callirrhoe began to fear that she would grow ugly as she grew older. She refused to sleep with Alcmaeon unless he gave her Harmony's dress and necklace, which guaranteed eternal youth. Alcmaeon had to go to Psophis and steal them from Arsinoe, the wife he had long ago abandoned – and on the way home he was ambushed by Phegeus' sons and killed. Arsinoe, now truly a widow, cursed her father Phegeus and her brothers, and prayed to the gods to kill them before the next moon waned. Phegeus punished her for this by locking her in a box and selling her into slavery.

Meanwhile, word reached Callirrhoe of Alcmaeon's death, and she prayed to **Zeus** that her baby sons might grow to manhood in a single day and avenge him. Zeus granted her prayer. The babies jumped out of their cradle, turned into grown men before they touched the ground, went to Psophis and killed Phegeus and his sons. Harmony's golden dress and necklace were given for safety to the priests of **Apollo**, and lay for centuries in one of the treasuries at Delphi.

ALCMENA
Europe (South)

Alcmena (Alkmene, 'mighty in anger'), in Greek myth, was the daughter of King Electryon of Argos, and the wife of his heir **Amphitryon**. Electryon's cattle had all been stolen, and his eight sons murdered, by King Pterelaus of the Teleboans, and Amphitryon set out to take revenge. While he was away, **Zeus** took advantage and seduced Alcmena.

There was more to this seduction than the lust which normally inspired Zeus' affairs on Earth. After the gods defeated the **Titans** and became lords of the universe, they had successfully defended themselves against **giants**, **monsters** and supernatural creatures of every kind. But Zeus knew that however powerful the Olympians were, **Mother Earth**'s relatives Ocean, Night and **Chaos** still lurked in the recesses of the universe, and that one day gods and mortals could be swept away just as Zeus and his brothers had displaced

the Titans. He had decided therefore to create a son, a **hero** who would combine the finest qualities of gods and mortals, who would act as the gods' champion, defy the world of darkness and keep its creatures cowed.

It was to be the mother of such a champion that Zeus chose Alcmena, the noblest of all mortal women. And since he knew that she would never betray Amphitryon to make love with anyone else, he waited until Amphitryon was far from Argos, fighting the Teleboans, then disguised himself as Amphitryon, pretended he had come successfully home from the expedition, and made love to Alcmena in Amphitryon's place. The love-making lasted for three mortal nights: Zeus made the **Sun** stable his horses and stay at home, while the **Moon** lingered and Sleep sealed mortal eyes. Human beings leapt up refreshed after their three-day sleep – and in the meantime the real Amphitryon finished his business with the Teleboans, hurried home and replaced Zeus in Alcmena's bed without anyone knowing that the ruler of the universe had ever usurped him there.

No one would have been any the wiser until the birth of the child, except that on the morning the baby was due Zeus boasted that everyone in Argos would be subordinate to the next prince born there. At once **Hera** realized what had happened. She sent **Ilythia**, goddess of **childbirth**, to hold back the birth, and Ilythia sat outside Alcmena's door and clasped her hands tightly round her knees. This spell prevented Alcmena from giving birth, and in the meantime Hera helped another Argive princess, Nicippe, to give

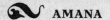

birth to a seven-months' child. (His name was **Eurystheus**, and as soon as he was born, Zeus' prophecy came true for him.)

There was still the matter of Alcmena's unending pregnancy. Hera meant to leave Ilythia sitting on guard until Alcmena and her unborn child died of starvation. But Alcmena's maidservant Galanthis ran in shouting 'A boy! A boy!' She was reporting Eurystheus' birth, but Ilythia mistook her meaning, jumped up and broke the binding-spell. Angrily she changed Galanthis into a weasel; but she was too late to stop Alcmena giving birth at last, to **twins**: **Iphicles**, the mortal son of Amphitryon, and **Heracles**, the son of Zeus.

*This was a favourite story in ancient times – but only in comedy. Comic dramatists and poets found irresistible the idea of two Amphitryons, one false one real, rushing round the palace and trying to get into Alcmena's bed, and several writers – notably Plautus, who wrote the most influential version of the story – treated it from the point of view of the confidential slave of the real Amphitryon, totally confused by having two masters he couldn't tell apart. In other versions **Hermes** muddied the waters still further by disguising himself as the slave in question, so that confusion was doubly confused: the origin of a thousand such mistaken-identity farces in later European drama.*

ALKLHA
Arctic

Alklha, in the myths of ancient Siberia, was the darkness of the **sky**. It was a

universe-filling **monster** whose wings and body were impenetrable blackness and which fed itself by gnawing and swallowing the **Moon** each month – and the **Sun** whenever it got the chance. Since both heavenly bodies were hot, they seared Alklha's gullet and guts, and the monster regurgitated them. We can see the gashes of Alklha's fangs on the Moon, and they would also be visible on the Sun if we could bear to look at it. ⋙→ **light and dark, monsters and dragons**

ALVIS
Europe (North)

Alvis, in Nordic myth, was a dwarf who rashly asked to marry **Thor**'s daughter Thrud. Normally Thor challenged all Thrud's suitors to trials of strength, and easily defeated them. But in Alvis' case, Thor challenged him to a riddle-contest. He spent the whole night asking him questions until day dawned, the rising Sun turned Alvis to stone and Thrud remained unmarried.

AMANA
Americas (South)

Amana, in the myths of the Caliña people, was the first being in the universe. Her **sea**-kingdom was the Milky Way, and its fish, whales, seals, otters and other **water**-creatures danced with her through the waters, while she rode on Turtle's back with her mermaid-tail streaming behind her like weed in the vastness.

The floor of Amana's kingdom was not sand but darkness, the gulf of space. From time to time volcanoes erupted from it, and the streams of spat-out rock floated in space as planets. Amana covered them with plants and creatures. All would have been serene and calm if it had not been for her very first creation, **Sun**. Eternal enemy of water, he fought to destroy both Amana and her creatures wherever she made them. He scorched life from most of the planets – we can still see the ashes of the cosmic fire which engulfed the **Moon** – and was prevented from destroying the most beautiful of all, Earth, only because Amana waited until he attacked in a huge fireball, then trapped the fireball in ocean. The fireball has seethed under the surface ever since, occasionally erupting in geysers and volcanoes sending their serpents of fire to scorch the land. To keep Sun's power at bay, and to allow herself to sail her sky-ocean without taking heed of Earth, Amana made two warriors, **Tamusi** (Light) and **Tamulu** (Darkness), and sent them to look after it.

≫→ creation, light and dark

AMATERASU
Asia (East)

Amaterasu's birth. Amaterasu, goddess of the **Sun** in Japanese myth, was Izanagi's daughter (see **Izanami and Izanagi**). When Izanagi came back to the world of light from **Yomi**, the **Underworld** (where he had gone, in vain, to bring his sister Izanami back from death), he stripped off his clothes and washed to remove the dust of the grave. When he took off his clothes twelve deities were created, when he scrubbed his body ten more appeared, and when he washed his face three great gods

were born (in some accounts from the water-drops which fell back into the basin, in others as points of light from the mirror he used to see what he was doing): **Susano** the storm-god from his nose, **Tsukuyomi** the **Moon** from his right eye and Amaterasu from his left eye. Izanagi gave Susano the sea to rule, and made Tsukuyomi and Amaterasu rulers, respectively, of night and day. Amaterasu's symbol of office was a necklace of light, the Milky Way, and her clothes (which she wove herself: the first garments ever made) were sewn with jewels, her radiance made into precious stones.

Amaterasu and Susano. Susano, furious at being supplanted by his sister, raged about the Earth so violently that seas dried up and mountains withered. Izanagi banished him to the Underworld, granting him just one favour before he left the world of light: to say goodbye to Amaterasu in **Heaven**. Susano now tricked Amaterasu. He pretended to be attacking Heaven, and when she reluctantly armed herself to fight him, said innocently that she was the aggressor, that he'd come in peace and that they should both perform wonders to prove their good faith. If her magic proved stronger than his, he'd go to the Underworld. If his proved stronger than hers, he'd stay with her in Heaven forever. He handed over his sword, and she gave him a hairband of five strung stars. Amaterasu broke the sword in three, chewed the pieces in her mouth and spat them out; they turned into three goddesses who (because they were made from Susano's sword) were sent to spend eternity on Earth. Susano washed the five stars in the Heaven-well of Eternal Life, crunched them in his mouth and spat out five gods; since these were made from Amaterasu's stars, they became rulers in Heaven.

Amaterasu and the Seasons. Amaterasu was by nature gentle and retiring. Her main activities were farming silkworms and spinning and weaving the resulting thread – skills she introduced to human beings. She was happy to let Susano racket round Heaven, so long as he left her and her maids in peace. But Susano wanted more attention. He hammered on the doors and howled through the windows of the weaving-house. When Amaterasu went to celebrate the feast of first fruits, Susano hurried to the temple ahead of her, and fouled the entire floor with dung. Finally, seeing Amaterasu alone in the weaving-house with her servant – or, in some accounts, with her sister the dawn-goddess Wakahirume – he killed one of the Horses of Heaven, flayed it and threw the carcass in the air so that it crashed through the roof and flopped to the floor. Amaterasu's servant jumped back in terror, and the shuttle of her loom stabbed her in the vagina and killed her. Driven out of patience at last, Amaterasu barricaded herself in a cave and refused to come out.

Amaterasu's exile deprived the universe of light – and with it, of growth and life. The eight hundred myriad gods tried unsuccessfully to persuade her to come out. They held a council on the banks of the Heaven-river, and Omoigane, god of wisdom, suggested a trick. He told the Heavenly Jewelmaster to make a star-necklace two metres long, the Heavenly Coppersmith to make a polished mirror and the others to plant *sakati* trees outside the cave-mouth and hang on the branches not only the necklace and mirror but strips of coloured cloth, prayer-scrolls and precious stones. Finally, he told **Uzume** the dancer to perform, and the other gods to make as much noise as they could. The gods sang and stamped their feet, Uzume's dancing grew more and more lascivious, the gods laughed louder and louder, and eventually Amaterasu moved aside one of the boulders blocking the cave-entrance – the light which emerged was the origin of the first dawn-light each day – and asked how they could be so happy when light was denied the world. Omoigane answered that it was simple: they'd found a god more radiant than she was, and were celebrating. Amaterasu pulled away a few more stones, saw her own reflection in the mirror hung on the tree, and came a little way out of the cave to see more. At once the Strong God dragged her fully out, the other gods strung a rope across the entrance to stop her going back, and two of the Elder Gods took her hands and begged her never to leave again.

Amaterasu's return brought light and **fertility** back to the world, and she marked it by showing human beings how to grow and cook rice. As for Susano, the Court of Heaven fined him, cut off his beard, fingernails and toenails and banished him to Earth.

Amaterasu and the Imperial Family. Susano's departure restored peace to Heaven. Although the time which then passed was the blink of an eye to gods, on Earth it took many

human generations, during which Susano's half-human, half-**monster** offspring ruled. Then Amaterasu
decided that Heavenly calm should
be given to Earth as well, and asked
her son Amenoosimasa to go there
and rule. He refused, saying that he'd
just had a son of his own and had
responsibilities in Heaven. Amaterasu
sent another god, Amenohohi, and
when no news came back of him
she asked his son Amenowakahiko
to find out what had happened. But
Amenowakahiko married one of Susano's descendants, and paid no more
attention to Heaven. Amaterasu sent a
pheasant-**messenger** to ask for news,
and he shot it dead. Finally Amaterasu
sent **Ninigi**, and gave him the mirror
and necklace the gods had made to
entice her from the cave, and the
Heaven-sword Kusanagi. Carrying
these emblems, Ninigi was escorted
to Earth in majesty, and was accepted
as ruler. He founded the Imperial
dynasty – and with their coming,
the story ends, the period of myth
ended and the cycle of history began.

*The Amaterasu story lies at the heart of
the symbiosis of Shinto worship and the
politics and social order of Imperial Japan. Scholars from outside Japan see it
as an amalgamation of ancient myths –
among the very few in the world in which
the Sun is not male but female – legend and
straightforward annalistic history. But in
Japan, the interpenetration of religion
and history was for centuries so powerful
that heads of the Imperial family continued
to be regarded by many people as gods,
direct lineal descendants of Amaterasu,
until Emperor Hirohito renounced this status after the Second World War. The cen-
trality of Amaterasu makes her story one of
the most often illustrated in all Japanese art,
with a wealth of iconography – peacocks,
pigs, gambolling monkeys, symbolic patterns of pebbles on the ground and
branches on the trees – not present in
myth-illustrations of other kinds.*
⫸ **Great Goddess**

AMAZONS
Europe (South)

The Amazons, in Greek myth, were
warrior women, descended from **Ares**
god of war. Their name either means
'without a breast', and refers to their
(alleged) custom of cutting off one
breast so that they could more easily
sling their quivers (they were expert
archers); or it means 'without cereal
food', and refers to their (alleged) cannibalism. The Amazons lived on the
shores of Ocean, the river which girds
the Earth, and waited for unwary sailors.
When the ships landed, they welcomed
the sailors, had **sex** with them, killed
them and ate them. Very few heroes in
myth, apart from **Heracles** and **Theseus**, visited them and lived to tell the
tale.

The Amazons seldom visited the
rest of the world, and when they did
they were usually defeated. Princess
Penthesilea, for example, fought on
Priam's side in the **Trojan war** until
she was killed by **Achilles**, and Princess **Antiope** (whom Theseus had
taken to Athens as his mistress)
called an Amazon army to attack
Athens and kill Theseus after he
abandoned her for **Phaedra**, but the
Athenians defeated them.

AMBALIKA
India

Ambalika, in Hindu myth, was a queen whose husband Vichitravirya died before he could give her children. (She was senior to her fellow-queen **Ambika**.) As custom was, she agreed to let his brother father her child instead. She expected to entertain her handsome brother-in-law **Bhisma**, but instead found **Vyasa**, a filthy hermit, in her bed. She turned pale with horror – and consequently conceived an albino son, **Pandu** ('pale').

AMBIKA
India

Ambika, in Hindu myth, was a queen whose husband Vichitravirya died before he could give her children. (She was junior to her fellow-queen **Ambalika**.) As custom was, she agreed to let his brother father her child instead. She expected her handsome brother-in-law **Bhisma**, but instead found **Vyasa**, a filthy hermit, in her bed. At the moment of penetration she shut her eyes – and consequently the son she conceived, **Dhritarashtra**, was blind.

AMBROSIA
Europe (South)

Ambrosia ('**immortality**'), in Greek and Roman myth, was the food of the gods, as **nectar** was their drink. It gave and guaranteed **immortality**. The sweetness of its smell and its taste surpassed all earthly foods, and although mortals often tried to make it for themselves (for example by mixing honey, wine and herbs), they never succeeded. The gods not only ate it, but distilled it into perfume and used it as ointment, rubbing themselves down with it after exercise and dropping it into wounds to heal them instantly.

AMERICAN MYTH

At some time between 35,000 and 10,000 years ago, during the last Ice Age, humans from Asia crossed the frozen Bering Strait into the American continent, and spread over its entire area. Over the succeeding millennia some 2000 individual peoples arose, some of them small communities (for example the fishers of Patagonia), others large empires or language-groups. (In its heyday, the Andean Inca empire was twice the size of the contemporary Frankish empire in Europe; at the same period the Iroquois-speaking confederacy dominated a vast area of what is now the Eastern United States.)

Despite such diversity, the strands of myth remained remarkably consistent throughout the continent. The idea, for example, that the Earth was created from mud drawn from the bottom of the primordial ocean, sometimes after an all-engulfing **flood**, was common to peoples from Canada and Argentina, the Great Lakes and the Amazon basin, Central America and – perhaps most tellingly of all, since there was unlikely to be any way in which they can ever have seen the **sea** – the Great Plains and Desert of the Central and Southwestern United States.

In the majority of these cultures, the Earth, home of human beings, was one of three worlds, the others being homes respectively of gods and spirits and of demons and the Dead. Usually the god-world was above the Earth and the demon-world below it. The gods were led by a bodiless entity, creativity made manifest, usually given a name such as Great Spirit, Maker, Nothing Lacking or Ancient One. Sometimes this Spirit remained concerned in and active for its own creation, but often it withdrew from activity, remaining in the universe but not of it, the object of speculation rather than of worship. The other gods were more manifest: offspring (usually in giant human form) of the Great Spirit, embodiments of such natural phenomena as Famine, **Lightning**, **Mother Earth**, **Rain** or **Sun**; rulers of the Dead. Animals were important. Many myth-systems – particularly those of the forests of the North and the Amazon basin – said that the Earth was originally the home of giant animals, which had the abilities to move freely between the three worlds, to take off their animal identity and hang it up like a skin on a peg, and to work magic (for example, many helped in the details of **creation**). This idea gave rise, first, to the adoption by many peoples of animals as guardian and guiding spirits (*totems*) and, second, to thousands of myths and folk-tales in which animals – Beaver in Canada, Coyote in the Southwest and California, Hare in the Great Lakes, Panther in Amazonia, Raven in the Pacific Northwest – were both archetypal **tricksters** and creation-gods. Other animals, particularly the Water-**snakes** (which ruled all rivers on Earth and were hostile to the Sun) and Thunderbirds (which controlled the weather), were common to cultures throughout the continent.

In Central America and the Peruvian Andes – and nowhere else, suggesting perhaps a common ancestry for this area – cosmologies of a different kind arose. These were present not only in the myths of such enormous empires as those of the Aztecs, Inca and Maya, but in smaller systems and individual stories from elsewhere. In all of them, the Sun and Moon predominated as original gods and creators. There was eternal conflict between **Light** and **Dark** (often embodied in a pair of warring god-**twins**), and human survival depended on keeping Dark (standing for evil and death) at bay and encouraging Light (standing for good and life). The lesser gods, those of harvest, rain, sickness, war and so forth, all tended towards one sphere of influence (usually that of their parent, good or bad), and had to be seduced to help mortals by unceasing prayer and sacrifice. The gods often mated with mortals to produce new warrior-gods or **fertility**-spirits, and many gods also chose to spend time as mortals, manifesting themselves in human society as empire-builders or glorious rulers.

Societies whose myths centred on the regular reappearance of the Sun and **Moon**, or on the cycle of the seasons, often immersed themselves in ritual to the point where observance itself began to seem to be what kept life going, not the gods in whose names the observances were made. Mayan myths, and the religious practices arising from them, depended on meticulous calculations of time, based on subdivisions of the year. Inca myths were obsessive in a similar way about spatial geometry, the location of each place or journey being exhaustively described. Aztec society drew from its myths (which hardly now seem to bear such a weight of interpretation) a system of rigorous ritual, sacrifice and self-denial which consumed its people's lives – and, if Spanish conquerors are to be believed, also their bodies, since holocausts of human victims, and cannibalism, were claimed to be standard practice at the shrines of even the most genial-seeming Aztec gods.

The question of biased description is one facet of a major problem for anyone investigating the myths of the Americas: transmission. However sophisticated the societies which gave rise to the myths, they were all non-literate, and what survives today is therefore largely a matter of what other people chose (and choose) to codify from an enormous, amorphous mass of ritual and oral storytelling. In the cases of the Incas, and particularly the Aztecs, the Spanish conquerors who were the first to write down their myths had a vested interest in making them seem as barbarous and bloodthirsty as possible. (The Maya survived this process by retreating into the jungle or the mountains, with the result that their myths, very recently rediscovered, are among the most dispersed and fragmentary of all major systems.) Similar disruption by Europeans of the culture of other societies (in North America in the sixteenth-nineteenth centuries CE, in Amazonia· at this precise moment) have led to myth becoming, for many native peoples, a crucial factor in the survival of tribal identity – and consequently to its politicization. In one area, the Caribbean, native myth has all but disappeared, replaced by the Christianity of eighteenth-century plantation-owners from Europe, the myths of the African people they shipped in as slaves, and systems (such as the Voodoo religion in Haiti) which draw on both.

➤➤➜ **Myths of the Arctic:** Aulanerk, Disemboweller, Eeyeekalduk, Igaluk, Kadlu, Nanook, Pinga, Sedna, Torngarsak

➤➤➜ **Myths of the Northwest coast:** Amotken, Copper Woman, Enumclaw and Kapoonis, Five Sisters, Komokwa, Kwatee, Nagaitcho, Nocoma, Qamaits, Raven, Sisiutl, Snoqalm and Beaver, Wishpoosh

➤➤➜ **Myths of the Northeastern woodlands:** Adekagagwaa, Ataentsic, Dajoji, Flying Head, Ga-oh, Gendenwitha, Gluskap, Gunnodayak, Hahgwehdiyu and Hahgwehdaetgah, Hinu, Ioskeha, Kitshi Manito, Nanabush, Nokomis, Onatah, Oshadagea, Tawiskaron, Underwater panthers

➤➤➜ **Myths of the Northern forests:** Amotken, Baxbakualanuchsiwae, Gluskap, Malsum, Michabo, Nipinoukhe and Pipinoukhe, Underwater panthers

➤➤➜ **Myths of the US/Canadian plains:** Ictinike, Maheo, Na'pi, Pah, Poia, Tirawa, Uncegila, Wakan Tanka, Wakonda, Wheememeowah, White She-Buffalo

➤➤➜ **Myths of the Southeastern US:** Asgaya Gigagei, Corn Woman, Dayunsi, Esaugetuh Emissee, Kananeski Amaiyehi, Unelanuki, Utset

➤➤➜ **Myths of the Southwestern US (desert):** Ahsonnutli, Atsehastin and Atseestan, Black God, Dzoavits, Estsanatlehi, Humanmaker, Nayenezgani and Tobadzistsini, Szeukha, Tonenili, Tsohanoai

➠ Myths of the Southwestern US (Pueblos): Awonawilona, Doquebuth, First Made Man, Kloskurbeh, Kokyangwuti, Payatamu, Poshaiyankayo, Star Country, Ten Corn Maidens, Umai-hulhlya-wit, Wonomi, Yanauluha

➠ Myths of the California coast: Chinigchinich, Gudratrigakwitl, Kodoyanpe, Kumokum, Kumush, Owiot, Quaayayp, Wonomi

➠ Myths of Central America (including Aztec and Mayan): Chac, Chalchihuitlicue, Cihuacóatl, Coatlicue, Coyolxauhqui, Ehecatl, Gucumatz, Hunab, Hurukan, Ilamatecuhtli, Itzamná, Itzpapalotl, Ixchel, Ixtab, Ixtlilton, Kanassa, Kasogonaga, Kukulkan, Macuilxóchitl, Mayauel, Mictlan, Mixcóatl, Ometecuhtli, Quetzalcóatl, Temazcalteci, Tezcatlipoca, Tlaloc, Tlazoltéotl, Tochopa and Hokomata, Tonatiuh, Xipetotec, Xiutecuhtli, Xochipili, Xochiquetzal, Xólotl, Yacatecuhtli

➠ Myths of the Caribbean (including Voodoo): Agwe, Annency, Azacca, Bossu, Damballah, Erzulie, Ghede, Legba, Mait' Carrefour, Mama Brigitte, Ogoun

➠ Myths of South America (including Inca): Ah Puch, Aiomum Kondi, Amana, Ariconte and Tamendonare, Auchimalgen, Aunyainá, Bachue, Bochica, Catequil, Ceucy, Chantico, Chiminigagué, Chonchonyi, Coniraya, Cupay, Ekkekko, El Dorado, Ellal, Guecufu, Guinechen, Huitzilopochtli, Ilyap'a, Inti, Kilya, Kononatoo, Kuat, Kururumany, Mama Quilla, Manco Capac, Mani, Pachacamac, Page Abe, Parawa, Pillan, Sinaa, Tamusi and Tamulu, Tupan, Uaica, Vaimatse, Valedjád, Viracocha, Wahari and Buoka

➠ general: Coyote, Thunderbirds

AMfORTAS: *see* Pelles

AMITABHA
Asia (East); India

Amitabha, in some Buddhist myth and belief, is **Buddha**'s manifestation as God. He sits in his Western Paradise, enthroned on a lotus-flower, and welcomes all who truly believe in him and repent their sins. His Chinese name is Emituofo, and he is attended by **Avalokiteshvara**, who appears in Chinese in female form as **Guan Yin**, goddess of mercy.

➠ supreme deity

AMMA
Africa

Amma, in the myths of the Dogon people of Mali, existed before the world. In some accounts, he was the disembodied principle of **creation**, and made the universe by conceiving an infinitesimally small particle, the nucleus of the atom of a seed, which grew and swelled to make the primordial egg. The egg was double-yolked, and its hatchlings, **Ogo** and Yasigi from one yolk, and the Nummo from the other, created all that exists.

In other accounts, Amma was the spirit not only of creation but of maleness. Desperate with sexual longing, he tried to make a female by moulding clay in two earthenware bowls. Having shaped **Mother Earth**, he threw the spare lumps of clay and the bowls into the sky – where the lumps became stars and the bowls the **Moon** and **Sun**. He tried to mate with Mother Earth, but her clitoris (a termite-hill) got in the way, so before he could penetrate her he had to circumcise her. From this union three children were born: Ogo and the Nummo twins (Yasigi does not feature in this account). Ogo was all-wicked, and to produce good creatures to counteract his evil Amma sacrificed the Nummo and scattered their blood on Mother Earth (to make her grow plants and animals), then reconstituted them and gave them new life: the first humans. (It was because they had died and come to life again that human beings are mortal.) The Nummo's children, Amma's grandchildren, were four males and four females. Each couple stood for one of the four elements (air, earth, fire, water), for one of the four cardinal compass points and for one of the four 'great skills': farming, magic, marketing and medicine.

⫸ civilization

AMMUT
Africa (North)

Ammut ('corpse-eater'), in Egyptian myth, stood by the scales which weighed the sins of the Dead in the **Underworld**. She had a hippopotamus' back legs, a lion's body and a crocodile's head, and her job was to eat the hearts of the wicked.

⫸ animal-gods, monsters and dragons

AMOTKEN
Americas (North)

Amotken, in the myths of the Salish-speaking peoples of the Pacific Northwest coast and interior US and Canada, created the world and everything in it. He made himself daughters, from five hairs from his head, and offered each of them any gift she asked. The first asked to become Mother of Evil, the second Mother of Good, the third Mother of Earth, the fourth Mother of **Fire** and the fifth Mother of **Water**. Amotken gave them their gifts. He decreed that Mother of Evil should rule the others for a day and a night, then Mother of Good, then Mother of Earth and so on. In the eyes of the gods, each of these periods of rule was short – but human time is different, and we are still labouring under the first reign of Mother of Evil, waiting for the second age to dawn. Benign and indifferent, Amotken sits in the sky like a doddering elder. His **messenger Coyote** carries his wishes to us on Earth, but the flow of information is one way only, and Amotken has no idea how we suffer under his daughter's tyranny.

⫸ creation, five sisters

AMPHION AND ZETHUS
Europe (South)

Amphion ('of two lands') and Zethus (Zetos, 'seeker'), in Greek myth, were **twin** sons of **Zeus** and Princess **Antiope** of Boeotia. They built the city of **Thebes**, Zethus laying out the streets with mathematical skills taught him by **Athene**, Amphion (a pupil of **Hermes**) by playing his lyre so skilfully that stones leapt into place of their own accord to form the walls. They called the city after Zethus' wife Thebe, and ruled it together.

Amphion and Zethus both died as a result of sorrow caused by their own children. The children of Amphion and his wife **Niobe** were so beautiful that Thebe was jealous. She crept into the palace nursery one night to murder them, and in the darkness made a mistake and cut the throat of her own son Itylus. The gods turned her into a nightingale, forever singing mourning songs – and next morning, when Thebe's husband Zethus found out what had happened, he killed himself from grief. For her part, Niobe began boasting that her children outdid in beauty even **Apollo** himself and his sister **Artemis** – and Apollo responded by shooting them dead. Amphion, driven mad by grief, gathered an army and marched on Delphi to sack the holy shrine – and although Amphion was Zeus' own son, Zeus punished him for challenging the gods by taking away his **immortality** and banishing him to the **Underworld**.

AMPHITRITE
Europe (South)

Amphitrite ('embracer', that is, the **sea**), daughter of **Proteus** the Old Man of the Sea, in Greek myth, swore eternal virginity. But **Poseidon** chose her sister **Thetis** as consort – and when he was told that she was fated to bear a son who would be greater than his father, he abandoned her to a mortal, **Peleus**, and courted Amphitrite instead. Amphitrite would have nothing to do with him, and withdrew in an enormous tidal

wave to the Atlas Mountains in Africa. (In some accounts, the wave drowned the continent of Atlantis.) Instead of raging after her, Poseidon sent an ambassador to woo her: Delphinus, king of the dolphins.

Charmed by Delphinus' antics – instead of speaking, he turned cartwheels, somersaulted and leapt in the air to convey his message – Amphitrite returned to the sea-kingdom to share Poseidon's bed. To her regret, she found that sending Delphinus was the one gentle thing Poseidon ever did for her. As soon as she married him, he returned to his former arrogance and lasciviousness, so that she spent much of her time in a fury, lashing herself into rages with storms and waves. Only Poseidon and her father could ever calm her, the one by threatening her with his trident, the other by lulling her asleep with warm West winds and soothing words.

AMPHITRYON
Europe (South)

Amphitryon ('harassing on each side'), son of Alcaeus and Hipponome in Greek myth, was a prince of **Thebes**. His elder sister had married King Electryon of Argos, and when Amphitryon grew up he married their daughter **Alcmena**. Electryon and his eight sons were cattle-lords, owning herds as far as the eye could see, and the cattle caught the eye of King Pterelaus of the Teleboans, who decided to steal them. He had one immortal hair, and unless it was discovered and plucked out of his head, he could not be harmed. Armed with this protection, Pterelaus raided

Argos, killed Electryon's sons and stole Electryon's cattle. Electryon planned to raise an army and go to punish the Teleboans, leaving Mycenae in Alcmena's care. But Amphitryon argued with him, saying that it was pointless to attack a man who could not be killed. He dashed his stick on the ground to emphasize what he was saying; the stick hit a stone, bounced up and killed Electryon.

Since this was an accident, Alcmena said that Amphitryon should not be banished for murder. But she refused to have anything more to do with him until he defeated the Teleboans and avenged the deaths of her eight brothers. Amphitryon went to Thebes to ask for help, and the Thebans offered him an army on condition that he rid their countryside of a monstrous fox: it was fated never to be caught or killed, and each month it ate or carried off a Theban child. Amphitryon hunted the fox with the famous dog Laelaps. This was a present given long ago by **Zeus** to **Europa**, and was fated always to catch and kill the animals it chased. So the hound which always caught its prey hunted the fox which could never be caught. In the end, to avoid breaking the laws of **Fate**, Zeus turned the pair of them to stone.

As soon as the fox was dealt with, the Thebans gave Amphitryon his army, and he went to fight the Teleboans. He was not at all sure how he was going to beat Pterelaus, who was still protected by his immortal hair. Fortunately, the gods made Pterelaus' daughter Comaetho fall in love with Amphitryon, and she plucked out the hair while her father slept and gave it to Amphitryon as a love-gift. Next day Amphitryon challenged Pterelaus to single combat, killed him, executed Comaetho for treachery and marched back to Argos driving his father-in-law's stolen cattle.

While all this was going on, Zeus, back in Argos, disguised himself as Amphitryon and made love to Alcmena – love-making which led to the birth of **Heracles**. As soon as Amphitryon arrived home he, too, made love to Alcmena, and their son Iphicles was born immediately after Heracles, as the hero's mortal twin.

AMRITA
India

Amrita ('immortal') was the food of the gods. In early Vedic accounts, by the Aryan people who invaded India in the seventeenth century BCE, it was the same thing as *soma*. But in later, Hindu myth it was created by the gods themselves. As the result of a curse laid on them by the wizard Durvasas, the gods' powers, and their ability to resist **demons**, began to decline. **Vishnu** said that they should make a truce with the demons, and join with them in creating a food which would guarantee strength and **immortality**. They should fill the primordial **sea**, the Sea of Milk, with seeds and plants of all kinds, and with the sperm of every animal; then, using a mountain as pole and the serpent **Vasuki** as cord, they should churn the mixture. To anchor the mountain in the void of non-being, Vishnu turned himself into a huge turtle, **Kurma**.

As the gods and demons churned, Vasuki writhed, groaned and spat out streams of poison, which **Shiva** swallowed before they could destroy **creation**. Gradually the mixture began to take on a rice-pudding-like texture, and beings were born from it: Surabji the sacred cow who grants all wishes, the wine-goddess **Varuni**, **Soma** the **Moon**-god, **Lakshmi** goddess of luck, **Parijata** the paradise-tree and **Dhanvantari**, doctor of the gods, holding a precious cup of *amrita*.

The battle for amrita. As soon as *amrita* appeared, gods and demons began squabbling for it. The demon **Rahu** snatched the cup and sipped – and if Vishnu had not sliced off the demon's head before *amrita* could flow through his whole body, he would have become ruler of the universe. As it was, the head remained immortal, a snarling, gaping thing which rolled round the heavens ever afterwards and tried to eat the stars. The quarrel continued, until the beautiful moon-goddess **Rohini** appeared and offered to settle it. She sat the gods and demons in long lines, facing one another, then took the cup of *amrita* and walked between them, letting each god taste it. The demons thought that when she reached the end of the row, she would turn round and start feeding them – but instead she revealed herself as Vishnu in disguise and disappeared, taking the *amrita*.

Battle flared once more, but now the gods had drunk *amrita* and outmatched the demons. They defeated them easily, and banished them underwater or into the crevices of dark where they have lurked ever since. The gods now owned *amrita* exclusively, and it guaranteed immortality to them and to anyone they allowed to taste it. But if the supply was to be renewed, it was essential that mortals make regular sacrifice to the gods. Each sacrifice had to be made according to exact ritual – and the demons lay waiting in the shadows each time, knowing that if the slightest ritual slip were made, the sacrifice would be void and a tiny drop of *amrita* would be subtracted from the heavenly store and descend to them.

AMUN
Africa (North)

Amun ('secret god'), or Amon or (Greek) Ammon, in Egyptian myth, was originally a god of the air, born with other deities from the voice of **Thoth**. He was protector of the area round Thebes (modern Luxor), and although he had no shape – he was all-pervasive and all-encompassing – he was worshipped as a curly-horned ram married to the goose which symbolized the River Nile. In the twentieth century BCE, when Thebes became Egypt's capital and a new royal dynasty was established, Amun was promoted to become god of gods, ruler of the universe, and the pharaohs added his name to their own as a symbol of authority: the founder of the Theban dynasty, for example, ruling from 1991-1961BCE, was Amunemhat ('Amun leads').

Amun's supremacy led him to take in the powers, myths and even names, of other gods. In particular, priests of his huge temples at Thebes and Karnak constructed an elaborate cult in his honour, taking over the **creation**-myth originally centred on **Atum**, and claiming that the Sun-god, **Ra**, was Amun's engendering power made manifest. (In this version, the Sun was renamed Amun-Ra.) These changes to the mythology gave Amun authority not only as creator and sustainer of the universe but as father and ruler of all gods – and his cult became so all-engulfing, in the next two millennia, that it was able to contain two mutually incompatible versions of his nature and power, and of the nature of the divine. In one, there were many gods, and Amun was the leader of a ruling trinity which also included **Ptah** and Ra. In the other, there was only one god, Amun, who was able to take any shape he chose – so that all other gods were merely his emanations, aspects of the One.

During the first 1400 years of Amun's hegemony, a ram was kept in the temple of Thebes. It was the god incarnate, and every year, in a glittering festival, it was carried across the Nile to visit Amun's relatives on the far bank (in what became the Valley of the Kings). Its companion in the divine barge (a model of the Sun-ship in which Ra sailed the sky each day) was the pharaoh, Amun-Ra's son and ruler of mortals as he ruled the gods. Thebes was sacked in the seventh century BCE, and physical power moved elsewhere (notably to Yunu or Heliopolis, now part of Cairo). But Amun-worship, as a focus of Egyptian nationalism, lasted a further six centuries, until the temples at Thebes and Karnak were damaged by earthquakes, and other gods, notably **Aset** and **Osiris**, became predominant.
⋙→ **supreme deity**

AN
Asia (West)

An or Anu ('**sky**'), in Mesopotamian myth, was the child either of Apsu ('fresh **water**') and **Tiamat** ('salt water'), or of Anshar ('light') and Kishar ('horizon'). He threw dice with his sons **Ea** and **Enlil** for kingdoms; Ea won the **sea**, Enlil dry land and An the sky. An then divided the universe among them, creating the regions each had won. At first, after this, he was benevolent and interested in his own creation. But **Marduk** the **Sun**-god attacked him, flayed him, cut out his heart and beheaded him – after which An withdrew from the universe and became an invisible entity: space, all-embracing but uninvolved. (In some accounts, this aloofness made him an ideal judge, before whom quarrelling gods and mortals could plead their cases; but although he appeared to listen to such oratory, there was only one occasion, in the case of **Adapa**, when he stirred himself actually to issue judgement.)

*Despite – or perhaps because of – An's aloofness, he was thought to personify infallibility and omniscience. His shrines were oracular centres, the seven judges of the **Underworld** were called Annunaki ('An's children'), and kings often legitimized and dignified their reigns by incorporating his name into their own.*
⋙→ **justice and universal order, prophecy**

ANANDA
India

Ananda, in Buddhist myth and legend, was born at the same moment as

Buddha, was his inseparable childhood companion and became his first disciple and follower after Buddha attained enlightenment. Some accounts make Ananda the same person as Buddha's half-brother **Nanda**.

ANANSI
Africa

Anansi ('spider'), in the myths of many West African peoples, was a **trickster**. He began his career as a creator-god, spinning the entire world at the request of the Great Sky-spirit, and was a **shape-changer**. Then he became one of the **messengers** between the Sky-spirit and human beings, teaching such things as how to pound corn in a mortar, how to use **fire** and how to tell stories.

The Sky-spirit had several messengers, all shape-changers, and there was constant bickering between them. Anansi and one of his rivals organized a contest, saying that whichever of them appeared in greatest splendour before the Sky-spirit would be his principal messenger thereafter. Anansi appeared first, turning himself into the yellow of a tiger's eye – and his rival matched him exactly. Anansi made himself the blue of sky reflected in a water-hole, the grey of the membrane on a lizard's eye, the pink of the blood-vessel in an antelope's ear – and was matched each time. Finally, exerting all his skill, he became the iridescence of sunlight in a dew-drop caught in a spider's web, and his rival turned into an entire rainbow and filled the sky. Anansi, defeated, wove a rope, let himself down from the Sky-spirit's hut and settled on Earth forever, leaving the carrying of messages to his successful rival: Chameleon.

*Mythographers suggest that this story is a folk-tale memory of the displacement of ancient deities by newer gods. It is also one of the very few tales in which Anansi is outwitted. Thousands of Anansi-tales survive, and all have the same pattern. Having decided, usually just for the fun of it, to trick someone, Anansi sets up a situation by boasting – for example that he will buy the songs of the Sky-spirit by fetching him a panther, a hornet, a ghost and his own self, or that he will bundle up the **Sun**, **Moon** and Darkness and bring them to Earth in a bag – and then fulfils each of the conditions by a trick. In some tales, he benefits other creatures – for example, he escapes from a bushfire by hiding in Antelope's ear and whispering to her the best way of escape, then rewards her by weaving a web to hide her fawn from marauding lions. But usually his tricks are done for their own sake, and the stories are invented simply for the pleasure of telling them, for the ingenious ways Anansi carries out each boast.*

*This insouciance marks a major difference between Anansi and the tricksters of such other areas as Australia and North America. In those parts, the tricksters (**Gluskap**; **Manabozho**; **Spider Woman**) are full-blown gods, with a serious and solemn role in the creation and continuance of life, and their folk-tale existence is distinctly secondary. Anansi's presence in the world, by contrast, not to mention his exploits, are almost all frivolous and told solely for entertainment.*

In the Caribbean islands to which many West Africans were taken as slaves in the eighteenth century CE, Anansi is known as **Annency**.

ANANTA: *see* Shesha

ANAT
Asia (West)

Anat ('mountain-lady'), in Canaanite myth, was the sister and consort of **Baal** the storm-god. In some accounts she was not his sister but his mother, but this may be no more than a poetic way of referring to the story of how she rescued him from the **Underworld** after he rashly said that he could defeat anyone, even Mot god of the Dead. She herself was defeated only by one being, the mortal Aqhat. He owned a miraculous bow (the arch of the **sky**) made for him by the blacksmith-god Kothar. Anat coveted it, and when Aqhat refused to give it to her at any price, not even for **immortality**, she killed him. Aqhat's corpse fell into the Underworld, and his bow sank into the **sea** – and at once the darkness of chaos engulfed the Earth and plants and animals died. Anat was forced to beg help from **El**, king of **Heaven**, and he allowed her to rescue Aqhat from the Underworld, to give him back his bow (so propping the sky above the Earth once more) and to restart **creation**.

Anat is the Canaanite name for the goddess known in other West Asian myth-traditions as **Astarte**, **Cybele**, **Inanna** and **Ishtar**. She travelled to Egypt as consort of **Seth** and protector of the pharaohs when they rode into battle, and into European myth as the Greek **Artemis** and then the Roman **Diana**.
≫→ **fertility**

ANCHISES
Europe (South)

Anchises ('associate of Isis'), in Greek and Roman myth, a distant cousin of King **Priam** of Troy, was the most handsome human being ever born, and **Aphrodite** herself was filled with lust for him. She disguised herself as a mortal princess, and seduced him, revealing her true identity only after he made her pregnant. She swore Anchises to secrecy, on pain of punishment from **Zeus** himself. But when Anchises' son **Aeneas** was born, he had inherited his mother's beauty as well as his father's, and Anchises found it almost unendurable to have to pretend that the child's mother was a mortal. Finally, he got drunk at a banquet and blurted out Aeneas' true identity – and Zeus hurled a thunderbolt which lamed him and turned him in an instant from handsome youth to wizened old man.

*In Virgil's **Aeneid**, one of whose main themes is Aeneas' sense of duty to **Heaven** and his family, Anchises is given somewhat more dignity than in this original myth. Aeneas carries him on his shoulders from the ruins of Troy, showing him no less respect than the statues of the ancestral gods, and when Anchises dies on the journey south (in Sicily) celebrates a huge funeral games in his honour. Later, he visits Anchises in the **Underworld**, where the old man, now a dignified sage and prophet, shows him the destiny of Rome and the generations of **heroes** and princes still unborn.*

ANDRIAMAHILALA: *see*
Andriambahomanana and
Andriamahilala

ANDRIAMBAHOMANANA AND ANDRIAMAHILALA
Africa

Andriambahomanana and Andriamahila-la, in Madagascan myth, were the first human beings. After they had lived for many centuries, and peopled the world, the **Sky**-spirit said that it was time to end their mortal existence, and asked where they would like to live in future. Andriam-bahomanana chose to spend some time underground and some on the surface, and the Sky-spirit made him a banana plant, being born, flourishing and dying each year. Andriamahilala chose to live on the **Moon**, and the Sky-spirit sent her there, where she is born, grows to maturity and dies every month.

ANDROMACHE
Europe (South)

Andromache ('battle of men'), in Greek myth, was the wife of Prince **Hector** of Troy, and the mother of his son and heir **Astyanax**. As senior princess of Troy, second in rank only to Queen **Hecuba**, she led the women throughout the **Trojan War**, and when the city fell never wavered in her dignity and re-straint despite being raped, enslaved and losing Astyanax (who was torn from her arms and thrown from the battlements). Together with her broth-er-in-law, the prophet **Helenus**, she was allocated as war-spoils to **Neoptolemus** and taken to Epirus. **Menelaus**, whose daughter **Hermione** had been promised in marriage to Neoptolemus, tried to kill her, but the gods (or some say **Peleus**) prevented it. After **Orestes** killed Neop-tolemus and married Hermione, Andro-mache married Helenus and they spent the rest of their lives as king and queen of Epirus.

The bare bones of the Andromache myth were fleshed out by many writers, who made her one of the most long-suffering and dignified characters in European litera-ture. In Homer's Iliad *she is the picture both of a princess and a noble wife and mother: in antiquity, her farewell to Hector as he goes to fight* **Achilles** *(Iliad Book 24) was considered one of the finest passages in all Greek poetry. Euripides made her a lead-ing character in* Women of Troy *– where she stoically endures the seizure and death of Astyanax – and the main character of* Andromache, *which dramatizes the strug-gle between her and Hermione. In more modern times, Racine's* Andromache *made her an emblem of royal duty and maternal devotion, maintained through great suffer-ing – a picture followed by most subsequent writers. Ancient vase-painters and sculp-tors, with their penchant for showing beau-tiful women in mourning, regularly depicted the moment when she surrendered Astya-nax to the Greeks who were to throw him from the battlements; a few more adventur-ous artists depicted her bravely facing Hermione and Menelaus as they tried to kill her in Epirus.*

ANDVARI
Europe (North)

Andvari ('fire-worker'), in Nordic myth, was a dwarf who crafted a magic ring, building into it the power endlessly to create more gold. He became master of all the gold in the universe, until **Loki** demanded that he hand it over to **Regin** and **Fafnir** to pay for Loki's murder of their brother **Otr**. Andvari offered all the gold except the magic ring, intending to use it to restock the dwarf-hoard. But Loki insisted on taking the ring as well, and Andvari cursed it, filling it with power to bring about the death of all who owned it.

In Wagner's Ring of the Nibelungs, Andvari becomes Alberich. The gold-hoard is the treasure at the bottom of the river Rhine, and he renounces love in order to possess enough of it to make the magic ring. This variant from the original relates to the common myth-idea that dwarfs are immortal but unable to reproduce: they can craft anything they like, with wondrous skill, except their own offspring.

»→ **crafts, smiths**

ANGERONA
Europe (South)

Angerona ('raiser') was one of the most revered but least trumpeted goddesses in Rome. She guarded the city's secret name, an identity which the gods alone knew and which would cause the city's downfall if it were ever revealed to enemies. For this reason her statues showed her gagged and with her hand clutching her mouth to stop the name escaping by mistake. She had another secret skill, as her name suggests: she knew the raising-spell which made the **Sun** rise from its torpor at the end of the winter Solstice, and used it once a year at her festival on 21 December.

ANIMAL-GODS

In several cultures, particularly those of the Christian, Islamic and ancient Nordic worlds, animals were thought to exist on a lower rung than humans on the ladder of creation. But in many others they held an equal or higher place. They had skills and abilities which humans both lacked and coveted. In many myth-traditions, the gods and spirits who created the world were **shape-changers**, and assumed the forms not only of men or women but of such animals as coyotes, dogs, eagles, kangaroos, lizards, ravens, snakes and spiders. The power of the sky was often embodied as a **bull**, the nourishing power of **Mother Earth** as a **cow**, the primordial ocean as a **snake**. These animal-spirits, and thence all subsequent generations of animals, were thought to own part of universal wisdom, to know secrets denied to humans. Perhaps because of this, many cultures also told myths of animal-human hybrids – some beneficent (skilled, for example, in healing and **prophecy**), others **demons** and **monsters**, nightmares fleshed. Animal deities were especially common in mystery-cults, and sacrificing and consuming the cult-animal was thought to share its knowledge and power among all worshippers. But a proviso applied to all animal-myths: animals and animal-gods never entirely revealed their whole natures. Many were **tricksters**, and all kept some of their secrets, so that animal-gods and spirits could be dangerous as well as fascinating.

»→ **(Africa): Itherther and Achimi, Ogo; (Australia): Bagadjimbiri, Kurukadi and Mumba, Marindi and Adnoartina, Minawara and Multultu, Tjinimin and Pilirin; (Americas):**

Coyote, Dayunsi, Gluskap, Michabo, Nanabush, Raven, Sinaa, Thunder-birds, Underwater Panthers, Wish-poosh, Xólotl; (Egypt): Ammut, Anubis, Bastet, Hap, Heqet, Khepri, Serqet, Tefnut; (Greece): Pan; (India): Balin, Ganesh, Garuda, Hanuman, Jambavan, Jatayu, Kurma, Matsya, Narasimha, Varaha; (Oceania): Areop-Enap and Rigi, Nareau, Totoima; (Rome): Faunus; (Tibet): Dorje Pahmo, sPyan-ras-gzigs

ANJANA
Indian

Anjana, in Hindu myth, was an **apsara** cursed with monkey shape. She lived alone in the forest, pining for a son. In some accounts a kite dropped a cake in her lap, and **Shiva** appeared before her and told her to eat it. When she did so, she became pregnant with **Hanuman**, the future monkey-king. In other accounts, **Vayu** the wind-god either raped her or blew the cake into her lap, to make her pregnant.

≫→ **beauty**

ANNENCY
Americas (Caribbean)

Annency, in the myths and folk-tales of Jamaica, Trinidad and Haiti (where he is also known as 'Ti Malice) is a **trickster** and **shape-changer**. He is able to take on any shape he pleases, but usually appears as human or spider. He is the African trickster-god **Anansi**, taken to the Caribbean by West Africans enslaved for plantation work.

ANNWN
Europe (North)

Annwn, or Anwfn ('not-world'), in Celtic myth, was the **Underworld**. Its other names included Affan ('invisible'), Affwys ('gulf') and Anghar ('loveless'). It was a mirror-image of the mortal world, replacing substance with emptiness, being with nonentity, time with infinity. Its ruler was **Arawn**, and its inhabitants were fairies, **demons** and goblins. In Annwn, they were serene and vacuous, shapes without identity; it was only when they spilled into the mortal world that they took on recognizable characteristics, usually mischievous or malign to humans who encountered them. Human beings who strayed into Annwn (for example by joining its inhabitants as they danced in the mortal world in a fairy ring) had the identity sucked out of them, and became wraiths, of neither one world nor the other. The only creatures able to pass easily in and out of Annwn were pigs: **shape-changers** who could assume, shed or mask their identity at will.

*Although in Christian times Annwn became sidelined, featuring chiefly in children's stories and fairy tales, its earlier importance in myth survives in two accounts above all others. In The **Mabinogion**, the story of **Pwyll** prince of Dyfed tells how Arawn persuaded Pwyll to change identities with him and win the throne of Annwn from its previous ruler Havgan. In the poem The Spoiling of Annwn, by **Taliesin**, King **Arthur** led a raiding party into Annwn to steal the Cauldron of Plenty, the never-failing source of* *the Underworld's prosperity and its inhabitants' inspiration and **immortality**.*

ANTERO VIPUNEN
Europe (North)

Antero Vipunen ('old Vipunen'), in Finnish myth, was a **giant** who spent his existence sleeping just under the surface of the land, using the topsoil as a blanket. He slept for so long that whole forests seeded themselves, grew, reseeded themselves and died above him. He knew every song and magic spell ever made, and when **Väinämöinen** failed to find in the **Underworld** the binding-spell he needed to finish his magic boat, a shepherd directed him to Antero Vipunen. Väinämöinen tried to wake the giant, unceremoniously poking his stick down Antero Vipunen's gullet. But Antero Vipunen yawned, swallowed him and went back to sleep. It was not until Väinämöinen made a smithy in the giant's belly and started working iron that Antero Vipunen woke up, vomiting, and spewed out both the hero and the binding-spells Väinämöinen had come to find.

ANTIGONE
Europe (South)

Antigone ('in place of a mother' or 'against her birth'), in Greek myth, was the eldest child of **Oedipus** and **Jocasta**. When Oedipus blinded himself and was sent into exile, she accompanied him, and eventually took him to Colonus near Athens where the gods received him into the **Underworld**. Antigone then went back to **Thebes**, just before her brothers **Eteocles** and **Polynices** quarrelled over the kingship, and Polynices gathered the army led by the **Seven Against Thebes** to win himself sole power.

When the Seven were defeated and the war was won by Thebes, Antigone's uncle **Creon**, regent of the city, proclaimed that all the dead Thebans, including Eteocles, were to be buried with honour, but that all the dead attackers, including Polynices, were to be left on the plain to rot. Antigone refused to accept the decree. Claiming to obey the laws of the gods, which said that all kin were to be treated with equal honour, whatever their crimes, she buried her brother Polynices, and faced arrest and punishment with a combination of innocence and determination which outraged Creon. He had her walled up in a cave to starve to death.

*The bare bones of this myth give no hint of its enormous fecundity in classical and later times. Beginning with Sophocles' Antigone, which sets Antigone (embodiment of honour, duty and radiant trust in God) against Creon (embodiment of unyielding and self-destructive political arrogance, authoritarianism turned into a tragic flaw), the story has travelled throughout the world, engendering more than 20,000 known versions, derivatives and variants. Of all surviving literary works from ancient Greece and Rome, only Homer's Odyssey and Virgil's **Aeneid** have come close to it in influence. Some scholars believe that the reason for this is entirely Sophocles' genius, the power of his arguments and the characterization of Antigone and Creon in his play; a few go further, and say that he invented the story himself to articulate his themes, embroidering a* *myth-original even scantier than the outline given here.*

ANTIOPE
Europe (South)

Antiope ('set face'), daughter of **Ares** in Greek myth, was princess of the Amazon city of Themiscyra. When **Heracles** came to the country of the **Amazons** to steal the golden belt of **Hippolyta**, one of his companions was **Theseus**. They besieged Themiscyra, and Antiope saw Theseus from the walls, fell in love with him, and gave him the keys of the city as a love-gift. He took her back to Athens and they had one child, **Hippolytus**. But then Theseus made a dynastic marriage with Princess **Phaedra** of Crete, and Antiope gathered a band of Amazon warriors and broke into the wedding-feast, trying to kidnap or kill the bride. Theseus fought her off and killed her – a crime for which the gods punished him by making his innocent Cretan bride, Phaedra, fall in love with his son Hippolytus.

In some versions, Antiope is confused with Hippolyta (possibly her sister).

ANUBIS
Africa (North)

Anubis, son of the **Underworld** gods **Osiris** and **Nebthet** in Egyptian myth, was originally the god of putrefaction, and took his shape – a crouching dog or jackal – from the animals which scavenged in burial-grounds in the time before deep grave-shafts and pyramids were built. In later myth his role changed round completely. He became the jackal which protected the dead against robbers and marauders (and was often depicted as a dog on guard); in the Underworld, he supervised the weighing of dead people's hearts before Osiris' judgement-seat. When bodies were embalmed, the priest who supervised the workers wore a jackal-mask to signify Anubis' presence.
➤➤ **animal-gods**

APHRODITE
Europe (South)

Aphrodite ('foam-born'; Latin Venus), in Greek and Roman myth, was created from the foam arising when **Cronus** threw the severed penis of **Ouranos** (Father **Sky**) into the **sea**. She was **beauty** incarnate, and the West Winds gathered her up and carried her to Cyprus, where she first appeared on Earth. She was the goddess of desire, and won gods and mortals by seduction. In **Heaven**, she had love-affairs with **Ares** (their offspring was **Eros**), **Dionysus** and **Hermes**; on Earth, she slept with **Adonis** and **Anchises**. But she was capricious, and hurt people more often than she helped them. She bribed **Paris** of Troy to judge her the most beautiful goddess in **Olympus**, and started the **Trojan War**. When the women of Lemnos forgot to worship her, she made them first reject and then slaughter their husbands. When Eros fell in love with **Psyche**, she made all-but impossible conditions before Psyche could enter **Heaven** and find happiness.

In Greece, Aphrodite was depicted quite differently by fine artists and writers. Artists showed her as the archetype of serene female beauty, while writers depicted her as usually charming but sometimes spiteful and sulky. In Rome, because she was the mother of **Aeneas**, founder of the Roman state, she was worshipped as 'Genetrix' ('mother [of the state]'), and was honoured less as a flighty young girl than as a mature and dignified woman, as benignly aloof from her people as a Roman aristocratic mother was from her children.

⟫⟶ beauty, Idun, sex

APOLLO
Europe (South)

Apollo (Apollon, 'destroyer'), in Greek myth, was the son of **Zeus** and **Leto**, and the **twin** brother of **Artemis**. They were born on the island of Delos, and the Sun flooded the island with its radiance, covering it with gold (hence the name Delos, 'shining'). Jealous of their birth, **Hera** summoned a gigantic serpent to hunt Leto to her death across the world. But four-day-old Apollo begged a bow and arrows from **Hephaestus**, cornered the serpent in the sacred cave at Delphi and shot him dead. (Later, the Pythian Games were held every four years in Delphi to celebrate this event. In some accounts, killing the serpent was what gave Apollo skill at **prophecy**: until then **Gaia**, **Mother Earth**, had been the only being able to foretell the future, and the serpent was one of her servants.) Next Hera sent a giant, Tityus, to hunt Leto. Once again Apollo, helped this time by Artemis, protected her with arrows, and at last Zeus hurled Tityus down into the **Underworld**, pegged him there on the rock floor and sent a pair of vultures to feast daily on his liver.

Apollo was the light of the **Sun** made manifest, and had the power either to sear to **death** or to give sudden illumination. He was thus both a bringer of disease and a healer, both a hunter and a rescuer, and a prophet whose oracles were ambiguous but always true. Throughout his youth he was fierce, quickly angered and unforgiving. For example, when people claimed that the singing and flute-playing of the satyr Marsyas was finer than anything Apollo could manage, Apollo challenged him to a contest: playing and singing at the same time. This was easy for Apollo, playing the lyre, but impossible for Marsyas – and Apollo punished him by skinning him alive and nailing his hide to a pine tree.

Apollo was equally merciless to women who refused to have **sex** with him. One was **Cassandra**, princess of Troy. He cursed her by giving her true knowledge of the future, and then arranging that no one would believe a word she said. Another was the **Sibyl** of Cumae in Italy. He offered her **immortality** if she slept with him; she refused and asked instead to be allowed to live as many years as she held grains of sand in her hand. Cruelly, he granted her wish – but she had forgotten to ask to remain young and beautiful, and shrivelled until she spent the rest of her life as a withered husk hung up in a bottle.

In the end Apollo's wildness angered even Zeus. Apollo's son **Aesculapius**, a skilful healer, brought back to life Artemis' mortal servant **Hippolytus**, something forbidden even to a god – and when Zeus punished Aesculapius by dashing him down to the **Underworld**, Apollo set arrows to bow and began killing the **Cyclopes** who made Zeus' thunderbolts.

Only the pleading of Apollo's mother Leto saved him from being sent to the Underworld himself. He remained resentful of Zeus, and joined **Hera** and **Poseidon** in a revolt against his power – for which he was punished by being forced to serve for a year as slave to a mortal, King **Laomedon** of Troy.

Apollo served his punishment and learned his lesson. He became one of the calmest and most dignified of all the gods, the senior male **Olympian** as **Athene** was the senior female. His favourite proverbs were 'Know yourself' and 'Moderation in all things', and his oracle at Delphi gave this advice to many enquirers. He spent his time healing gods and humans, and making music (a skill taught him by **Hermes**). He led the **Muses** in playing and singing, and danced on Mount Parnassus with **Dionysus** and his followers. When he played his lyre, the whole of creation stopped to listen, awestruck, and the syllables he sang – 'Ee-eh Pa-ee-an' – were the only examples ever heard on Earth of the language of the gods, sounds to haunt every listening ear. He kept aloof from mortals (though he sometimes desired individual men and women as much as they longed for him, and had brief affairs with them). But his main contact was by oracles, when he revealed, through the mouth of his priestesses the Sybils, the secrets of past, present and most especially future.

Apollo was one of the gods most often represented in ancient Greek sculpture and painting. He was shown as a handsome, serenely smiling young man ('kouros' in Greek), the ideal of male beauty as **Aphrodite** *was the ideal of female beauty. In literature he appears as a somewhat forbidding guide and guardian or (in pastoral poetry) as the leader of the Muses and sweetest singer ever heard. Euripides, alone of surviving writers, concentrates on his deviousness, asking how human beings can cope with a god who never lies but who often blurs or only partially reveals the truth. In more modern times, critics of the arts liked to make a distinction between the 'Apollonian' impulse, based on rationality and classical control, and the 'Dionysian', derived from emotion and romantic self-indulgence.*

➣➤ **archers, disease and healing**

APSARAS
India

The *Apsaras* (or *Apsarasas*, 'essences of water') were the dancers of the gods. They were created from the mist which rose at the churning of the **Sea** of Milk (see **amrita**) or from fragments of **Prajapati**'s body, and there were (in some accounts) 'seven times six thousand' of them, or (in others) 35 million. They took many forms – doves, gazelles, butterflies, rainbows – but their favourite shapes were clouds or beautiful women. As clouds, they hovered in trees, waiting to seduce the unwary and draw them into fairy time. As women, they danced for the gods, and made love eagerly with the **Gandharvas**, the celestial musicians. As goddesses of **fertility**, they were always welcome at weddings, and they also had the power to bring good luck for their favoured mortals, in dice and other games of chance.

➣➤ **beauty, Graces, nymphs, shape-changers**

ARACHNE
Europe (South)

Arachne ('spider'), in Greek myth, was the finest weaver in Athens. She was also a fool, and challenged **Athene** (goddess of weaving) to a contest of skill. Athene warned her by weaving a tapestry showing scenes of mortals who were punished for challenging the gods. But Arachne took no notice, and wove a tapestry full of scandalous scenes of the gods' love-affairs. Athene tore it to pieces and thrashed Arachne with her own shuttle. Arachne hanged herself in mortification, and Athene changed her into a spider, condemned to weave for the rest of time, and to use threads from her own body to do it.
≫→ crafts

ARAWN
Europe (North)

Arawn, in Celtic myth, was a prince of **Annwn** the **Underworld**. He was ambitious to rule it, but was not powerful enough to kill Havgan its overlord. He persuaded the **shape-changer Pwyll** to take his identity for a year and kill Havgan, then took his place as ruler of the Underworld. He spent his time roistering and racketing, and every so often, on stormy nights, led his **demon** followers in a riotous chase through the mortal world, riding black horses with hunting-dogs yapping at their heels.

ARCHERS

Archers are a small but select band in world myth, and their stories are among the most imaginatively detailed. Arrows were often identified with the sunshaft, which could kill, send flashes of prophetic insight, cause or cure disease. They were also linked with sexual ejaculation, so that (male) gods of lust were often archers, and human or heroic archers were notably lustful. Both associations linked archers and archer-gods with hunting (if male) and procreation and **childbirth** (if female); in such cases, a female god, by practising archery (with its male sexual associations), desexed herself, combining her role as patron of **fertility**, birth and the newborn with uncompromising chastity.
≫→ (China): Jang Xien, Yi; (Greece): Apollo, Artemis, Eros, Heracles, Philoctetes; (India): Arjuna; (Japan): Raiden and Raiju, Yamasachi, Yuriwaka; (Nordic): Ull

ARDHANARISHVARA
India

Ardhanarishvara, in Hindu myth, was a form of **Shiva** in which the left half was female (creative, impulsive, violent) and the right half was male (industrious, reflective, calm). The balance between them was a generative and constructive force – and that is what Ardhanarishvara represented.

AREOP-ENAP AND RIGI
Oceania

Areop-Enap ('old spider'), in the myths of the islanders of Nauru, searched for food in the darkness at the beginning of **creation**. She found an enormous clam, but before she could stun it, it swallowed her and snapped shut again.

Exploring the clam's insides, Areop-Enap found a tiny snail (or, in some accounts, a Triton's Horn shellfish). Instead of killing it, she asked it to climb to the hinge of the shell and prise the clam open. As the snail moved across the clam's flesh, it left a phosphorescent trail, in the light of which Areop-Enap saw a white worm (or some say a caterpillar), Rigi. Ignoring the snail, Areop-Enap put a strength-spell on Rigi, and persuaded him to try to snap the clam open.

Time and again Rigi set his head against the upper shell and his tail against the lower, and heaved. The clam resisted, and sweat poured from Rigi, making a pool in the lower shell, then a lake and finally a sea. The saltiness finally forced the clam open, and it lay there dead. Areop-Enap made its lower shell Earth and its upper shell Sky. She set the snail high in the sky-shell, where it became the Moon. She made islands from clam-flesh, and clothed them in vegetation made from her own web-thread. Finally she turned to Rigi, and found him drowned in his own sweat, killed by his own exertions. Areop-Enap wrapped him in a cocoon of silk and hung him in the sky: the Milky Way.

≫→ animal-gods, Nareau

ARES
Europe (South)

Ares ('fighter'), in Greek myth, was the son either of **Zeus** and **Hera**, or in some accounts of Hera alone without a male partner: her rage made into a god. He was the god of war, brawn without brains, anger beyond restraint, force without control, and spent his time swaggering round **Heaven** and Earth with his followers Deimos ('dread'), Enyo ('fierceness'), **Eris** ('quarrel') and Phobos ('terror'). His war-cry laid mortals dead in heaps, and gave the gods such headaches that they kept trying to find ways of throwing him out of **Olympus** – in vain, for none dared directly to challenge him, or his mother Hera. Sexually insatiable, he raped **nymphs**, goddesses, **Titans**, even rocks and trees, and fathered a gang of brutish **heroes** who lorded it on Earth as brainlessly as he did in Heaven. His only weakness was his love for **Aphrodite**, on whom he fathered **Eros** (and, some say, **Priapus**).

Although Ares was later identified with the Roman **Mars**, their characters were completely different.

ARETHUSA
Europe (South)

Arethusa ('waterer'), in Roman myth, was a **hunting-nymph**, a virgin follower of Diana (see **Artemis**). One day she went swimming in the river Alpheus, and the river-god tried to seize her and rape her. She picked up her clothes and ran – and the god assumed human form and ran after her. He was just about to snatch her when Diana hid her in a cloud. Alpheus tried to part the cloud-wisps with his hands, but when he had dispersed it all he found nothing: Arethusa had changed to water inside it, and slipped away into a crack in the ground, far out of his reach.

Alpheus, a river, was easily able to follow Arethusa underground. But as soon as she slipped below the surface the spirits of the **Underworld** led her by secret channels to Sicily, where she bubbled up in a stream of pure water near the town of Syracuse. Alpheus wandered in despair along the river-channels and streams of the Underworld for a thousand years, until the gods at last took pity, guided him to Syracuse and filled Arethusa's heart with love for him. She and he mingled their streams, and have been together ever since.

This folk-tale, typical of hundreds, was said to have been devised to explain a curious phenomenon: when offerings were thrown into the river Alpheus in Greece, they vanished underwater, only to reappear days later in Arethusa's Spring in Sicily.
≫→ **water**

ARGONAUTS
Europe (South)

The Argonauts, in Greek and Roman myth, were fifty **heroes** chosen by **Jason** to help him steal the **Golden Fleece**. Their name comes from their ship, *Argo*, built for them by Argus. There are many different lists of their names: each Greek state liked to claim that one of its ancestors had taken part in the expedition. Apart from Jason and Argus, the Argonauts most commonly listed include sixteen sons of gods (among them **Aesculapius**, Calais and Zetes, the **Dioscuri**, Echion, **Heracles**, **Nauplius** and Periclymenus), the musician **Orpheus**, two dozen heroes including Admetus, Euryalus, Idas and his twin Lynceus, **Laertes** and **Peleus**, one woman, **Atalanta**, and one boy, Heracles'

page **Hylas**. Most were chosen for their bravery, but some had special skills as well: Echion was a herald, Lynceus the sharpest-eyed man who ever lived, Nauplius a navigator and Periclymenus a **shape-changer**.

The adventures of the Argonauts, and the way each contributed to the expedition in his own specialized way, were comprehensively described in Apollonius of Rhodes' Homer-inspired epic Argonautica *(The Voyage of Argo). It is from this that all later accounts, from tragic dramas to children's fairy-tales, are derived.*

ARGUS (HUNTING DOG)
Europe (South)

Argus (Argos, 'eager'), in Greek myth, was **Odysseus**' old hunting-dog. For twenty years, while his master was away fighting in Troy or travelling home, Argus had been neglected, and now he lay on the dung-heap, aged and full of fleas. But when he saw Odysseus, who had returned to Ithaca disguised as a beggar, he lifted his head, flattened his ears and wagged his tail. He was the first living creature to recognize Odysseus returned, and (as Homer puts it in the *Odyssey*) 'he no sooner recognized his master than he gave himself up to death's dark hand.'

ARGUS (WATCHMAN)
Europe (South)

Argus (Argos, 'eager'), in Greek myth, was a **giant** with a hundred eyes (or in some accounts, a thousand). When **Hera** wanted to hide **Io** from **Zeus** (who was eager to seduce her), she changed her into a cow, hid her in the divine herd and set Argus on guard. He was the ideal choice, because even when most of his eyes closed in sleep, some always remained alert. Zeus asked **Hermes**, god of **tricksters**, to steal Io, and Hermes played Argus a tune on his lyre so sweet that all Argus' eyes closed at the same moment – whereupon Hermes snatched Io and cut Argus' head off to prevent him telling. When Hera found the head, she gathered Argus' eyes and set them to decorate the peacock's tail.

ARIADNE
Europe (South)

Ariadne ('purity'), in Greek myth, was the daughter of King **Minos** of Crete and sister of **Phaedra**. She fell in love with **Theseus**, and showed him how to find his way out of the **Minotaur**'s lair in the Cretan Labyrinth (by rewinding a spindle of wool which he had unwound on the way in). After he had killed the Minotaur, she sailed with him for Athens, hoping to become his queen. But on the way they landed on the island of Naxos, and Theseus deserted her. In some accounts, this was because he already had a wife in Athens (the **Amazon** princess **Antiope**); in others it was because **Dionysus** fell in love with Ariadne and put a spell on Theseus to make him forget her.

What happened next is also disputed. Some versions say that Ariadne was so broken-hearted at losing Theseus that she hanged herself, others that married King Onarus of Naxos and lived many happy years as his queen. The most common story says that Dionysus took her into **Heaven** and made her his consort in his revels and dances across the universe, that he or **Aphrodite** gave her a crown of seven stars, and when she died – for he was unable to give her **immortality**, that possession of gods alone – the star-crown was placed in the sky forever as her memorial: the Corona Borealis or Northern Crown.

ARICONTE AND TAMENDONARE
Americas (South)

Ariconte and Tamendonare, in the myths of the Tupinamba people of Brazil, were **twins** but with different fathers – their mother (a mortal) was raped by a god at the exact moment when she was having **sex** with her mortal husband. Some time later she was eaten by cannibals, and the twins set out to avenge her murder and then to find their father. They cornered the cannibals on an island, and shifted the river-flow to swamp it; at the last moment the cannibals turned into panthers and escaped into the jungle.

In a lonely village the twins found an old, wise man, and asked him who their father was. He said that they could prove their identity by undertaking supernatural tests. They shot at targets, but their arrows vanished in thin air. They leapt between the two halves of a huge boulder, Itha-Irapi, which crashed together like snapping jaws. One twin was crushed, but the other reconstituted him and breathed new life into him. For the third test, they were told to steal bait from the demon Agnen, who fished food to feed the dead in the **Underworld**. The twins succeeded – but not before one of them was torn to pieces by Agnen and had to be remade and revived by his brother.

So each twin died and was reborn with his brother's help. They went back to the village wizard, who told them that he himself was their immortal father, Maira Ata. Their mortal father, Sarigoys, had died or disappeared long ago. Maira Ata had no idea which twin was mortal and which immortal, and Ariconte and Tamendonare spent their rest of their time on Earth sharing adventures, testing and watching each other, neither daring to kill the other or let him die in case he was the god.

Modern mythographers have given this story a neat (not to say wished-for) psychological explanation: Ariconte and Tamendonare are the two halves of each human being's nature, perpetually in rivalry but neither able to exist without the other. The Italian writer Italo Calvino reworked the story in his short novel The Cloven Viscount. In this, a medieval crusader is sliced in two, and the two halves roam the world, each a separate identity, yearning for the moment when they can meet and unite again, letting the man who is compounded of both of them end his days in peace.
≫→ animal-gods, creation

ARISTAEUS
Europe (South)

Aristaeus (Aristaios, 'best'), son of **Apollo** and the mountain-**nymph Cyrene** in Greek myth, was the god of bee-keeping. A hunter like his father, he was following his hounds one day when he saw **Orpheus'** wife **Eurydice** bathing.

Filled with lust, he leapt into the water to rape her, and when she fled she trod on a **snake** and was killed. Her **nymph**-sisters punished Aristaeus by killing all his bees, and he wandered the world trying to find new swarms. His mother advised him to ask **Proteus**, the Old Man of the **Sea**, and Proteus told him to sacrifice four bulls and four cows in Eurydice's memory, but to leave the carcasses to rot instead of burning them. Aristaeus did so, and swarms of bees rose from the carcasses to fill his hives.

Apart from this one lapse, Aristaeus was gentle and kindly. **Zeus** gave him charge of the infant **Dionysus**, to whom he taught love of the countryside. He married Princess Autonoe of **Thebes** (sister of Dionysus' mother **Semele**), and settled with her on Mount Haemus. Their son, Actaeon, grew up to be a hunter like his father and grandfather before him − only to anger **Artemis**, Apollo's sister, and die for it.
≫→ farming, Zosim

ARJUNA
India

Arjuna, in Hindu myth, was the son of **Indra** and Queen **Kunti** of **Bharata**. He was the third-born of the five **Pandava** brothers, each of whom had a different god for father. He was a master **archer**, and his skills were crucial in the huge war between the Pandavas and their cousins the **Kauravas**. But he was a thoughtful and peaceable man, and tried to find reasons why he should kill not merely his own cousins (who had been friends and companions throughout their boyhood), but also countless hundreds of soldiers he'd never even met. His charioteer, the god **Krishna**, resolved his doubts, explaining that only the gods understand the pattern of each individual human destiny. Our duty is not to question but to have faith in God, obedience and willingness – and only this surrender will bring us true fulfilment.

*Arjuna's adventures are told in the **Mahabharata**, the sixth part of which, the Bhagavad Gita ('Song of the Lord') contains his dialogue with Krishna, a main text in both Hindu philosophy and Sanskrit poetry.*
≫→ archers, heroes

ARTEMIS
Europe (South)

Artemis ('pure water-spring'; Latin Diana), in Greek and Roman myth, was the daughter of **Zeus** and **Leto**, and the twin sister of **Apollo**. When Zeus slept with Leto, to prevent **Hera** finding out he changed both himself and her into quails. Leto therefore bore her children with as few birth-pains as a mother quail suffers when it lays an egg. Ever afterwards women in **childbirth** used to pray to Artemis to ease their labour-pains. She brought to the childbed a pine-torch blazing with the light of life; its warmth and radiance were symbols of security for the newborn child. She shielded infants and baby animals from harm until they grew out of helplessness and could fend for themselves. She was the goddess of women's monthly cycle, protected innocence and virginity, and was herself untouched by god or mortal; in her honour her followers swore lifelong virginity.

As Apollo symbolized the sunshaft, so Artemis symbolized the moonbeam. She was a hunter, using a silver bow and arrows made for her by **Hephaestus** and a pack of immortal dogs bred for her by **Pan**. Sometimes her prey was human: when sudden death came to a mortal its cause was an arrow from Artemis, punishment for some crime of which the guilty person might not even be aware. She also punished mortals in other ways: for example, when **Agamemnon** mistakenly shot one of her sacred deer, she ordered him to pay for it by sacrificing his daughter **Iphigenia**. But her usual prey was deer and other wild animals. She hunted them either in a silver **moon**-chariot pulled by two horned hinds, or on foot with her company of **nymphs** and her pack of dogs.

Although Artemis and her nymphs would have nothing to do with males, they were among the most beautiful and graceful of all the immortals, and many gods and men pursued them and tried to have sex with them. This made Artemis shy of being seen by males at all, and merciless to any who came on her unawares. When Actaeon caught sight of her bathing naked in a river, she set his own dogs on him. On another occasion, on the island of Chios, when Orion surprised her in a forest clearing, she conjured from the ground a giant scorpion which stung him dead.

In Greek myth, although Artemis was terrifying, she was a comparatively minor goddess. Roman Diana, by contrast, was one of the main protectors of the stability of the state, and was worshipped both at huge public festivals and in secret **mysteries**, available to women alone.

Artemis/Diana was shown as a young, beautiful woman, either in hunting dress or robed as a princess. Her companions were dogs, lions and panthers, and she was sometimes shown with wings arching above her head to symbolize the path of stars in the night sky. Her temple at Ephesus (which held a many-breasted statue, symbolizing **fertility** *– said by some to be the* **Palladium** *of Troy) was one of the most important pilgrimage sites of the ancient Roman world – as Saint Paul acknowledged when he chose to preach a sermon there saying that the old gods were dead and Christianity had replaced them.*

≫→ archers, Great Goddess

ARTHUR
Europe (North)

Arthur's birth and accession. The 'once and future king', in Celtic myth, was originally one of the most ancient gods of Northern Europe, Artos the Bear, brother of the war-goddess **Morrigan** (or **Morgan le Fay**). When Christianity came to Britain, the Celtic gods abandoned the world of mortals for the sky, and Artos became the constellation Arcturus. But from time to time he felt a longing to return to Earth, and slipped into a mortal woman's womb at the moment of conception. He did this when **Uther Pendragon** made adulterous love with Queen Ygern of Tintagel, and was brought up in secret as Uther's son. He succeeded to the throne by

magic, pulling the sword **Excalibur** from a stone (or, some say, being given it by the **Lady of the Lake**).

The Round Table and the Holy Grail. The early years of Arthur's reign were happy and successful; with the help of wizards and **shape-changers** (such as **Merlin**) he made war on the Romans and united all Britain under his rule. He married Princess **Guinevere** and established a magic court at **Camelot**, a Round Table where **giants**, wizards and mortal warriors lived peaceably together. The Round Table was a force for good in the world, and existed in fairy time, untroubled by aging or mortality. But when the **(Holy) Grail** began to disappear from the mortal world, King **Pelles** of Carbonek sent his grandson **Galahad** to Camelot, and one by one Arthur's courtiers agreed to join Galahad in a quest to find the Grail. This Christian ambition upset the placid life of Camelot, dragging its warriors into the mortal world. Some returned, but most were killed, and the harmony of Camelot was destroyed forever.

The end of Arthur's reign. Soon after the Grail-quest, several of Arthur's courtiers, including his son **Modred**, conspired to snatch his throne. They told him that he was being cuckolded by **Lancelot**, his oldest friend and noblest warrior. Arthur banished Lancelot, and Modred and the others seized their chance and declared war. One by one Arthur's surviving courtiers were killed in the fighting, and finally the old king faced his son in single combat. Arthur killed Modred, but was so severely wounded that he had to withdraw once more from the mortal world. He went to the land of **Avalon**, the island of the blessed where the golden apples of **immortality** grew, and neither he nor Camelot were ever seen again. Still, today, the myth ends, Arthur and his warriors lie sleeping under a mountain, and when the need is great and the horn blows to waken them, they will gallop to restore the Golden Age.

The Arthur story is a confection, made in early Christian times from several elements of Celtic myth. In medieval fable, it was further elaborated, incorporating stories from France (Lancelot and the Lady of the Lake) and Germany (Percival or **Parsifal**). *In the fifteenth century Malory, in his Morte d'Arthur, gave it prescriptive literary form, the romance of Christian chivalry and betrayed love and friendship in which it is still best-known today. These versions concentrate on the events of Arthur's youth, before and after he won his throne, on the tragic effects of the love of Lancelot and Guinevere, and on Arthur's battle with Modred and his death. In between these events, they often depict Arthur as the typical medieval roi fainéant, the figurehead-king who sits in royal state, inactive and characterless, while his lords have all the adventures. This does nothing for Arthur, but greatly assists the problem of assimilating many different legends and folk-stories into a single narrative.*

The story of Arthur – and the ideas of chivalry and knight-errantry grafted on to it – have gripped the European imagination for fifteen hundred years. Scholars have conducted quests for the 'real' Arthur, identifying him as a Celtic prince who fought the Romans and excavating many of the sites of his supposed activities (including several different versions of Camelot). *Literary works range from the anonymous medieval poem Gawain and the Green Knight, through complex allegorical epics by such Christian apologists as Chrétien de Troyes and Malory (who gave the story, perhaps, its most definitive form) to such twentieth-century works as Steinbeck's translation/adaptation of Malory,* The Acts of King Arthur and His Noble Knights *and T.H. White's novel-trilogy* The Once and Future King. *In fine art, Pre-Raphaelite painters in Britain took Arthurian legend as a main source for their vision of a pure, simple and elegant medieval world, and their work in turn influenced other art-works of all kinds, ranging from a clutch of Hollywood swashbucklers (not to mention such Disney extravaganzas as* The Once and Future King, *an animated version of T.H. White's novel, and the comedy* A Spaceman at the Court of King Arthur, *drawing on Mark Twain's novel* A Connecticut Yankee in King Arthur's Court) *to Bresson's brooding film* Lancelot du Lac *and the stage musical* Camelot.
⋙ **heroes**

ARUNA
India

Aruna ('rose-coloured'), in Hindu myth, was god of the morning **sky**. He was hatched from the same clutch of eggs as **Garuda**, and would have been the most handsome god in **Heaven** except that his mother, eager to see him, broke the shell before he was fully formed, so that he had no feet. He was able to soar in the sky, but not to walk, and was barred forever from the gods' feasts and sacrifices.

ASCANIUS
Europe (South)

Ascanius (Askaneios, 'tentless'), in Greek myth, was the son of **Aeneas** and Creusa. When the Greeks captured Troy, Ascanius followed his father into exile, sailing with him to Sicily, Carthage and finally Italy. During the battles which followed the Trojans' landing near the mouth of the Tiber, Ascanius fought bravely, and when the war was won Aeneas declared him his heir. Shortly after this Aeneas died or disappeared, and Ascanius became king. He ruled for 30 years from Lavinium, his father's former city, then founded a new community, Alba Longa, on the site of the future Rome.

In the time of the Emperor Augustus, who was a member of the Julian (or Iulian) dynasty, enormous propaganda was organized to link the imperial family with the heroic founders of Rome and with the gods who were parents or ancestors of those founders. As part of this work, Livy and Virgil changed Ascanius' name to Iulus, borrowing the name of a later, less distinguished king of Alba Longa. This muddied the historical record, made the imperial descent seem even more distinguished, and caused the near disappearance of the name Ascanius from Julian circles, if not from myth, from that time on.

ASEGEIR
Europe (North)

The Asegeir, in Nordic myth, were twelve seers and scholars who set sail in a boat to try to convert all Scandinavia to wisdom instead of **war**. They were beset by a storm, but the god **Forseti** rescued them and steered their boat safely to the island of Heligoland, where they lived happily ever afterwards.

ASET
Africa (North)

Aset (or Eset, 'throne'; Greek Isis), in Egyptian myth, was the daughter of **Nut** and **Geb** and sister of **Osiris**, **Set** and **Nebthet**. She and Osiris had a dual function as **fertility** gods: she oversaw **love** and union, he was the god of growth. They ruled Egypt as wife and husband; he taught his subjects the rule of law and respect for the gods; she taught them marriage, household management and medicine.

After Osiris was drowned and dismembered by their jealous brother Set, Aset used her medical skills first to impregnate herself with the last drop of semen in her consort's penis, and then to reassemble the corpse and bring it back to life. The first magic worked, and she became pregnant with **Horus**. But the gods refused to let Osiris return to the world of mortals, and he went to rule in the **Underworld**, leaving Aset vowing revenge on Set. Instead of fighting him herself, she encouraged Horus to take every chance to try to kill him, and when this proved impossible she arranged for Horus to humiliate and disempower Set. In some accounts this happened when Horus castrated Set in a duel, fit punishment for Set's crime of cutting off Osiris' penis and throwing it into the Nile.

In other accounts, Set was defeated by a trick. Horus went to Aset, complaining that in one of their wrestling-bouts Set had raped him, and producing drops of the god's semen to prove it. Aset asked Horus to masturbate over a lettuce-bed, and when the lettuces were grown took the choicest to Set, who ate them greedily. Then she handcuffed him and took him before the court of the gods, claiming that he'd stolen what belonged to Horus. Set protested that he'd not stolen the lettuces but had been given them – at which point Horus' semen began flying out of his mouth like a flock of finches, returning to its creator.

*In a society most of whose gods concerned themselves with the sky or the Underworld, Aset was one of the few great powers identified exclusively with life on Earth. She was worshipped throughout Egypt as a queen in royal robes (paralleling the depiction of her brother Osiris as a king in the Underworld). She wore either a throne-shaped crown (symbolizing royal power) or cow's horns enfolding the Sun-disc, and carried a talisman, the tyet, a knotted girdle symbolizing the interconnectedness of life and sometimes made from red jasper to symbolize menstrual blood. In other representations she was shown as a pregnant sow or as a cow of plenty (either the goddess **Hathor** or – in Thebes – the cow which **Ptah** fertilized and which gave birth to **Hap**, the sacred bull).*

*Under the Greek name of Isis, Aset was worshipped particularly in the Greek-Egyptian towns of the Nile Delta, where she was regarded not as one of a pantheon of goddesses but as the **Great Goddess** herself. In the Delta myth-cycle, Isis tricked Ra into giving her his powers and his obligation to keep the universe in balance. She did this by a trick. Ra's power depended on*

*his true, secret name, known to no other being in creation. But although he was immortal, he was subject to aging, and one day Aset/Isis gathered some of the spittle he'd drooled into the sand and moulded a water-snake which bit him in the ankle. Racked with pain, he begged her to use her medical skill to cure him – and she agreed only if he told her his secret name. He told her a whole litany of false names, but each one made the snake-venom torment him even more, until at last he spoke the true secret name and was cured. Devotees of the **Mysteries** of Isis, a popular cult in Greek Egypt and Rome from the first century BCE to the time of the Christian Empire (fourth century CE), believed that knowledge of the name made Isis the most powerful deity in the universe – and furthermore, that when they themselves were told the name on their initiation into the cult, it gave them a (limited) share of the goddess' magic: power to defeat illness, aging and even death.*

⇛→ justice and universal order

ASGARD
Europe (North)

Asgard ('home of the **Aesir**'), in Nordic myth, was the realm of the gods, in the highest of the three levels of existence, above **Midgard** (home of human beings) and **Niflheim** (home of the Dead). It was not so much a citadel as an entire fortified country. The gods owned palaces, farms, meadows, forests and lakes. They spent their days as prosperous human landowners did in Midgard, tending their crops and animals, ruling their followers and meeting each other to enjoy hunting, feasting in their banqueting-hall Gladsheim ('joy-home') and listening to the songs of bards. Every morning they gathered in council at the Well of Urd, where the three **Norns** guarded one of the roots of **Yggdrasil**, tree of the universe.

Asgard was connected to Midgard by **Bifröst**, the rainbow bridge. But the gods, although they looked down into Midgard and supervised mortal lives, seldom visited it, and no mortal ever passed from Midgard to Asgard except the souls of dead **heroes**, carried by the **Valkyries** to **Valhalla**. The **giants**, by contrast, were always trying to invade Asgard, hoping to steal the golden apples of **immortality**. Against their attacks the Aesir surrounded Asgard with an enormous wall. It was built by immortals and could be destroyed only by immortals. During the war between Aesir and **Vanir**, the entire wall was smashed, and a giant master-mason offered to rebuild it. He demanded as price the **Sun**, the **Moon** and **Freyja**, guardian of immortality, and the gods tried to cheat him by setting a time-limit too short for the work to be done. But the giant was helped by his magic horse Svadilfari, and it was only when **Loki** disguised himself as a mare and seduced Svadilfari away from the work, three days before the deadline, that the gods both got their wall and kept their immortality.

Ever after this, the myth ends, since both Asgard's defences and the gods' continuing immortality depend on a trick, they have been imperfect and are therefore doomed. At **Ragnarök**, the end of the universe, the forces of evil will rise to do battle with the powers of light, and Asgard will be overwhelmed. Its walls, rebuilt not by gods but by a mortal giant, will fall and it and its inhabitants will pass from existence as if they had never been.

⋙➤ **Heaven**

ASGAYA GIGAGEI
Americas (North)

Asgaya Gigagei ('red person' or 'red man of lightning'), in the myths of the Cherokee people of the Southeastern US, was a healing spirit which indicated sympathy by assuming the same sex as the person who asked for its help.

⋙➤ **disease and healing**

ASHUR
Asia (West)

Ashur (or Ashshur or Assur), in Mesopotamian myth, was the chief god of the Assyrian people of what is now Kurdistan. In **Heaven** he was the principle of **justice and universal order**, and his defeat of chaos kept the universe in being. On Earth he was the guarantor of **fertility** (symbolized by his appearance in art as a goatherd), or a warrior, protector of the city named after him, and depicted either as a king standing on a bull or, even more symbolically, as a bow or thunderbolt enclosed in a winged **Sun**-disc.

⋙➤ **supreme deity**

ASHVATHAMAN
India

Ashvathaman, in Hindu myth, was the son of **Drona**, one of the **Kaurava** generals in their war with the **Pandavas**. The gods had told Drona that he and humans, involved in the Trojan War. They then propelled this story forwards, generation by generation, until they linked Aeneas to **Romulus and Remus**, sons of Mars and founders of the city of Rome – and from them, by a process which gradually blended myth into legend and legend into 'real' history, to the current ruling dynasties of the city and the Empire. Virgil and Livy are the best-known authors involved in this process, but they were not inventing what they wrote so much as codifying what every educated Roman, and many uneducated Romans, already knew.

In this book, to save unnecessary duplication, where the same stories are told both about Roman-named characters and characters from other traditions, they come under the participants' original names – usually Greek, though characters from more remote traditions such as **Cybele** and **Mithras** make appearances. Roman names appear in the index, and refer to these entries: thus, for example, Latona is referred to the article on **Leto**, Pluto to **Hades**, Venus to **Aphrodite**. Other main parallels are as follows (article-headword in brackets): **Aesculapius** (Asclepius), Aurora (**Eos**); Bacchus (**Dionysus**), Ceres (**Demeter**), Cupido (**Eros**), Diana (**Artemis**), Juno (**Hera**), **Jupiter** (**Zeus**), Mars (**Ares**), Mercurius (**Hermes**), Minerva (**Athene**), Neptunus (**Poseidon**), Saturnus (**Cronus**), Terra (**Gaia**), Uranus (**Ouranos**), Venus (**Aphrodite**), Vulcan (**Hephaestus**). ⟫⤖ Achates, *Aeneid*, Anchises, Angerona, Baucis and Philemon, Bellona, Cacus, Dido, Epona, Faunus, Flora, Fortuna, Hersilia, Horatius Cocles, Lar, Latinus, Lavinia, Lucretia, Mania, *manes*, *Metamorphoses*, Mors, Nisus and Euryalus, Penates, Picus and Canens, Pomona and Vertumnus, Psyche, Pylades, Pyrrhus, Saturnus, Tiber, Troilus and Cressida, Turnus

ROMULUS AND REMUS
Europe (South)

Two brothers in Roman myth, Numitor and Amulius, ruled the town of Alba Longa, founded twelve generations before by Trojan settlers led by **Ascanius**, son of **Aeneas**. Numitor was the lawmaker, Amulius the warlord. After several years' joint rule, the brothers quarrelled, and Amulius deposed Numitor and took full control. To prevent the rise of a rival royal dynasty, he imprisoned Numitor and made Numitor's daughter Rhea Silvia a Vestal Virgin, sworn to eternal celibacy.

The gods, however, had other plans for Alba Longa. **Mars** raped Rhea Silvia on the banks of the **Tiber**, and in due course she gave birth to **twins**, Romulus and Remus. Amulius was furious. He killed Rhea Silvia by burying her alive (a standard punishment for spoiled Vestals), and ordered that Romulus and Remus be drowned in the Tiber. But the river-god floated the babies to safety in a basket, washing it up on the shore under a fig-tree (later called Ruminal) beside a grotto (later called Lupercal). A she-wolf found and suckled the twins, until they were rescued and brought up by the royal shepherd Faustulus and his wife Larentia. When Romulus and Remus were fully-grown, Mars appeared to them and told them the story of their birth. They led an uprising of shepherds and farmhands, killed Amulius and restored their grandfather Numitor to the throne.

Rome. In the next few years, overcrowding in Alba Longa led Romulus and Remus to found a new town, on the shores of the Tiber where they had once been left to die. While Romulus marked out boundaries, ploughing furrows to mark the line of new fields and walls, Remus and his men went hunting. On Remus' return, the brothers quarrelled. One account says that Remus mocked the new 'walls', jumping scornfully over them, and Romulus or one of his followers killed him. Another says that the brothers took bird-auguries to decide who would rule the new city. Remus saw six vultures on the right (the favourable side), Romulus twelve on the unlucky left. The brothers argued about which augury was better, there was a skirmish and Remus was killed. The new settlement was named Rome, and Romulus was its king.

Rape of the Sabines. Despite early military and mercantile success, Rome seemed doomed to die in a single generation. It was a town of men, without women. Romulus invited the people of neighbouring towns and villages to a festival in honour of Neptune (see **Poseidon**), declaring (as at all religious events) a sacred truce and welcoming women and children as well as men. But when the signal was sounded for the Games, instead of lining up to race the young Romans took out concealed weapons and abducted the visiting women. This incident – known ever afterwards as the Rape of the Sabines, after the most numerous of the visiting peoples – led to several years of inter-communal war, ended only when the women marched between their Roman husbands and their parents and insisted that peace be made.

Romulus' departure from the world. Romulus ruled for forty years. He was presiding one day at an athletics festival when the gods shrouded the area with cloud and took him up to **Olympus**. He was made immortal – some say as the war-god Quirinus, a follower of Mars whose temple was on the Quirinal Hill in Rome – and was worshipped throughout Roman history as creator and protector of his people.

The main surviving sources for this story are the Roman writers Livy and Ovid. Livy was a historian, concerned – in the manner of his time – to tell the story of his people from mythical times, and to give legitimacy to contemporary rulers and practices by finding, or inventing, precedents in the distant and supernatural past. Ovid was more interested in telling a good story, but projected contemporary habits of speech, dress and custom back on the people of the past (rather as Shakespeare did later). The origins of the myth – it is akin in some details to the wolf-children stories characteristic of Northern and Central Europe, and in others to many world myths about quarrelling twins – are thus lost under a later Roman gloss. Subsequent tellings, and all depictions in art, take Livy or Ovid as their starting points.

The she-wolf suckling human babies became a main symbol of the city of Rome, and a statue of the scene (not all of which is authentic) survives to this day in the Capitoline Museum. Ancient Roman artists, however, avoided later events of the myth, preferring to depict Romulus in his godly transformation, and Remus hardly at all – and more modern artists, for examples Rubens and the Pre-Raphaelites, followed this trend, so that the part of the story most favoured in art is the Rape of the Sabines, with its opportunities for showing huge panoramas of warrior males in uniform and nubile females half (or more) undressed.

ROSMERTA
Europe (North)

Rosmerta ('great provider'), in Celtic myth, was the goddess of plenty. Originally a goddess of **fertility** and harvest, when the Romans conquered Celtic lands she was made the consort of Mercury (see **Hermes**) god of markets, and became the guarantor of success in business.

RUAUMOKO
Oceania

Ruaumoko, in Maori myth, was the youngest immortal child of **Rangi** (Sky) and **Papa** (Earth). When the gods split Rangi and Papa apart, and turned Papa face down so that Rangi would not see her face from above and weep oceans of tears for her, Ruaumoko was still an infant, suckling at Papa's breast. He fell into the darkness of the **Underworld**, and his brothers, gods of the Upper World, were unable to rescue him. But they pitied his crying, and Tawhiri the windlord took a **lightning**-bolt from his brother Tu, god of **war**, and blew it down to the Underworld to warm Ruaumoko. This lightning was the ancestor of all Underworld fires, and when Ruaumoko grew up he spent his time stoking them, causing **earthquakes** and sending molten rock and flame streaming through vent-holes to the world above.

RUDRA
India

Rudra's birth. Rudra ('howler' or 'red') came to India with the Aryan invaders of the seventeenth century BCE. In some accounts he was the son of **Prajapati** the creator and **Ushas** the dawn. Horrified that Prajapati and Ushas should have committed incest, the gods gathered the most terrible attributes of each of them and gave them to Rudra. The child began to cry, and his father immediately named him 'Howler'. This was a mistake, as one of the Rudra's first acts was set arrow to bow and shoot him. In another account, Rudra was the joint child of Ushas and her four brothers **Aditya**, **Agni**, **Candramus** and **Vayu**. When the brothers saw Ushas for the first time, they became so sexually excited that they spilled semen across the universe – and Prajapati gathered it and made from it a power with 1000 eyes and 1000 feet: Rudra. In yet another version, Rudra was **Brahma**'s son, born in an explosion of anger from his father's forehead.

Rudra's nature and powers. Rudra was the god of storm-winds, thieves and murderers, and raged through the universe in imitation of **Agni**, god of fire. His food was corpses, and he drank the blood of bulls. To appease him, people worshipped him as *shiva*, 'kindly' – and this led to his later merging with the god **Shiva**, who took over his attributes and powers. Like most gods of disease, he was his own mirror-image, healer as well as killer, and he was also worshipped as the scouring heat of the **Sun** and as the wind of artistic inspiration. His children, sometimes called Rudras after him, were the **Maruts** or storm-winds.

Rudra usually appears in art as a blue-necked man with many red faces, a black belly, innumerable arms and legs and a furious temper. He wears shaggy animal-skins, rides a wild boar, spits with rage and shoots arrows of death at anyone in his path. In some paintings and sculptures he is shown as a huge, roaring bull.

»+ **disease and healing, Rudrani**

RUDRANI
India

Rudrani ('red princess') came to India with the Aryan invaders of the seventeenth century BCE. She was **Rudra**'s wife, bringer of **death** and disease, a monster who gorged on the blood of battle and lapped it from the edges of sacrifice. (In later, Hindu myth she became identified with **Durga**.) She ended the gods' **fertility**. When she and Rudra first mated, they were locked together for so long that the gods, alarmed at the kind of monster such a union might produce, begged Rudra to withdraw without ejaculating semen. He did so, and swore that he would never have **sex** again. Rudrani cursed the gods with infertility – and they never again had offspring. The only exception was **Agni**, who was not there when Rudrani made her curse.

»+ **disease and healing**

RUGIEVIT
Europe (East)

Rugievit was an ancient **war** god of the Western Baltic, particularly associated with the island of Rügen. He was chiefly remembered for his savagery, symbolized by his wearing seven swords and brandishing an eighth, and by the savage glances from his seven faces.

RUHANGA
Africa

Ruhanga, in the myths of the Banyoro people of Uganda, was the god of **fertility** and prosperity. He gave people health and happiness, and in his kindness even promised that they would be immortal, rising from the grave – on condition that no one ever mourned for a dead relative, but put on festive clothes and danced. The whole human race accepted this condition except for one woman, who refused to dance and sing when her daughter (or in some accounts, her pet dog) died – and Ruhanga had no choice but to make **death** the end of our existence.

RUKMINI
India

Rukmini, in Hindu myth, was one of the avatars of **Lakshmi**. When **Vishnu** went to Earth as **Krishna**, Lakshmi followed him, becoming Rukmini, sister of Prince Rukmin of Vidarbha. Rukmin wanted to marry his sister to the **demon**-prince **Sisupala**, a sworn enemy of Krishna, but Rukmini wrote Krishna a letter begging him to rescue her, and he kidnapped her from the wedding-ceremony and married her himself. She became the first and most important of his 16,108 wives, and bore him a mortal son: Pradyumna, an avatar of the love-god **Kama**.

RUSSALKI, THE
Europe (East)

The Russalki (plural of Russalka) were the souls of unbaptized babies or of young girls who had accidentally drowned or died on their wedding nights. (Some mythologists associate the name with Rosa, the Latin for 'rose', and say that the Russalki were named after the wedding-garlands they wore.) They sang seductively over ponds and rivers, luring male hearers to disaster. In Southern Slavic lands the Russalki were long-haired and beautiful, nesting in trees hanging over the water, dancing in water-meadows to make the ground fertile, and tickling their prey to death. In Northern Slavic lands they were ugly and cold, roosting like bats in lakeside trees.

≫→ **water**

RUWA
Africa

Ruwa, creator-god in the myths of the Djaga people of Kenya, made human beings and planted a paradise-garden for them to live in. He gave them **immortality**, on condition that they avoided picking or eating the fruit of just one plant in the garden, a yam called Ukaho. Every morning and evening he sent an angel to make sure that this condition had been kept. One night, as the angel came down to Earth, he smelled yam cooking – not just any yam, but Ukaho itself. In the cool of the afternoon **Death** had visited the garden and told the people that Ruwa had made a special exception: for him, and him alone, they could prepare Ukaho. The angel took Ukaho's remains, in their pot, back to Ruwa, who reconstituted Ukaho in **Heaven** for the gods alone. He left mortals their garden, but they were now Death's prey.

*This myth is one of the oldest in all Africa, and predates the **Adam and Eve** story in the Bible. The similarities between them – and indeed the prevalence of myths in which immortality is contained in a fruit forbidden to mortals – have suggested to some mythographers that all such stories have a common ancestor, and the possibility is that it came from this region of Kenya, where the human race first evolved.*

*In another Djaga myth, also of a type common throughout Africa, Ruwa told mortals that they could keep ever-young by taking off their aged hides as **snakes** and other reptiles sloughed their skins. The method worked until a young girl who knew nothing of it burst in by accident on her grandfather while he was half-undressed, and the spell was forever broken.*

Satan and the Rebel Angels (*William Blake, 18th century*)

SADKO
Europe (East)

Sadko, originally a pagan **water**-god in Slavic myth, was reinvented in Christian times as one of the *bogatiri* associated with the city of Novgorod. He was a merchant trading overseas. One day his boat was becalmed in mid-ocean, and Sadko took three cups, filled one with gold, one with silver and one with jewels, and floated them on the sea-surface on a plank, for the servants of the Tsar of the Sea to carry to their master. But the plank stayed where it was, and Sadko realized that the Tsar demanded human sacrifice. He and his crew drew lots, and Sadko himself was chosen. He took his *gusli* (a string instrument) – and in more pious accounts, an icon of Saint Nicholas calmer of storms – climbed on to the plank and was drawn down to the Sea-Tsar's underwater palace. He played his *gusli*, and the Tsar was delighted and began to dance, faster and faster until the sea boiled overhead. Realizing that it was about to drown the world, Sadko broke the strings of his *gusli*, took firm hold of Saint Nicholas and escaped to the surface.

The storm had left Sadko penniless. For twelve years he worked as a barge-hand on the river Volga, eating nothing but bread and salt. Then he decided to go back to Novgorod, and at the end of his last day on the Volga he gave the river a gift of salted bread and a prayer of thanks. The river-spirit answered, asking Sadko to take a greeting to its brother, Lake Ilmen. Sadko did so, and the lake-spirit told him to cast fishing-nets in the deepest part of the water. Sadko hauled in three huge nets, bursting with fish – and when he carried them back to land they turned into silver coins, making him rich again.

This favourite story is best-known outside Russia in the form of Rimsky-Korsakov's opera Sadko, and the 'symphonic picture' he derived from its music.
≫→ heroes

SAGARA
India

Sagara, in Hindu myth, was a mortal king ambitious to become a god. By prayer and sacrifice he won the gift that one of his wives would have one son, the other 60,000. The first son was conceived by sexual intercourse in the normal way, the others when Sagara masturbated over a gourd held by his second wife and containing 60,000 seeds. However the sons were conceived, they were all worthless, as Sagara had forgotten to ask that they be noble or heroic.

Sagara set out to dethrone **Indra**. He planned to sacrifice the celestial horse which symbolized the strength of the universe, and so to gather that strength for himself. Indra hid the horse deep in the womb of **Mother Earth**, and Sagara set 60,000 of his sons to dig down and find it. Mother Earth complained to the gods, and they turned the sons into burrowing termites before they could do more harm. Indra said that the sons would come back to human form if, and only if, the river Ganges left **Heaven** and flowed down to Earth. This was equivalent to saying 'Never' – but Sagara persisted. He ruled for 30,000 years, perpetually sacrificing and praying to **Brahma** to order the Ganges down to Earth. Brahma at first refused to listen, but after Sagara's surviving son, grandson and great-grandson also plagued his ears with prayers and sapped his will with sacrifice, he agreed. He intended the Ganges to fall like a meteorite and destroy the Earth, but **Shiva** took the river's weight on his head and made it flow more gently.

Sagara is the personification of ocean, and his 60,001 sons are the world's various seas and lakes. He asked for the Ganges to flow on Earth to make sure that his own strength was constantly replenished – and Shiva's weakening of the flow of the Ganges was essential to prevent Sagara/Ocean from brimming up and swamping all creation.

SAHADEVA
India

Sahadeva, in Hindu myth, was one of the twin sons of the **Ashvins** and the mortal **Madri**, second wife of King **Pandu**. (His twin brother was **Nakula**.) Sahadeva fought with his **Pandava** brothers in their war against the **Kauravas**, and was famous as much for his peppery pride as for his fighting skill.
≫→ heroes

SAKTASURA
India

Saktasura, in Hindu myth, was a **demon** who tried to kill the infant **Krishna** by crushing him. The child was lying in the shade under a wagon. Saktasura took the form of a dove and alighted on the wagon – and just as he did so, changed back to his full size and mountainous weight. The cart collapsed, but Krishna underneath lifted one tiny foot and kicked it up so that it rolled on top of Saktasura and killed him.

SALMONEUS
Europe (South)

Salmoneus ('loved by the goddess Salma'), in Greek myth, was the son of **Aeolus** the wind-lord and the mortal Enaratta. His brothers were **Athamas** and **Sisyphus**. He ruled in Thessaly, with extreme cruelty, until he was forced out by his people, after Sisyphus his brother claimed that he had slept incestuously with his own daughter Tyro. Salmoneus went to Elis, where he founded a new city, Salmonia. Here his arrogance reigned unchecked, until one day he went too far, announcing that he was no longer a mortal but had changed into **Zeus** himself and was ready to receive his people's worship. He drove through the streets in a chariot, dragging a bundle of copper cooking pots: their clattering, he claimed, was how Zeus made **thunder** in the sky. For thunderbolts he lit oak-branches at a brazier in the chariot and hurled them at his subjects. In the end Zeus hurled a real thunderbolt at him and dashed him to the **Underworld**.

SAMBA
India

Samba, in Hindu myth, was **Krishna**'s son. He inherited his father's delight in pranks and tricks, but had none of the god's compassion or common sense. Rather than win a bride in the usual way, for example, he chose the adventurous method of abduction, kidnapping the daughter of the **Kaurava** prince **Duryodhana** and so prolonging the huge war related in the *Mahabharata*. His impishness eventually led to his own father's departure from Earth. He dressed as a pregnant woman and taunted some Brahmins, asking which of them would admit to being the baby's father. They cursed him: he was to bear an iron club which would kill his father. In due course the club was 'born', and Samba immediately had it broken up and thrown in the sea. But a fish swallowed one piece of it, and when the fish was caught the fragment was found and made into an arrowhead – the very one by which, later, Krishna was accidentally killed.

SAMPO, THE
Europe (North)

The *sampo*, in Finnish myth, was a magic mill demanded by Princess **Louhi** of **Pohjola** as the bride-price for her daughter. She said that whoever made the mill would marry the girl. **Väinämöinen**, who had originally courted Louhi's daughter, forgot this condition, and asked his brother **Ilmarinen** to make the *sampo*. Ilmarinen threw into his furnace swansdown, milk from a barren cow, sheep's wool and barley, and sang moulding-spells as he worked the bellows. On the first day a golden bowl appeared, on the second a copper ship, on the third a cow with golden horns and on the fourth a plough made of precious metals. Each was a guarantor of prosperity, but Ilmarinen threw them back into the furnace and waited.

On the fifth day the *sampo* appeared: a mill shaped like a pyramid. Out of the first side came endless supplies of salt, out of the second flour and out of the third gold.

Ilmarinen took it to Louhi and duly married her daughter. The *sampo* brought prosperity to Pohjola, and Väinämöinen coveted it for his own people in Finland. His chance to steal it came when Ilmarinen's wife died and her mother Louhi refused to let Ilmarinen marry her younger sister. Väinämöinen, Ilmarinen and **Lemminkäinen** sailed to Pohjola, made the people fall asleep by playing music on a magic zither, and stole the *sampo*. On the way home, their ship was battered by a storm sent by Louhi, and the *sampo* was smashed and washed overboard. But Väinämöinen managed to rescue enough of the pieces to take home to Finland, and their magic made his country the prosperous, peaceful place it remains to this day.

SAMSON
Asia (West)

Samson (Shimshon, 'Sun-man'), in Hebrew myth, was a **giant** trapped in a normal-sized human body. His superhuman strength (which he used to fight the Philistines) depended on strict devotion to **Yahweh**, and was symbolized by his refusal to drink alcohol or cut his hair. The Philistines sent Delilah to seduce him, and when he got drunk and told her his secret she cut off his hair so that the enemy soldiers could lead him away, as helpless as a child. They blinded him, chained him between the pillars of their temple, and set him to work the mill like an animal. He endured this until his hair grew again, then exerted all his strength and pulled down the pillars and the temple, killing his enemies and himself.

Mythographers regard this story as a devotional reworking of an original Sun-myth, now otherwise lost. Samson is the strength of the Sun, and his long hair symbolizes its rays at midday. Cutting the hair and blinding are forms of emasculation – a humiliation Sun-men undergo in myths of all cultures. Samson's devotion to Yahweh and ritual forms of self-denial, the heart of the story to the Hebrew teachers who reworked it, are regarded by myth-experts as pious embroideries.

SANDHYA
India

Sandhya, in Hindu myth, was **Brahma**'s daughter. She was so beautiful that her own father lusted after her. In some accounts, Brahma got drunk and raped Sandhya, and **Shiva** punished him by cutting off his fifth head. In others, Sandhya was Shiva's wife, and Shiva prevented the rape by turning her into a doe and shooting her before Brahma (now changed into a stag) could mount her.
≫→ **beauty**

SANJNA: *see* Surya (Sun)

SAOSHYANT
Asia (West)

Saoshyant ('saviour'), in ancient Iranian myth, was the saviour whose coming would inaugurate the last age of the world, the Golden Age restored when **Ahura Mazda**, spirit of light, finally routed the power of darkness (**Ahriman**). He has not yet come.

SARANYU
India

Saranyu, in the Vedic myths of the Aryans who invaded India in the seventeenth century BCE, was the daughter of the smith-god **Tvashtri**. She married **Vivasvat**, god of the rising **Sun**, and bore him twin children, **Yama** and Yami, the first human beings. Then, afraid of her husband's dazzling radiance, she hid among the clouds, leaving in her place an exact replica of herself (some say fashioned by her father). Vivasvat fathered **Manu** on this clone before she told him who she was. Vivasvat searched **Heaven**, Earth and Middle Air for Saranyu, and eventually found her in the shape of a mare. He became a stallion and reared to mount her, but was so excited that he prematurely ejaculated. His semen spilled from the clouds onto **Mother Earth**; Saranyu sniffed it and at once became pregnant. In time she gave birth to the twin **Ashvins**.

SARASVATI
India

Sarasvati ('she who flows'), in Hindu myth, was originally a river-goddess, and devotees still sometimes claim to see her at the confluence of the rivers Ganges and Yamuna, the most sacred place in India. Her other names include Brahmi ('[female] first principle'), Shatarupa ('hundred-formed'), Savitri ('life-giver') and Vac ('speech').

Sarasvati and Brahma. In one version of the Hindu **creation**-myth, Sarasvati was the first being created by **Brahma**. Either he divided himself in two, making her the female half, or she was born in a gush of **water** from his side and turned at once into a goddess. She was so beautiful that he lusted after her – the first lust ever felt. Shyly she drew back, walking slowly round him in a circle; or, some say, she danced round him in delight at being in his presence. As she walked, or danced, he remained sitting where he was, but grew a second, third and fourth face to gaze at her with eyes of love. She soared above him, and he grew a fifth face on top of his head to see her. (This was later burned off by the rays of **Shiva**.) Sarasvati and Brahma retired into seclusion for 100 divine years (147,688,000 mortal years), and during that immortal honeymoon they created everything which exists.

In another, far less complimentary myth, Sarasvati was originally one of the three wives of **Vishnu**, the others being **Lakshmi** and **Ganga**. But the three squabbled ceaselessly, and Vishnu gave Sarasvati to Brahma and Ganga to Shiva, keeping Lakshmi for himself. In this myth, Sarasvati was vain and lazy, and Brahma took a second wife, Gayatri, who was more interested in intellectual pursuits. Sarasvati insisted that she was the senior wife, but the dispute between intellectuality and **beauty** in females has – males say – never been resolved from that time to this.

Sarasvati and the arts. Sarasvati is the goddess of the arts, particularly poetry and **music**, and inspires all science and scholarship. She invented writing, and put order into musical sounds. When Brahma's four faces gave birth to the four *Vedas* (sacred writings), she took charge of them. Sarasvati forms Brahma's inspirations and gives them to humans. She is worshipped with gifts of flowers, fruit and incense, and her shrines are often found in libraries.

Sarasvati is second only to Lakshmi in the beauty of the art she has inspired. She is usually shown as a voluptuous, serenely-smiling woman sitting on a lotus, riding a peacock or swan, or gazing enraptured at Brahma. Her skin is ivory, her forehead is a crescent moon, and her four arms hold objects connected with the arts or with **beauty***: a musical instrument, a pen, a necklace, a perfume-box.*
≫→ civilization, fertility

SATAN
Asia (West)

Satan (Shaitan, 'adversary'), in Hebrew myth, was originally an angel, a lord of light. (Later Christian theologians, writing in Latin, identified him as Lucifer, 'light-bringer', the morning star.) But he despised **Yahweh**'s son **Adam**, not only refusing to honour him but tempting him to disobey his creator by eating the fruit of the Tree of All-knowledge in the Garden of Eden. Yahweh punished Satan for this by hurling him from **Heaven** to Hell, where Satan became Prince of Darkness just as Yahweh was Prince of Light. His original courtiers were other fallen angels (for example Azazel, who lusted after a mortal and fathered on her the monstrous Asmodaeus), but he soon gathered an army of imps and **demons** (many of them spawned from matings between angels and humans, angels and animals or animals and humans), and began using them to tempt or torment the human beings he hated.

On this simple myth-foundation Jewish and Christian writers built an enormous philosophical and psychological edifice, in which Satan became not merely an embodiment of evil but the Other, the negative image of ourselves with which, with God's help, we must come to terms. In the Middle Ages, however, ordinary people in Europe sidestepped such intellectual ideas and reverted to the idea that Satan was a physical rather than a spiritual adversary. Satanic cults and demon-worship became endemic and a vast literature of rituals, spells and prophetic utterances, much of it in numerological code, began to be compiled. This literature and the practices it serviced, in their turn, richly fed the imagination of tale-tellers, painters, playwrights and writers: everything from Hieronymus Bosch's depictions of Hell to such stories as Faust *or* Little Red Riding Hood, *at one level, and at another the whole horror-genre from* Dracula *or* Doctor Jeckyll and Mr Hyde *to such films as* Friday the Thirteenth *or* Nightmare on Elm Street, *sucks power from it.*

SATI
India

Sati, in Hindu myth, was the daughter of **Daksha**. She was in love with **Shiva**, but her father opposed the marriage, until Sati forced his hand by throwing a bouquet of flowers into the air at a betrothal-banquet – for Shiva to catch.

Afterwards, Daksha lost no opportunity of insulting Shiva, and finally Sati grew so angry that she threw herself into a sacrificial **fire** and died. The grief-stricken Shiva took her body and began dancing – his dance of death which would destroy the universe. Vishnu hastily brought Sati back to life, reincarnating her as **Parvati**, and she spent the rest of eternity as Shiva's beautiful, playful and loving wife.

Some authorities say that the myth of Sati's self-sacrifice for love was devised to explain the custom of wives throwing themselves (actually or symbolically) on their dead husbands' funeral-pyres – a custom named sati (or 'suttee') after her.

SATURNUS
Europe (South)

Saturnus ('sower'), in Roman myth, was one of the oldest of the gods. When the Romans incorporated their myths with those of the Greeks, they identified him with **Cronus**, and the stories of Cronus' mutilation of his father **Ouranos** (Roman Uranus or Coelus) and his battle with his children (led by **Zeus**, Roman **Jupiter**) were told of Saturnus too. The main change was at the end of the story. Instead of sending Saturnus with the other **Titans** to punishment in the **Underworld** or to live in the Islands of the Blessed in the Far West, Jupiter allowed him to escape to Italy, where he ruled jointly with **Janus**. Saturnus taught the Italians such skills as **farming**, architecture and engineering, and during his reign the world enjoyed peace and prosperity unknown before or since. (It was the first of the **Five Ages**: the Golden Age.) At the end of his time on Earth he went to live forever in the sky: the planet Saturn.

Because Saturnus was pardoned by Jupiter, he was the patron god of freed slaves, and his temples were full of miniature manacles and leg-chains of gold and silver, thank-offerings from grateful freedmen. He supervised the Saturnalia, held at the turn of every year: a carnival during which slaves and owners symbolically changed places for a day or two, there was a legal amnesty, a series of bank holidays, no business was carried on and there was eating, drinking and high-spirited enjoyment. The celebrations climaxed on December 25 – the day accordingly chosen by the early Christians as Christ's official birthday.
≫→ civilization

SATYRS
Europe (South)

Satyrs (Latin Fauni, 'fauns' or Silvani, 'forest-people'), in Greek and Roman myth, were the offspring of mountain nymphs and goats. From the waist up they were human, from the waist down goat, and some had horses' tails into the bargain. They served **Dionysus**, and were famous for drunkenness and the lasciviousness of their dancing.
≫→ Faunus, Pan, sex, Silenus

SAULE
Europe (East)

Saule, the **Sun** in Baltic myth, was courted by **Sky** but then became the consort of **Meness** the **Moon**. The stars and Earth were their children. However, Saule still spent half of each day with Sky, and there was constant bickering between her and Meness. What mortals called an eclipse was when she and Meness had just made up, and hung a sheet of darkness to hide them from the world while they made love. They would have separated except that they couldn't decide who should have custody of Earth, their favourite child. In the end **Pyerun** said that he would chase away whichever of Sky and Moon lingered too long with her. Saule got up so early that Meness got bored and went to make love with the Morning Star.

Every morning, Saule left Moon's bed and harnessed her gleaming copper chariot. She rode across Sky to the sea, where she washed her horses and then either sat on the Sky-hill or sailed a copper boat across the sea. Sometimes she wept, and her tears turned to red berries and fell to Earth.

In some Baltic traditions, the sexes of Saule and Meness are reversed.

SAVITRI (GOD)
India

Savitri (or Savitar, 'life-giver'), in the Vedic myths of the Aryans who invaded India in the seventeenth century BCE, was **Aditi**'s son and the god of movement: he caused the rotation of day and night, supervised the seasons and managed the turning year. He was the morning and evening **Sun**, and was shown as a fire-haired prince riding a golden chariot pulled by white horses whose manes streamed **fire**.

SAVITRI (PRINCESS)
India

Savitri, in Hindu myth, was a mortal princess named after the goddess **Sarasvati**. She fell in love with Prince Satyavan, who lived as a forest hermit with his blind father, exiled King Dyumatsena. She married Satyavan, despite being told that he had only one year to live. At the end of the year she went with her husband into the forest, where **Yama**, judge of the dead, was waiting. Savitri followed Yama as he dragged Satyavan towards the **Underworld**. Three times Yama turned, praised her faithfulness, and promised to reward it with any gift she asked. First, she wished that Dyumatsena's sight would be restored. Second, she wished that Dyumatsena be restored to power. Third, she wished that she might become the mother of a thousand children – and when Yama agreed, pointed out that this would be impossible unless her husband came back to life. Yama, as amused by her trick as he'd been charmed by her devotion, granted her wish.

⟫→ **beauty**

SCAMANDER
Europe (South)

Scamander (Skamandros, 'twisted'), son of the Cretan priest Corybas in Greek myth, was a worshipper of **Cybele**, goddess of **fertility**, whose followers danced themselves into ecstatic trances during which they mutilated themselves with knives. Scamander sailed from Crete to take the rites of Cybele to other countries, and settled at the foot of Mount Ida (near the future site of Troy). He began to teach the local people Cybele's worship, and was demonstrating the ecstatic dance when he fell into the river Xanthus and drowned. Cybele granted him **immortality** on Earth, making him god of the river (whose name she changed to Scamander after him) and giving him the power to ensure the fertility of any young female who bathed in his waters. Ever afterwards, farmers used to dip their sheep and cattle in the water, young women used to swim there on the night before their marriages – and when **Aphrodite**, **Athene** and **Hera** were preparing to appear before **Paris**, asking him to say who was most beautiful, they made sure to bathe in Scamander first.

≫→ **water**

SCYLLA AND CHARYBDIS
Europe (South)

Scylla (Skulle, 'bitch') and Charybdis ('sucker-down'), in Greek myth, were **sea-monsters**. Scylla was the daughter of the sea-god Phorcys and the witch-goddess **Hecate** (or, some say, the monster **Lamia**). She was originally a beautiful sea-sprite, but **Poseidon** had **sex** with her, and his jealous wife **Amphitrite** filled Scylla's favourite pool with poisonous herbs, so that the next time Scylla bathed there she was turned into a revolting monster. In another version of the story, the transformation was worked by **Circe**, who was jealous because the sea god Glaucus preferred Scylla to herself. But whoever changed Scylla, the result was the same. From the waist up she kept human form, but from her waist sprouted twelve dogs' legs and six yapping heads with razor teeth and snaky necks. Charybdis was the daughter of Poseidon and a sea-**nymph**, and was as beautiful as Scylla until she, too, offended the gods.

Scylla and Charybdis went hunting together, eating seals, sealions, dolphins and anything else that came their way. But one day they went too far, attacking and eating the herd of cattle **Heracles** had stolen from **Geryon**. It was time for the gods to punish them. Heracles killed Scylla, and her father Phorcys quickly burned the body and boiled the ash, to bring her back to life. He gave her a new home, in a cave on a cliff whose peak pierced the skies and whose sides were washed glass-smooth by waves. Zeus stole Charybdis' beautiful body from her, leaving her nothing but a toothless, ravenous mouth just under the surface of the sea.

The lairs of Scylla and Charybdis were on opposite sides of the narrow sea-channel between Italy and Sicily. Three times a day Charybdis opened her gullet and swallowed the sea overhead and anything in it. Scylla waited on guard above, reaching down and eating alive whatever passed her way: seagulls, fish and – as the crews of **Odysseus** and **Aeneas** found to their cost – human beings.

SEA

The sea and its gods played an equivocal part in many myth-traditions. The sea was often thought to have existed before the rest of the universe, as the primordial ocean from which all life began. But **creation** itself was usually done by **Sky** and Earth, and their gods took precedence over those of the ocean. In some traditions Sea then fought Sky and Earth for a share of power, or they divided it by agreement. In others, sea-gods lived aloof from the rest of the pantheon, rulers of an element filled with beings like no others in creation, and endowed with knowledge of the universe's primordial secrets, predating all other gods and the source of a power as overwhelming as it was mysterious.

≫→ (Americas): Komokwa, Pachacamac; (Arctic): Aulanerk; (Celtic): Lir, Manannan MacLir; (China): Four Dragon Kings; (Egypt): Nun and Naunet; (Finnish): Ahto; (Greece): Amphitrite, Nereus, Poseidon, Proteus, Telchines, Thetis; (India): Tara; (Japan): Tide Jewels; (Mesopotamia): Tiamat; (Nordic) Aegir, Njörd, Ran; (Oceania): Tangaroa

SEDNA
Arctic

Sedna, or Arnarquagssaq, or Nerrivik, or Nuliajuk, in Eskimo myth, was the daughter of the creator-god Anguta and his wife. In some accounts she was so huge, and so hungry, that she ate everything in her parents' home, and even gnawed off one of her father's arms as he slept. In others, she refused to marry the suitor Anguta chose for her and instead took a dog for husband. (Their children were all the human beings and animals on Earth.) Some accounts go on to say that she was then kidnapped by Petrel, and when her father rescued her in a canoe, Petrel sank it in a storm. Others say that her father was so angry at her marrying a dog that he threw her overboard. She clung to the sides of the canoe, and he chopped her fingers off one by one until she sank to the depths. She lives there still, queen of all the **monsters** and **demons** of the **Underworld** – and her huge fingers are the origin of seals, sea-lions and whales.

≫→ **giants**

SEKHMET
Africa (North)

Sekhmet (or Sakhmet, 'powerful'), in Egyptian myth, was consort of **Ptah** the craftsman-god and daughter of **Ra**, the Sun. She was lion-headed and carried a fire-spitting cobra. When she was at rest, she was a figure of calm, royal dignity. But when she was angry, she transformed herself into the Eye of Ra, and became a war-goddess so fierce that even the world-snake **Aapep** cowered before her. Fire-arrows darted from her eyes, she breathed flames, and searing heat – the parching winds of the desert – radiated from her body. She charred her enemies' bodies and gulped their blood.

Ra and Sekhmet. In the beginning, Ra created the world and all its people. He was the Sun, but he also took human shape, as the pharaoh, so that humans could see him and worship him. But human shape also meant that, although he was immortal, he was subject to aging. He began to wither and stoop, as the Sun does at evening, and his people turned away from him and worshipped Aapep instead. Enraged, Ra sent Sekhmet his Eye (or some say Sekhmet and **Hathor**) to punish mortals. Sekhmet raged across the land, parching the crops, searing the earth and greedily feasting on human blood. She slaughtered all Aapep's followers, and then turned on the innocent. The Nile foamed red with blood; the human race seemed doomed.

Not even Ra could control Sekhmet in her rage. The only way to stop her was trickery. While she was rampaging in the Delta, Ra sent servants to the island of Elephantine, to gather red ochre or, some say, pomegranates. Meanwhile, other servants fetched beer from the royal cellar. They mixed the red ochre (or the pomegranate juice) with the beer, and poured it over the land – seven thousand jarsful. When Sekhmet came hissing and snarling down the sky, she took the red mess for blood, lapped it up, and became so fuddled that her fires were banked, her eyes closed, and she laid her lion's muzzle on her paws and slept like a cat.

Sekhmet the healer. From the time of this 'taming' onwards, Sekhmet turned her rage mainly on Egypt's enemies, particularly the Nubians: their dark colour was caused by the searing of her breath, and she reduced their country to desert. For her own people she became a healer, using her skill in sorcery (learned because no darkness was too great for her piercing eyes to search out) and scorching with her fire-arrows the disease-**demons** that attacked humans. She ruled with her husband Ptah and son Nefertem in Memphis, where her priests formed a centuries-long dynasty of healers (specializing, some authorities say, in diseases of the heart), and she was worshipped everywhere in statues of black basalt, which can still be found all over Egypt.

≫+ **Bastet, disease and healing**

SELA: *see* Mwambu and Sela

SELENE
Europe (South)

Selene (Latin Luna), 'Moon', in Greek and Roman myth, was the third child of the **Titans Hyperion** and Theia. Unlike her brother **Helius** (**Sun**) and sister **Eos** (Dawn), she was secretive and shy. She loved the darkness of Night, and galloped through it on horseback or in a chariot pulled by pearl-white horses or silvery oxen. Soundless and aloof, she soared above the clouds. She hoarded her light: it was often pale and thin, and sometimes she veiled her face altogether and let Night's darkness rule.

In some accounts, Selene was not born shy, but withdrew from the world after her abortive love-affair with the mortal **Endymion**. In others, the reason for her shyness was that human beings were always trying to catch her and pull her down to Earth. In particular, people thought that if her reflection could be trapped in water, like a fish in a pool, she would become the slave of whoever caught it, and that if you prayed quietly enough she would creep nearer and nearer to hear you, and you could pick the right moment to snatch her from the sky. For this reason, her true worshippers banged cymbals and drums, shrieked and blew trumpets, to drown out her enemies' whispered prayers.

In most accounts, Selene is a different goddess from **Artemis** (Diana), but some myths treat them as the same.

SEMELE
Europe (South)

Semele ('Moon', Latin Luna), daughter of **Cadmus** and Harmonia in Greek myth, caught **Zeus**' eye, and he sent word that he wanted to sleep with her, promising in the name of the river **Styx** to give her any reward she asked. **Hera** intercepted the message, took the form of Semele's aged servant Beroe, and told her to demand a high price: she would submit to Zeus only if he came to her in all his immortal glory. Semele made her demand, and Zeus was forced to grant it, as not even gods can swear by Styx and break their word. He appeared to Semele in full glory – it was as if the sky itself were bearing down on her – and entered her in the form of a thunderbolt. Semele was scorched to ashes, and Zeus just had time to snatch up the embryonic child in her womb, **Dionysus**, before **Mother Earth** gaped open and Semele's remains disappeared into the **Underworld** forever.

SERAPIS
Africa (North)

Serapis, in Egyptian myth, is the Greek form of the name Osirap, 'Osiris-Hap'. Until the time of Alexander the Great, he was a **fertility**-god, a merging of the bull-god **Hap** and the **Underworld** ruler **Osiris**. But when Alexander the Great was on his deathbed, in 323 BCE, he called out to Serapis (the only deity he invoked), and after his death Ptolemy, who inherited power in Egypt, began a Serapis cult, centred on a statue which he claimed had miraculously fallen from the sky and which he

housed in a grandiose temple in Alexandria. In the time of Ptolemy's descendant Cleopatra, when all things Egyptian fascinated the Romans, Roman army officers were drawn to the Serapis cult, and took its **mysteries** to Rome. Serapis' initiates claimed that the god was able to cure all illnesses, and gave his worshippers easy passage between the worlds of Life and **Death**.
⋙→ **disease and healing, Mithras, mysteries**

SERQET
Africa (North)

Serqet (short for *Serqet hetyt*, 'she who lets the throat breathe'), the scorpion-goddess in Egyptian myth, was named to ward off evil: scorpion-venom paralyses the breathing instead of easing it. One of **Aset**'s serving-maids, she helped to reassemble **Osiris** after **Set** cut him to pieces. She was an expert bandager, and was given the task of helping with the embalming of bodies for burial. (She was quickly promoted from bandage-nurse to chief embalmer of entrails.) In some accounts, the gods sent her to fasten the coils of the world-snake **Aapep** in a multiple S-bend pattern which would stop him moving fast enough to attack the Sun-ship.
⋙→ **animal-gods**

SESHAT
Africa (North)

Seshat ('queen of the bookroom'), in Egyptian myth, was the wife of **Ptah** god of **writing**, and the divine archivist. She noted the passage of time and the movements of the stars, made blueprints for temples and palaces, and kept a tally of all taxes, gifts and war-spoils in **Heaven** and on Earth. Her priests – unusually for Egypt, women as well as men – were site-engineers, historians and mathematicians; above all, they kept records of land-holdings and the annual levels of the Nile-floods.

SET
Africa (North)

Set (or Seth or Seti; Greek **Typhon**), in Egyptian myth, was the storm-god son of **Geb** and **Nut**. He was so impatient to be born that he ripped himself from Nut's womb before he was fully formed, and consequently had no fixed shape. To give himself body he borrowed pieces of animals, or inhabited animal bodies as a hermit-crab takes shells. Most often he had an ant-eater's head, donkey's ears and a scorpion's tail, or appeared as a hippo with a crocodile's jaws and tail; he also entered the bodies of unwary humans, and drove them mad.

Ra made Set watchman on the prow of the Sun-ship, where he fought and killed **Aapep** every evening. But he was jealous of the gods of light and lusted after their women, causing havoc in **Heaven**. In particular, he killed his own twin brother **Osiris** and then fought a prolonged battle with Osiris' son **Horus**, ending only when Horus and **Isis** humiliated him in front of the celestial court. Castrated and impotent, he gave up his ambitions to be anything more than a slave of the light-gods, Ra's figurehead, and spent eternity harassing the mortal world instead.

➤ **light and dark, twins**

SEVEN AGAINST THEBES
Europe (South)

The throne of Thebes. In Greek myth, after **Oedipus'** banishment from **Thebes**, his brother-in-law **Creon** became regent while Oedipus' sons **Eteocles** and **Polynices** grew up. As soon as the princes were old enough, they began a bitter quarrel for the throne. They could have ruled Thebes jointly, but neither would agree to share. Eteocles (the eldest) proposed that they should take turns, ruling for one year each and spending one year in exile. Polynices refused, saying that he could never trust Eteocles to hand over the throne when his year was up. He went to Argos and asked King Adrastus for help to win the throne. Adrastus gathered an army, led by seven champions, the Seven Against Thebes: Adrastus and Polynices, Amphiaraus, Capaneus, Hippomedon, Tydeus and Parthenopaeus.

Seven Against Thebes. The Seven marched their army up and ringed Thebes with spears. There were seven city gates, and each champion led the attack on one of them. Inside the city, seven Theban champions led the defence: Actor, Hyperbius, Lasthenes, Megareus, Melanippus, Polyphontes and Prince Eteocles. There would have been an eighth champion, Creon's son Menoeceus, taking Eteocles' place while Eteocles led the whole defence. But just before the battle, the prophet **Tiresias** said that the Thebans would win if a royal prince sacrificed his own life for the city, and Menoeceus jumped from the battlements and killed himself.

The battle began, and Capaneus, fieriest of the seven Argive champions, was driven mad by blood-lust. He climbed a scaling-ladder, and was boasting that he would fall on the city like a thunderbolt, so hot that in comparison **Zeus**' thunderbolts would seem like rays of winter sun, when Zeus threw a real thunderbolt and toppled him. The omen encouraged the Thebans, who threw open four of the gates and surged out to attack. Two of the seven champions, Hippomedon and Parthenopaeus, were killed at once in the fighting, and a third, Tydeus, was wounded in the belly. His supporter **Athene** ran to save him, but at the last moment Amphiaraus cut off the head of the spears-man who had wounded Tydeus and gave it to him saying 'Suck the brains' – and when Tydeus sucked out his enemy's brains Athene hurried back to **Olympus** and left him to die. The Theban hero Periclymenus ran to kill Amphiaraus, who jumped into his chariot and fled. He prayed to Zeus to spare him the dishonour of being stabbed in the back, and Zeus split open the earth so that Amphiaraus and his chariot plunged headlong into the **Underworld**. When Adrastus saw this, and realized that with five of his champions dead the expedition was doomed, he leapt onto his winged horse (a gift from his father **Poseidon**), shook the reins and soared from the battlefield. The Argive army fled.

Eteocles and Polynices. Now, on the plain, only the brothers Eteocles and Polynices were left, facing each other in single combat. Before Oedipus left Thebes, he had cursed them, praying that they would decide their inheritance with iron and go to the Underworld on a single day, each killing the other – and in the same moment, after battering each other for hours, they lunged, dealt each other mortal wounds and fulfilled the prayer.

The Epigoni. In Thebes, Creon was now king. He issued an edict that all the dead Thebans, including Eteocles, were to be buried with honour, but that all the dead Argives, including Polynices, were to be left to rot. This proclamation not only set Creon against his own niece **Antigone** (who buried Polynices knowing that it would lead to her own death), but disgusted all Greece. King **Theseus** of Athens led an army against the city, executed Creon and saw that all the dead soldiers, on both sides, received equal funeral honours. This done, he left.

Enfeebled and powerless, the city of Thebes carried on a ragged existence for a couple of decades. But then another group of seven warriors, the Epigoni or Second Champions, descendants of the original Seven, decided that for honour's sake it should be obliterated forever. Led by Alcmaeon son of Amphiaraus, they were Aegialeus son of Adrastus, **Diomedes** (King of Aetolia), son of Tydeus, Sthenelus son of Capaneus, Polydorus son of Hippomedon, Promachus son of Parthenopaeus and Thesander son of Polynices. They set siege, intending to starve the people into submission. But in the night Tiresias warned the Thebans that their city was doomed, and they packed their belongings and crept away – so that next morning the Epigoni found the gates swinging open and the city deserted.

SEVEN GODS OF GOOD LUCK, THE
Asia (East)

The Seven Gods of Good Luck (*Schichi Fukujin*, 'seven happiness beings'), in Japanese myth, were Benzai goddess of love, Bishamon god of success in war, Daikoku god of wealth, Ebisu god of fishing, Fukurukoju god of good health, Hotei Osho god of generosity and large families, and Jurojin god of long life.

SEVEN SEERS, THE
India

The Seven Seers, in Hindu myth, were star-lords of the constellation of the Great Bear. They were **Atri**, Bharadwaja, Gautama, Jamadagni, Kasyapa, **Vashishtra** and **Vishvamitra**. They protected gods and human beings, and fought ceaseless wars against **demons**. But they were touchy, quarrelsome and unpredictable, and neither the gods, mortals, nor other Seers were safe from their bad tempered magic.

SEX

The sex-urge, the impulse to mate, appeared in two ways in most myth-traditions. At the beginning of the universe, it was a physical equivalent of the irresistible mental urge which started the process of **creation**, and it remained only just controllable, female spirits endlessly receiving and welcoming fertilization, males spraying **fertility** in unstoppable floods. (In some accounts, creation-gods were so fertile that whenever they stirred, or breathed, or moved, new life appeared.) Later, charge of the sex-urge was given to particular gods, who combined seductiveness with unpredictability and danger, and who oversaw the fertility of the gods, the universe and all creation except **demons**, **monsters** and creatures of the **Underworld**. In many accounts, sex-gods guarded or embodied **immortality** itself, and **giants** and others, deprived of it, were always trying to kidnap them or rape them. A rollicking side-branch of sex-myths concerned gods inadvertently trapped on Earth, who spent eternity obsessively mating with everything in sight, from trees to nymphs, from stones to horses – or, if all else failed, standing in endless erection as signposts, scarecrows or doorguards.

⯈ (Americas): Ghede, Tlazoltéotl, Wahari and Buoka; (Australia): Bildjiwuaroju, Miralaldu and Djanggawul; (Egypt): Min; (Greece): Aphrodite, Cybele, Eros, Pan, Priapus, Satyrs; (India): Kama, Rati, Shiva; (Mesopotamia): Inanna, Ishtar; (Nordic): Frey, Freyja; (Oceania): Kamapua'a; (Slavic): Yarilo

sGROLMA
Asia (Southwest)

sGrolma, in Tibetan myth, was **Mother Earth**, one of the two first beings in the world. She took the form of a rock-giantess and mated with the other primordial being, the monkey-god **sPyan-ras-gzigs**, and their offspring were all created beings.

SHAMASH
Asia (West)

Shamash ('**Sun**'), in Sumerian myth, was the son of the **Moon**-god **Sin** and brother of **Ishtar**, goddess of **fertility** and **war**. He lived in a palace called Efabbar ('shining house') with his wife Aya ('youth') and his sons Giru ('fire'), Kittum ('truth'), Mesharum ('justice') and Nusku ('light'). Because nothing could hide from the radiance which streamed from his eyes, he oversaw **justice and universal order**, using a knife (or in some accounts a saw or a sickle) to slice truth from lies. He and his sons spent their days riding their chariot across the sky, and at night they threw open a gate in the mountains and galloped into their palace to rest.

In art, Shamash was shown sometimes in symbolic form, as the Sun-disc or wheel of truth, and sometimes as a king sitting in splendour, wearing a four-horned crown and holding the staff of justice and the wheel of truth.

SHANG DI
Asia (East)

Shang Di ('great god'), in Chinese myth, was the supreme being. He personified the power which generates life and causes growth. This power energized the universe at the beginning of **creation** and keeps it in existence, by the continual rebirth of plants and animals. In the earliest times, Shang Di was regarded as a Heavenly equivalent of the Emperor on Earth, presiding over a vast court of functionaries and lesser gods. In Confucian times he was made more abstract, an august and somewhat disembodied power to whom no myths were attached. In Daoist times (in fact as late as the eleventh century CE) he was merged with a new figure, **Yu Huang**, to become the single supreme being in a monotheistic and largely philosophical system; anyone who didn't follow the Dao, however, continued to regard him as the benevolent ruler of a **Heaven** teeming with deities, the long-bearded, smiling grandfather so often shown in art.

»→ justice and universal order, supreme deity

SHANGO
Africa

Shango, in Yoruba myth, ruled the people in the days when gods still walked the Earth. He was the son of **Ogun** the **war**-god, a **lightning**-bolt in human form, and when he was angry **fire**-arrows shot from every orifice and burst through his skin. His wives were three rivers, Niger, Oba and Oshun, but not even their coolness could soothe his rage. In the end his temper made his people turn against him and banish him. Instead of leaving the kingdom, he hanged himself – and when the people went to bury his body all they found was an iron chain dangling from a hole. Priests interpreted this to mean that the king had become a god, but the people disagreed and there was furious argument until Shango settled it by sending a lightning-storm which destroyed the houses of everyone who'd refused to worship him. Ever afterwards he was revered as god of **thunder**.

Shango's animal-familiar was the lion, and when Yoruba slaves took his worship to Brazil in the nineteenth century CE, their Christian masters identified him as Saint Jerome (who also had a lion as his symbol) – a somewhat unexpected new role for the saint previously remembered chiefly for translating the Bible into Latin.

SHAPE-CHANGERS

At the beginning of the universe, the gods and spirits who oversaw **creation** were usually shape-changers, trying on different forms to find those they liked or were most suitable for their work. They were creative energy or intellectual thought incarnate, and to imagine a thing was to become it. Usually thereafter, when something was created it was given a stable form, and kept it; the exceptions were **tricksters** and wizards, who kept their shape-changing powers, sometimes to help human beings (especially as they roamed the world finishing the task of creation), sometimes as ways to discover new knowledge (for example what it was like to be an ant or a sea-current), and sometimes just for the fun of it.

After the coming of the great monotheistic religions, when the establishment of a scriptural canon involved much selection and editing of myth, shape-changing was allowed only to the supreme deity, and other shape-changers were downgraded – in some traditions into **devils** and **monsters**, in others into the fairies, goblins, sprites and witches of folk-tale. But in other traditions, including some of the most ancient, shape-changers were among the grandest and most awesome

deities in the pantheon: **Heitsi-Eibib**, **Tezcatlipoca**, **Odin** and **Zeus** are typical examples.

⫸ **(Africa):** Dxui; **(Americas):** Annency, Mixcóatl; **(Australia):** Wondjina; **(Celtic):** Cernunnos, Fintan, Lady of the Lake, Merlin, Morgan le Fay, Nimue, Pwyll, Uther Pendragon; **(China):** Erh Long, Five Emperors, Yu; **(Finnish):** Lemminkäinen; **(Greece):** Proteus, Telchines, Titans; **(India):** *apsaras, nagas* and *naginis,* Sisupala; **(Japan):** Ukemochi; **(Nordic):** Fafnir, Heimdall, Loki, Otr, Thiazi; **(Oceania):** Honoyeta, Kamapua'a; **(Slavic):** Vodyanoi, Volkh

SHASHTI
India

Shashti, in Indian myth, was the goddess of **childbirth**. **Demons** were particularly active on the sixth day after a child was born, trying to snatch it to the **Underworld** – and Shashti rode to the rescue on her sacred cat, or in cat-form herself, driving them off as a cat drives off snakes. In some accounts, she was one form of **Durga**, in others of Shri, goddess of prosperity.

⫸ **animal-gods**

SHATRUGHNA
India

Shatrughna, in Hindu myth, was the son of King **Dasaratha** and Queen **Sumitra**. He was a loyal supporter of his brother **Bharata**, and acted as his lieutenant in the same way as Shatrughna's twin **Lakshmana** served their elder brother **Rama**.

SHEN NONG
Asia (East)

Shen Nong, in Chinese myth, was the second of the **Three Sovereigns**, successor to **Fu Xi**. He was the son of a mortal princess and the Sky-dragon, and was a **shape-changer**. Usually he took the form of an ox-headed human, but he also made himself into the scorching wind which produces forest-fires – a shape which, in some accounts, earned him the honorary name Yen Ti ('burning emperor'). He taught human beings the 'slash-and-burn' technique of land-clearance, invented the plough and showed our ancestors the properties of all plants on Earth, distinguishing between those which nourished, those which cured illness and those which poisoned.

In some versions, Yen Ti was an entirely separate Emperor, Shen Nong's successor and the third of the Three Sovereigns. But no stories are told of him, and scholars now think that he and Shen Nong were the same individual. Accounts which try to give historical identities to myth-characters say that Shen Nong ruled from 2737-2697 BCE. Myth accounts, more exuberantly, claim that he ruled for seventeen mortal generations. The herb-lore of ancient Chinese medicine is still claimed to have been largely his invention – and myth says that he had a transparent stomach, and used it to test plants. The testing went well until one particularly poisonous herb shredded his insides and ended his mortal life.
≫→ disease and healing, farming

SHEOL
Asia (West)

Sheol ('pit'), in Hebrew myth, was the **Underworld**, a vast cavern filled with the dead of all creatures which had once lived in the Upper World. It was the mirror-image of the Upper World, except that its hierarchies depended on whether people had been 'good' or 'bad' in earlier lives. Instead of light its inhabitants had darkness, instead of body they had non-entity – and crucially, instead of knowledge-of-God they had absence-of-God.

SHESHA
India

Shesha ('all that's left'), also known as Ananta ('endless one'), in Hindu myth, was the huge **snake** which encompassed the universe. **Vishnu** slept on Shesha's coils, which floated on the primordial ocean, and the snake raised its thousand heads like a canopy to protect him. At the end of each cycle of existence, Shesha spews forth fire which destroys **creation**.

Shesha and Balarama. In some accounts, when Vishnu was incarnated as **Rama**, Shesha joined him, taking the human form of **Balarama**. When the time came for Balarama to die, Shesha turned back into a snake and wriggled out of his body, before cloning himself a thousand-thousand-fold to make every snake on Earth.

Scholars explain Shesha as the infinity of time.

SHITALA
India

Shitala ('shivering'), in Indian myth, is the goddess of skin diseases, particularly smallpox. She is the eldest and most virulent of seven unholy sisters (each of them manifestations of **Devi**, goddess of disease), and either flogs the skin of her victims raw with iron reeds, or creeps into their bodies and kisses the pestilence into them from inside.

⇒→ **disease and healing**

SHIVA
India

Shiva's origin and names. Shiva ('auspicious'), in Hindu myth, is one of the triad of gods who oversee **justice and universal order**. He is the destroyer, the force which sucks everything towards the centre; **Vishnu** is the preserver, the force which radiates outwards from a still centre; **Brahma** is the equilibrium between them. The name Shiva, in the Vedic prayers and poems of the Aryans who invaded India in the seventeenth century BCE, was a description of **Rudra** the storm-god, given him to placate his fury; Shiva became an independent god in the second century BCE. His own honorific names include Bhaivara ('who enjoys dancing' – a reference to his presence in cremation-grounds, dancing among the pyres), Digambara ('sky-clad' – that is, naked), Gangadhara ('upholder of the Ganges' – see below), Hara ('ravisher'), Ishvara ('lord'), Kala ('**death**'), Lingodbhava ('lord of the phallus' – see below), Mahadeva ('great god'), Nataraja ('lord of the dance' – see below), Natesa ('dancer' – when he slays **demons** by dancing on their heads) and Pashupa ('lord of animals').

Shiva's birth. Brahma and Vishnu were discussing which of them was the supreme power in the universe, when they were interrupted by the sudden appearance of a vast penis, a pillar which shone with star-brightness and whose roots were as far out of sight below as its tip was invisible above. Brahma changed into a wild goose and flew up to find the tip; Vishnu changed into a boar and grubbed in the **Underworld** to find the roots. Both gods returned, defeated – and a vagina-shaped opening appeared in the penis' side and gave birth to Shiva. Brahma and Vishnu, recognizing his power, at once accepted him as third member of the triad which ruled the universe.

Shiva's appearance and attributes. Shiva was the reconciliation of apparent opposites: he was a destroyer who created, a scatterer who unified, an implacable judge who showed mercy, and his twin attributes were meditation and ferocious dance. He sided with such outcasts as demons and **vampires** – and often slouched into **Heaven** as a matted-haired beggar, his body and head streaked with ash from the mortal funerals he enjoyed. Or he sat for years, brooding, and none of the gods dared approach him. He was knowledge, unflinching and essential: his third eye (see 'Shiva's weapons', below) and his fearsome dance banished ignorance and darkness because those things were part of him, because he understood them from within. His dance, which was Truth, so delighted the world-serpent **Shesha**, who saw it by chance one day, that he abandoned Vishnu for years and tried every kind of prayer and sacrifice to be allowed another glimpse.

Shiva's strength. Ceaseless meditation gave Shiva enormous strength – and he increased it by trickery. Demons once persuaded Brahma, by prayer and sacrifice, to give them three castles which could be destroyed only by a god, and then not unless he fired a single arrow. Safe in these castles, they made war on Heaven, and none of the gods had a bow powerful enough to fire such an arrow, or was strong enough to draw it if they had. They asked Shiva's help, and he offered to lend them half his strength. But none of them could control it, and he proposed instead that they pool all their own strength and lend him half. When the gods agreed, Shiva fired a single arrow and dealt with the demons — and then refused to return the gods' strength. Their strength combined with his made him the most powerful being in the universe.

Shiva's weapons. As eternity progressed, Shiva acquired a miscellany of weapons, into each of which he distilled some of his power, making them invincible. He was armed with a stubby mace whose tip was a skull, a sword and trident fashioned from thunderbolts, a bow made from a rainbow, and above all his terrible, third eye. Originally he had just two eyes, and their calm gaze illuminated the entire universe. But one day his wife **Parvati** crept up behind him and playfully covered his eyes. The universe went pitch-dark, and demons clambered eagerly out of the Underworld to take control. But Shiva opened a third eye in the centre of his forehead, and concentrated all his inner light to shine from it. It scattered the darkness and seared the demons dead. Ever afterwards the eye remained in Shiva's forehead. Usually it was closed, but at the end of each cycle of the universe he opens it as he dances, and destroys gods,

mortals, demons and everything in **creation**.

Shiva and the thousand atheists. A thousand seers once thought themselves so powerful that they had no need of gods. The gods asked Shiva to deal with them. He walked into the seers' stronghold, disguised as a naked tramp, and said, 'There are gods: worship them.' The seers combined their magic powers and made a tiger as big as a mountain — and Shiva extended the nail of one little finger, skinned it alive, threw the skin round him like a cloak and said, 'There are gods: worship them.' The seers conjured up a demon-dwarf of black rock, armed with a thunder-mace: ignorance personified. Shiva jumped on its head and began to dance — and the seers gaped at the beauty and terror of the dance. Then Shiva said, 'There are gods: worship them', and parted the sky to show the gods in Heaven, watching like spectators at a show. The seers fell to their knees in homage, and never questioned the gods again.

Shiva Gangadhara. All water in the universe came from the river Ganges, flowing eternally to fill the primordial ocean. At first, the Ganges watered only Heaven, making it green and lush, and there was no water at all on Earth. The ashes of the dead began to choke the land and destroy the world's **fertility**. A sage, **Bhagiratha**, persuaded Brahma to solve the problem by diverting the Ganges from Heaven to Earth. But the river was so powerful that if it fell from the sky it would shatter the Earth and drown it and everything on it. Shiva sat in meditation under Mount Kailasa in the Himalayas, and let the river wash over him. It spewed out of Heaven and became lost in the tangle of hair on top of his head. For seven years it wandered, trying to find a path through his matted locks – and finally ran to Earth, tamed, in seven broad streams, to water all the world. Shiva built himself a palace on Mount Kailasa, and it has been his home ever since.

Shiva and Daksha. Shiva's all-knowledge made him implacable: wherever he found wickedness, he punished it. On one occasion he went too far, cutting off one of Brahma's heads (see 'Shiva Linghodbhava' below), and the gods retaliated by banishing him from Heaven. This exile began a long quarrel, which flared up particularly in a feud between Shiva and Brahma's son **Daksha**. Daksha held a betrothal-feast for his daughter **Sati**, inviting all the gods except Shiva, and invited Sati to choose her future husband. Sati threw a garland into the air – and Shiva materialized in the middle of the room and caught it. Daksha shouted that Shiva was an outcast, mad, a dancer in cemeteries and a consorter with demons – and every time he saw Shiva or held another feast at which the god was not invited, he repeated these accusations.

Finally Sati could stand it no more: she threw herself into the sacrificial fire and was consumed. Shiva, furious with grief, sliced off Daksha's head, plucked demons out of his hair like lice and sent them scampering through Heaven, grabbed Sati's body and began dancing with it, his dance of destruction which would end creation. Vishnu hastily intervened, causing Sati to be reborn as Parvati, even more beautiful than before. In return, Shiva gave Daksha back his life. But the demons had stolen Daksha's head, and Shiva could only replace it with the head of the first creature which came along: a goat. This hardly improved Daksha's temper, and he continued to hold feasts without inviting Shiva – something which caused trouble whenever Shiva found out (see **Pushan**).

Shiva Lingodbhava. Two myths explain Shiva's title 'lord of the phallus'. One is the story of his birth: see above. (In some accounts, Brahma claimed to have reached the tip of the penis, and Shiva in a fury cut off one of his heads – the deed for which the gods later banished him from Heaven.) In the second myth, he was wandering in a forest when he saw the beautiful wives of a group of sages. He changed himself into a youth so handsome that all the wives began swooning with desire for him. The furious sages put a spell on him which caused his penis to wither away – and he retaliated by blighting the universe with darkness, until they hastily made an artificial penis, garlanded it with flowers and planted it in the ground for their wives to worship. From that moment the penis-column, or *lingam*, became one of Shiva's aspects, and the regeneration of his penis symbolized the springtime rebirth of fertility for all the world.

No gods are more often represented in art than Shiva, or in so many different forms. Sometimes he is a smiling prince with four arms and four faces (one of which contains the third eye); in paintings his skin is fair and his neck is blue (from the poison he sucked from **Vasuki**, *who tried to spit it into the* **amrita** *churned from the Sea of*

Milk); he wears a tiger-skin and a necklace of skulls and bones, or has snakes coiling round his neck or arching above his head to strike. Sometimes he rides Nandi, his milk-white bull; sometimes he is Yogeshvara, 'prince of ascetics', meditating, covered in ash, with his matted hair lank and strag-gling. As Lingodbhava, 'lord of the phal-lus', he is shown either as a man with a huge erect penis, or as a flower-garlanded penis jutting from the ground. In the com-monest image of all he is shown as Natar-aja, 'lord of the dance': surrounded by a ring of fire, with snakes fanning from his head, he stands with one leg raised in the dance. One hand holds a drum (or some-times a gazelle), another a flame (or some-times an axe), the third hand blesses, and the fourth points down towards the dancing foot, to symbolize salvation.

≫→ sex

SHI ZONG DI
Asia (East)

Shi Zong Di, in Chinese myth, was one of the ministers of **Shen Nong**, second of the **Three Sovereigns**. Shen Nong, lord of the scorching wind, travelled with such force over **Mother Earth** that he dried up the ground and parched vegetation without realizing it – and in the nick of time, before the whole of **creation** withered and died, Shi Zong Di poured water in a bowl, dipped a branch in it and scattered it over the Earth: the first **rain**. For this he was rewarded with **immortality** and the title Rain-Master. He was an important offi-cial in the celestial court until he rashly supported Qi Yu's *coup* against the Emperor **Huang Di**. The revolt was crushed and Shi Zong Di was

demoted. The administration of rain was given to others, and instead of dipping his branch to water the whole Earth, he was allowed to use it only to sprinkle the dust ahead of Huang Di as he walked in procession.

SHOU LAO
Asia (East)

Shou Lao ('star of long life'), in Chinese myth, was in some accounts the home of the Old Man of the South Pole, in others the god himself in the form of a star. He was a favourite figure in art, being shown as a smiling, bald old man carrying a peach (symbolizing long life) and a gourd (symbolizing prosperity), sitting on the ground or riding a stag and with a bat and crane in attendance. (Stags, bats and cranes were symbols of happiness.)

≫→ **Three Gods of Happiness**

SHU
Africa (North)

Shu ('air'), in Egyptian myth, was the son of **Atum** and brother of **Tefnut**. In some accounts he was born after Atum masturbated; in others (perhaps influ-enced by the sound of his name), he was sneezed out of Atum's nose. He and Tefnut mated to produce the interlock-ing **twins Geb** (Earth) and **Nut** (Sky), and Shu then separated them, leaving Geb floating in the primordial ocean and arching Nut's body high above as a pathway for the **Sun** to travel each day from horizon to horizon.

In art Shu takes two forms. As god of light, he is shown kneeling, facing us,

556

holding the Sky-arch on his shoulders and upraised arms. As one of the deities of darkness, he is leader of a gang of glee-fully-drawn demons who butcher the wicked in the Underworld.

SHUN
Asia (East)

Shun, in Chinese myth, was the fifth of the **Five Emperors**. From his birth, to humble parents, he was outstandingly sweet-natured and patient. His father, brothers and step-mother hated him and tried to kill him, but he gradually wore them down until, like everyone else, they loved him. The aged Emperor **Yao** was so impressed by tales of his uprightness that he married him to one of the Imperial daughters and then sent him, as royal son-in-law, to pass a series of tests – finding his way in jungle, adjudicating between quarrelling farmers, showing potters how to improve their work – and when they were done, he appointed the young man his heir, preferring him above his own legitimate sons.

As soon as Shun took the throne, the chaos always latent in nature rebelled. There were ten Suns in the sky, and every day they took the form of birds and flew up into the sky. Nine roosted in trees, and the tenth soared on high to warm the Earth. After Shun's enthronement all ten rose simultaneously, and their heat would have scorched Earth's inhabitants dead if Shun had not sent the archer **Yi** to shoot nine of the Sun-birds dead – which is why there is only one Sun today. Shun then sent **Yu** the Dragon Lord to control disastrous **floods** which were engulfing the

Earth, and as soon as the land was dry divided it into twelve administrative regions and ruled in peace and harmony until the day he died.

In some accounts, Shun is said to be the same person as **Zhuan Hu**, the second of the Five Emperors.

Shun's golden age, somewhat anodyne compared to the roistering of his predecessor Huang Di, was held to have taken place at the end of the third millennium BCE, and to have been a time of consolidation and order whose benefits stayed with China for thousands of years. Shun himself was a roi fainéant, setting a good example but leaving strenuous good deeds to others (such as Yi and Yu). He was, however, held in such reverence that when the list of Twenty-four Examples of Hsiao was compiled in historical times, his name came first. (Hsiao, the quality of acceptance and fulfilment of one's duty – as parent to child or child to parent, and as ruler to ruled or ruled to ruler – is akin to the Roman quality of pietas attributed by Virgil to Aeneas, and is therefore usually, and inadequately, translated as 'piety' in English.)

SIBYLS
Europe (South)

Sibyls, in Greek and Roman myth, were prophetesses. They were ordinary girls, taken from their families and trained for their work from infancy. When worshippers asked questions of the gods, the Sibyls put themselves in trances – for example by chewing sacred plants or allowing sacred snakes to bite them – and uttered sounds supposed to be the gods' words, which priests then wrote down and translated into prophecies.

The best known Sibyls served at shrines close to supposed gateways between **Heaven** and Earth or Earth and the **Underworld**. The Sibyl at Delphi, for example, presided at Mount Parnassus, a favourite bridge for the gods between Heaven and Earth. The Sibyl of Cumae guarded one of the entrances to the Underworld. The last Sibyl of Cumae was the most respected of all. Her birthname was Deiphobe ('god-fearing'), and she was so beautiful that **Apollo** not only told her the future but offered her any gift she chose if she would have **sex** with him. In some accounts she asked for **immortality**, in others to live one year for each grain of sand she was holding in her cupped hands. But in each case as soon as the wish was granted she refused to have sex, and Apollo punished her. She had forgotten to ask to keep her youth and beauty forever, and as the years passed she became ever more shrivelled, until in the end the priests hung her on the wall in a bottle, and when travellers asked 'Sibyl, what do you want?' she answered 'I want to die'.

*The Sibyl of Cumae was highly regarded in Roman myth and legend. When Aeneas visited her, she took him to the Underworld where his father **Anchises** showed him the whole future destiny of Rome, the generations of Romans yet unborn. (Roman writers computed that at this time the Sibyl was a mere 700 years old.) Later, she took nine books of prophecies to King Tarquin, saying that they contained every secret of Rome's future, that it would last forever, and offering to sell them to him if he agreed to take over her immortality and supervise that future. He refused, and she burned*

*three books before offering him the others at the same price. Once again he said no, and she burned three more. Tarquin bought the last three books, and the Sibyl disappeared and was never seen again. The prophecies in the books turned out to be gibberish, but none the less Tarquin had a temple built for them and the 'Sibylline verses' were ever afterwards consulted by the priests in times of civic trouble. But by allowing six of the original nine books to be burned, Tarquin had foreshortened not only his own life but the future destiny of Rome. Its glory was great but finite, and – the story ends – wherever the Sibyl now is, living out her agonized immortality, she has the dubious satisfaction of knowing that in this **prophecy**, as in all others, she spoke exact and literal truth.*

SIDDHARTHA GAUTAMA
India

Siddhartha Gautama, in Buddhist myth and belief, was the mortal prince who became **Buddha**. Born miraculously to **Maya**, he was kept from all the evil and misery of the world throughout his youth. He grew up rich, carefree and happy, married the beautiful **Yashodhara** and had a son. But one day by accident he saw an old man, and the sorrows of the world suddenly flooded his consciousness. He left his family and his palace to wander the world, and after six years, and five weeks' meditation under a *bho* (wild fig) tree, he achieved enlightenment about the causes of human misery, and how to avoid it.

Siddhartha (c563-479 BCE) was a historical figure, and artwork shows him as a typical prince of the time, riding his chariot, hunting, seated at court, surrounded by friends and servants. His face usually shows anxiety and alarm at the state of the world, in marked and deliberate contrast to the serenity which always characterizes Buddha.

⇛→ Ananda, Devadatta, Mara, Nanda

SIDO
Oceania

Sido, in the myths of the Kiwai and Toaripi peoples of Melanesia, was born to a pair of Siamese-**twin** goddesses, and as soon as he was born he separated them. Generative power sprayed from his penis like rain, clothing the naked Earth with plants. Sido's mothers taught him the secret of **immortality**: to slough his skin like a **snake** each night. But a group of children disturbed him halfway through the change, and the spell was broken. His spirit continued to wander the world, but his body rotted – and his mothers washed his skull and used it as a cup for the water of immortality (a gift available to every god but Sido, who was unable to drink from his own skull). Sido's restless spirit married a mortal girl (and gave her fire as a wedding-gift), and when she died it transformed itself first into a gigantic pig (which mourners ate at her funeral-feast) and then into the vast, dark House of **Death** where all mortals are doomed to go.

⇛→ fertility

SIEGFRIED: *see* Sigurd

SIf
Europe (North)

Sif the harvest-goddess, **Thor**'s wife in Nordic myth, had hair like ripe wheat, flowing to the ground. One night as she slept, **Loki** cut it all off for a prank, leaving her bald and the world grainless. Thor threatened to kill Loki unless he replaced the hair, and Loki went to the dwarf Dvalin, master-goldsmith, and promised him that if he made Sif a headful of new hair he would have the thanks and favour of the gods forever. Dvalin and his brother forged hair from gold, working it with rune-magic, and used the spare gold to make two other presents for the gods, an unerring spear for **Odin** and for **Frey** a ship big enough to hold all the gods, but which could be folded up like a handkerchief when not in use and kept in Frey's pocket.

Armed with these presents, Loki now bet two other dwarfs that they could never surpass them. If they did, he said, he'd let them cut off his head. The dwarfs set to work, and Loki realized at once that they were better goldsmiths even than Dvalin. The first dwarf stayed at the forge, working the bellows and keeping the fire at a constant temperature – essential for the magic – while the other went out of the room to cast his spells. When he left for the first time Loki changed himself into a fly and bit the first dwarf on the hand, trying to distract him. But the dwarf took no notice, and when his brother returned they pulled out of the fire the golden boar Gullinbursti, destined to be Frey's charger as he rode the sky. The second time, Loki bit the bellows-dwarf on the cheek, and again failed to distract him:

the treasure this time was a golden armlet for Odin which had the property of cloning itself eight times every ninth night. The third time, Loki stung the bellows-dwarf on the eyelid, and the dwarf let go the bellows for an instant to brush him away. The treasure this time, a golden hammer, was short in the handle and seemed imperfect. But when Loki took all six presents to the gods, they told him that the hammer, Mjöllnir, was in fact the greatest treasure of all, since Thor would use it to kill all their enemies. The dwarf-brothers now demanded Loki's head, as promised – and when he said they could have it so long as they didn't take any part of his neck (which was not included in the bargain), they sewed up his lips instead, using a magic awl to cut through his immortal skin.

The dwarfs now gave Thor his hammer, and sewed the golden hair to Sif's head, where it immediately began to grow. So the gods got protection from their enemies, mortals got back their harvest, and Loki got a twisted mouth and the laughter of all **Asgard**.

⟫→ crafts, fertility, smiths

SIGMUND
Europe (North)

Sigmund ('victory-mouth'), in Nordic myth, was the great-grandson of **Odin**'s son Sigi. Odin stuck a magic sword in a tree (some say in **Yggdrasil**), and declared that whoever pulled it out would be the greatest hero mortals had ever seen. Sigmund was the only man strong enough to perform the feat. He led his people to victory in battle after battle, and when the time came for

him to leave the mortal world for **Valhalla**, Odin smashed the sword to fragments. Sigmund's widow Hjördis gathered them and gave them to the smith **Regin**, to whom she also entrusted her and Sigmund's newborn son **Sigurd**. Regin was to foster Sigurd, and when the boy came of age he was to refashion the sword and give it to him, so that Sigurd would lead his people with the same bravery and distinction as Sigmund had done. (Unfortunately for Hjördis' plans, the gods had other ideas: see **Andvari**, **Fafnir**, **Regin**, **Sigurd**.)

⟫→ heroes

SIGNY
Europe (North)

Signy, Volsung's daughter and **Sigmund**'s **twin** sister in Germanic myth, was married to Siggeir, who had killed her other nine brothers and her father in order to seize the throne. Determined to bear a son who would be one of the greatest warriors ever seen on earth, she sent her firstborn for Sigmund to train in the arts of **war**. Sigmund found him an effeminate weakling, and killed him. Signy sent her second son – and Sigmund scornfully returned him, saying that he wasn't worth even the trouble of killing. At this point Signy decided that the fault must be Siggeir's and that he was unworthy to sire the grandson of Volsung. She changed her appearance by magic, took Sigmund to bed for three nights and days of continuous intercourse, and then disappeared, returning to her own shape. Nine months later **Sinfiotl** was born, and Signy claimed that he was Siggeir's son.

SIGURD
Europe (North)

Sigurd ('victory-peace'), in Nordic myth (or, in Germanic myth, Siegfried) was a member of the Volsung family, descendants of **Odin** and a mortal. He was the son of **Sigmund**, born after his father's death and brought up by the smith **Regin**, who reforged for him a magic sword which had symbolized his father's kingship until it was smashed by Odin. Using this sword, Sigurd killed Regin's dragon-brother **Fafnir** and stole his hoard of gold (the wealth of the universe). He also bathed in Fafnir's blood, which made him invulnerable except for one place, where a leaf fluttered down and stuck to the skin of his shoulder.

By eating Fafnir's heart, Sigurd acquired second hearing, the ability to understand the languages of birds, animals and insects. The birds told him that Regin intended to murder him and take the gold – and before this could happen he killed Regin. He took from the treasure a single gold ring (not realizing that it had been cursed by its dwarf-maker, **Andvari**, with the power to destroy all who owned it), and set out to find adventure. Crossing the rainbow-bridge **Bifröst**, he came to the hilltop where the **Valkyrie Brynhild** lay sleeping in a ring of fire, waiting until a hero braved the flames and woke her. Sigurd gave her the ring as a sign of betrothal, and continued on his journey.

In the land of the **Nibelungs**, Sigurd was given a magic potion to make him forget his promise to Brynhild, and prepared to marry princess Gudrun. Remembering only that Brynhild had his ring, he first sent Gudrun's brother Gunnar to exchange it for another, and then (when Gunnar was driven back by the fire-circle) disguised himself as Gunnar, agreed to marry Brynhild and exchanged rings with her. He gave the magic ring to Gunnar who married Gudrun. Brynhild, scorned and mocked, made her brother-in-law Guttorm murder Sigurd as he slept – and then, filled with guilt, threw herself on Sigurd's funeral-pyre and died.

These are the bare bones of the story, as told in the Norse Volsung Saga. *The German* Nibelung Poem *from the same period (thirteenth century CE) tells much the same story, changing some of the names (Andvari becomes Alberich; Gudrun becomes Kriemhild; Gunnar becomes Gunther; Guttorm becomes Hagen; Regin becomes Mime; Sigurd becomes Siegfried) and makes Brynhild (Brünnhilde) an Icelandic princess. Hagen kills Siegfried by stabbing him with his own sword, in the one vulnerable spot on his skin. The gold-hoard, including the baleful ring, is thrown into the Rhine and lost to mortals forever. The poem continues with Kriemhild leading her armies against Hagen, to avenge his murder of Siegfried, and ends with her death in battle.*

In the nineteenth century, the Volsung Saga *and* Nibelung Poem *inspired Wagner's four-part music-drama* The Ring of the Nibelungs. *Wagner took elements from both stories and added ideas from other Norse and Germanic myths – gods, dwarfs and other supernatural beings play leading parts, and Brünnhilde's (Brynhild's) suicide* triggers nothing less than Götterdämmerung (**Ragnarök**), the end of the universe. He also gave the characters psychological complexity, and used musical 'leading motifs' (tags of melody or harmony, each with a specific referent, for example 'love', 'destiny' or 'the sword') to weave webs of meaning and relationships latent in the myths, perhaps, but outside the scope of the medieval works which inspired him. In its way, the Ring is as 'definitive' a myth-based work as Homer's Iliad or Virgil's **Aeneid** – and our feeling that Wagner has taken more liberties than Homer or Virgil might vanish if we knew as much about their sources as we do of his.

⋙➜ heroes

SILENUS
Europe (South)

Silenus (Sileinos, 'moony'), in Greek myth, son of **Mother Earth** (or, some say, of **Hermes** or **Pan**) was renowned for his wisdom. He was made tutor to the young god **Dionysus**, and filled him with good advice. In return, Dionysus filled Silenus with his new invention, wine, and Silenus became a jovial drunk. He grew too fat to take part in ecstatic Dionysian dancing, preferring to sit on the sidelines swilling wine and urging on the dancers. In processions, he always rode last, on a donkey, crowned with flowers, holding a parasol or a wineskin in one hand and stroking his paunch with the other. He was Dionysus' good luck personified, and the gods honoured him by making him king of the **Satyrs** and giving him **immortality** so long as he stayed on Earth.

⋙➜ Faunus, Pan

SIMARGHU
Asia (West); Europe (East)

Simarghu (Iranian) or Simorg (Slavic) was a dragon who guarded the tree of life, on which could be found seeds of every plant on earth. This tree looked like all other trees, and Simarghu itself was invisible, so that no human could ever know which was the tree of life. To fell any tree at all was therefore dangerous. In Iran all trees were left standing until they collapsed of their own accord, in the Slavic forests tree-felling took place only after elaborate rituals to propitiate Simarghu.

⋙➜ monsters and dragons

SIMORG: *see* Simarghu

SIN
Asia (West)

Sin ('moon'), also known as Asimbabba, **Nanna**, Nannar, Suen and Zuen, was the **Moon**, son of **Enlil** (air) and father of **Ishtar** (**fertility**) and **Shamash** (the **Sun**). He was the power of the sky embodied in bull form. In some accounts, **demons** tried to nibble him to nothing, but **Marduk** stopped them before he was utterly destroyed, and Sin recreated himself, growing to full strength – a miracle repeated each month. This event began the process of time, and Sin was its guardian. In other accounts he was invisible, neither light nor dark. He sailed the sky in his ship (the crescent Moon) looking for demons, and when he found them he expanded the ship to a full light-disc and scattered them to the **Underworld**.

SINAA
Americas (South)

Sinaa, in the myths of the Juruña people of Brazil, was the creator-spirit, half man half jaguar. He made the world, propped the sky on a stick, and peopled Earth with creatures. Alone of all **creation**, he could defy time, taking off his skin (and with it age) every night to bathe, and being restored to youth. But he controlled human time – and he will end the world whenever he chooses, by kicking away the sky-stick.
»»+ animal-gods

SINFIOTL
Europe (North)

Sinfiotl, in Germanic myth, was the son **Signy** conceived with her brother **Sigmund**, and passed off as the child of her husband Siggeir. Determined to make the boy the bravest mortal ever born, she toughened him up from infancy, sewing his clothes to his skin each morning and ripping them off each night. The child's 'uncle' Sigmund taught him the arts of war and of shape-changing. Every night, the two of them changed into wolves and roamed the countryside slaughtering everything in their path.

When Sinfiotl was old enough, Signy persuaded him to murder his two elder brothers (Siggeir's legitimate children). Siggeir punished Sinfiotl by burying him alive, but Sinfiotl dug his way to freedom with a magic sword, and he and Signy burned the palace round Siggeir's ears. Signy, as was the custom, threw herself into the flames which were destroying her husband –

and as she died she shouted to Sigmund that he was Sinfiotl's true father. The story would have ended here, happily (at least for Sigmund and Sinfiotl), except that Sinfiotl had an argument with the brother of Sigmund's wife Borgild, and killed him – and Borgild retaliated by poisoning him.

This whole sequence of events was manipulated by the gods. Sinfiotl was, so to speak, no more than a first attempt at creating the greatest of mortal **heroes** – and he was clearly flawed. The gods therefore put it into Sigmund's mind to divorce Borgild for killing him, and marry a new wife. This wife was Hjördis, and the gods intended her and Sigmund's son **Sigurd** to be not only as heroic as Sinfiotl, but also just and pure. (Thanks to Sigurd's upbringing, these plans failed: see **Regin**, Sigurd.)

SIRENS
Europe (South)

The Sirens (Seirenes, 'binders'), in Greek myth, were the three daughters of the river-god **Achelous** and the **Muse** Calliope (or, some say, Melpomene or Terpsichore). They were beautiful girls with sweet voices (inherited from their mother), and served **Persephone**. When **Hades** opened the ground and stole Persephone to the **Underworld**, the Sirens failed to help her. In some accounts, Persephone's mother **Demeter** changed them into **monsters**. In others, they begged the gods to give them wings so that they could fly across the world to find her. Whatever the reason, they became birds with women's heads and lions' claws.

The Sirens lived on a barren island, one of the entrances to the Underworld, and whenever ships passed they sang, hoping to entice Persephone. Their singing was so beautiful that no human being could resist them, and sailed closer and closer to the lip of Hell. Each time, when the Sirens realized that Persephone was not on board, they swooped on the ship and its sailors, tearing them limb from limb and sending their souls unburied to the Underworld. The only mortal to hear them and live was **Odysseus**. He stopped his crews' ears with wax, and told them to keep on rowing whatever instructions he shouted at them in his desperation. Then he strapped himself to the ship's mast, heard the Sirens' song, and remained unscathed.

SISIUTL
Americas (North)

Sisiutl, in the myths of the Kwakiutl and Bella Coola peoples of the Northwest coast (Canada), was a water-**snake** with three heads: snake, human, snake. Its skin was so tough that no knife could pierce it: only a holly-leaf had sufficient magic. Sisiutl lived in a pool behind the home of the sky-goddess **Qamaits**, and could be seduced from it down to Earth by magic rituals – to help or harm human beings, depending on the kind of magic.

SISUPALA
India

Sisupala, in Hindu myth, was a **monster**: in some accounts, the son of **Shiva** and a mortal queen, in others, an avatar of the **demon Ravana**. He was born with four arms and three eyes, and the gods told his terrified mortal parents that these were signs of good luck, and that he would live happy and adored until he sat on the knee of the person who would kill him – at which point the extra eye and arms would shrivel away, and with them his luck. One day **Krishna** visited the palace, and the child Sisupala ran to sit on his knee. At once the extra arms and eye disappeared, and he was a child like all other children. His mother begged Krishna not to kill him but spare his life a hundred times, and Krishna promised.

From that day on, Sisupala spent all his time brooding about Krishna and plotting ways to kill him. His fury was not eased when Krishna stole his bride-to-be **Rukmini**. (She had written to Krishna, saying that she hated her future husband and begging him to stop the wedding – and Krishna rode to the rescue, kidnapping Rukmini from the wedding-procession and marrying her himself.) But whatever ambushes Sisupala prepared, and whatever disguises he assumed, he was no match for Krishna. A hundred attacks all ended in forgiveness, as Krishna kept his promise to Sisupala's mortal mother.

Sisupala's hundred-and-first attack came when Krishna was the honoured guest at a sacrifice held by King **Yudhishthira**. Sisupala insulted him before the crowd, calling him a cowherd and a yokel. He then drew his sword and went to kill Yudhishthira – and Krishna called down the discus of the Sun, which fell on Sisupala's head and split him in two from crown to toes. The two halves of the demon's body fell apart like segments from an orange, and Sisupala's soul gushed out in a pool of fire. It surged round Krishna's feet, and then was absorbed into the god's own being: Sisupala had spent so long brooding on his enemy that he had become inseparably part of him.

The details of this story were probably elaborated for moral teaching: however often you sin, if you keep God in mind at all times, you will eventually be freed from the trammels of mortality and be absorbed in him.

➤ shape-changers

SISYPHUS
Europe (South)

Sisyphus and Autolycus. Sisyphus (Sisyphos, 'too clever'), in Greek myth, was the son of **Aeolus** the wind-lord; his brothers were **Athamas** and **Salmoneus**. He was a cattle-farmer on the Isthmus of Corinth, and a rogue, rivalled only by his neighbour **Autolycus**. Autolycus asked his father **Hermes** (god of **tricksters**) for the power to make black seem white and white seem black. He used it to steal Sisyphus' cattle: when Sisyphus' men came looking for black cows in Autolycus' herds, they found only white ones, and vice versa. To prove who was stealing his cattle, Sisyphus had to think up a trick of his own. He branded all his cattle with his initial (C, the Greek capital S) – not on the hide, but on the underside of the hooves. The next time Autolycus' men raided Sisyphus' herd, a trail of Ss next morning led to Autolycus' byres, and the stolen cattle could be identified despite their colour-change.

Sisyphus and Salmoneus. Sisyphus won a kingdom by treachery. His brother Salmoneus was king of Thessaly. Sisyphus raped Salmoneus' daughter Tyro, and she was so ashamed that she killed her sons as soon as they were born. Sisyphus called the Thessalians together, showed them the bodies and said that they were Salmoneus' and Tyro's children, the result of incest. The people were so disgusted that they banished Salmoneus and made Sisyphus king. (In some accounts, he later claimed that the Delphic oracle had made him lie about the incest, to punish Salmoneus' crimes against his own people; but as he was just as much of a tyrant himself, this claim was hardly credible.)

Sisyphus and Zeus. In Thessaly, Sisyphus revelled in cruelty. His method of executing enemies – not to mention rich travellers rash enough to risk his hospitality – was to peg them on the ground and build stone-piles on top of them. In the end, he went too far and cheated **Zeus**. When Zeus stole the river-**nymph** Aegina from her father and hid her, Sisyphus was the only person on Earth who knew where she was, and he promised Zeus to keep it secret. But Aegina's father, the river-god Asopus, offered to pay for the information by creating a spring of pure water in Sisyphus' citadel; Sisyphus immediately broke his word to Zeus and told Asopus where to find the lovers. His reward from Asopus was the spring called Pirene; his reward from Zeus was death.

Even then, Sisyphus nearly managed to cheat **Death** himself. Zeus sent his brother **Hades** to make sure that Sisyphus actually reached the **Underworld**. Hades told Sisyphus to hold out his wrists to be tied. Sisyphus pretended to be fascinated by the knot, and asked Hades to show him how to tie it. Hades held out his wrists, and Sisyphus tied him up and locked him in a dungeon. For days, now that Hades was a prisoner, no mortal in the world could die. This was particularly awkward for **Ares**, god of war: all over the world men were being killed in battle, only to spring back to life and fight again. In the end Ares went to Thessaly and untied Hades, and the two of them frog-marched Sisyphus to the Underworld. On the way, Sisyphus called out to his wife that she was on no account to bury his body; then, when he reached the Underworld, he complained to **Persephone** that he had been dragged down to Hell alive and unburied. He asked her to allow him three more days in the Upper World to arrange his own funeral. Suspecting nothing, she agreed – and Sisyphus went back to Corinth and took up his old life exactly as before. Zeus realized that the only person who could outwit such a rogue was an even greater rogue, and sent **Hermes** himself to deal with Sisyphus. Hermes devised the cleverest trick of all: no trick at all. Sisyphus was expecting argument or lies, and was on his guard against words. But instead of speaking, Hermes simply took him by the scruff of the neck and bundled him down to Hell.

The judges of the dead gave Sisyphus a punishment to suit both his trickery and his method of killing people with boulders. They placed a huge boulder just above him on a steep hillside. The only way he could prevent it rolling back and crushing him was to push it up the hill, and they promised that if he ever reached the top and pushed it down the other side his punishment would end. With immense effort, time after time, Sisyphus heaved the boulder to the lip of the downward slope – and each time, just as one more push would have toppled it, it slipped out of his grasp and rolled all the way back down the hill. So he was doomed to make desperate efforts, and to be cheated, until the end of time.

SITA
India

Sita ('furrow'), in Hindu myth, was born fully-formed from **Mother Earth** when the mortal King **Janaka** marked out a line in the ground before sacrificing and asking the gods to send him children. Some accounts say that she was Mother Earth's own child, others that she was an avatar of **Lakshmi**, **Vishnu**'s wife, placed by the goddess on Mother Earth to share the earthly life of **Rama** (Vishnu's avatar) as she, Lakshmi, shared her husband's existence in **Heaven**.

Janaka treated Sita as his beloved daughter, and suitors flocked to court her from all parts of the country. Janaka set up a competition: she would marry whichever of them succeeded in bending a huge bow given him by **Shiva**. Prince Rama not only bent the bow but shattered it, and so Sita married him. Soon afterwards, the demon-king **Ravana** kidnapped her and carried her off to his fortress in Sri Lanka. Rama won her back after a huge war between **demons** and mortals. But his subjects refused to accept her as queen, saying that because she'd spent time in another king's harem, she was spoiled. Sita appealed to Mother Earth to prove her faithfulness, and the earth-goddess rose up, seated on a golden throne, took Sita in her arms and carried her from mortal sight forever.

≫→ Balin, beauty

SKADI
Europe (North)

Skadi ('hurt' or 'shadow'), in Nordic myth, was the daughter of the **giant Thiazi**, who stole **Idun** from the gods and was killed for it. Skadi went to **Asgard** to avenge his death – and the gods, unwilling to fight a female, asked her instead to take as a husband whichever of them she chose. Skadi, full of desire for **Baldur**, agreed, and the male gods lined up behind a curtain, only their bare feet showing, and asked her to choose. Unfortunately for Skadi, Baldur's feet were less beautiful than those of **Njörd**, the Old Man of the Sea, and she chose him instead.

The marriage was a disaster. Njörd refused to live in Skadi's icy mountain home, and Skadi refused to live in Njörd's sea-palace. They agreed to separate, and she went back to her skiing and hunting. In some accounts, however, they had sex just once before they parted, and their children were the **twins Frey** and **Freyja**, gods of desire. (In others, Frey and Freyja were born to **Nerthus**, the earth-goddess against whose shores Njörd lapped to comfort himself after Skadi left him.)

Alone in her mountain-lair, or on her rare visits to Asgard (to which, as Njörd's wife, she now had access), Skadi still pined for Baldur. When he was killed, as a result of **Loki**'s plotting, the gods took Loki to her fastness and pinioned him there with the entrails of his own son Narvi. Skadi hung a snake high in the roof above his head, hoping that its venom would drip into his eyes until **Ragnarök**, the end of time. Being a giantess, however, and not a god equipped with all-knowledge, she didn't realize that Sigun, Loki's faithful wife, had also crept into the cave, and now sat by her imprisoned husband, protecting him by catching the venom-drops in a wooden bowl.

SKANDA: *see* Karttikeya

SKILI
Americas (North)

Skili, in the myths of the Eastern Cherokee people of North Carolina, were witches that preyed on humans. They travelled at night, and often disguised themselves as owls.

SKRYMSLI
Europe (North)

Skrymsli, a **giant** in Nordic myth, was challenged by a mortal to a chess-game. If he won, he was to eat the mortal's son, unless the child could be hidden in such a way he could never find him. Skrymsli won the game, and the boy's father begged the gods to help hide his son. First **Odin** changed the child into a single grain in a field of standing corn – and Skrymsli mowed the field and ate the corn, grain by grain. At the last moment, **Honir** snatched the child, turned him into a feather and hid it in the down on a swan's head. Skrymsli took the swan and began eating it, down and all.

Loki now took a hand. He turned the child into one egg in the roe of a huge turbot, which he set swimming in a school of fish in the deepest part of the ocean. Skrymsli launched his boat and started fishing, and as soon as he was gone Loki set up a spiked trap in the boat-house, hidden in a pile of rope. Skrymsli fished his way through all the turbot in the ocean until he caught the one with the child in it. While he was picking through the roe, trying to find the child, Loki snatched the boy, changed him back to human shape, put him on shore and told him to run for safety. Skrymsli rowed back to the boathouse and fell over the hidden trap. At once Loki cut off his leg – but it grew again, twice as strong as before. Loki cut off the other leg, and this time, before it grew back, placed a spark of fire on the stump. Skrymsli bled to death, and the child was safe.

SKY

Sky, in most traditions, was the originator of **creation**: its arising from the primordial ocean and mating with Earth began the universe. Sky itself began as a god, but in most traditions gave way to its own offspring or was dispossessed by them, retreating to an elder-statesman-like serenity far beyond the squabbles of the rest of creation. The chief god in many traditions took over the powers of Sky, and ruled the entire world of **light**, usually in opposition to the powers of darkness and in uneasy alliance with the gods and spirits of the **sea**.

➤ (Africa): Olorun; (Americas): Ataentsic, Damballah; (China): Di Jun, Tian; (Egypt): Nut; (Finnish): Jumala; (Greece): Atlas, Ouranos, Zeus; (India): Aditi, Aruna, Dyaus; (Mesopotamia): An; (Nordic): Thor, Tyr; (Northern Europe): Num; (Oceania): Rangi; (Slavic): Dievas

SLAVIC MYTH

Slavs, migrants from Central Asia and such areas as Turkey, Iran and as far South as the Indus Valley, settled on the Western shore and hinterland of the Black Sea in the sixth century CE. In the next 200 years they spread in all directions: to Poland and the Baltic, Macedonia, the former Czechoslovakia, Russia and the Ukraine. Each of these regions developed its own distinctive language, and the peoples turned from being nomads to living in settled agricultural communities, but many of the ancient myths remained, a bedrock of universal Slavic culture. (There were, none the less, a few important additions, borrowed from neighbouring traditions. The Baltic god Perkunas (**Pyerun**), for example, has affinity with the neighbouring Norse god **Thor**; **Simorg** was the Iranian god **Simarghu** in Slavic dress.)

The pre-Christian Slavs had no knowledge of **writing**, and all we know about their myths is based on the writings of outsiders. When Christianity came (in the ninth century CE), missionaries brought a script and the new religious system it codified, and began organizing offensives against the ancient Slavic gods. Some gods disappeared; others changed their identity – Volos the farming-god, for example, became a shepherd figure identified with Saint Vlas; others again were downgraded into the folk-heroes known as *bogatiri*. (Notable examples were **Ilya Muromets**, originally the **war-god Pyerun**, **Miktula**, **Potok-Mikhailo Ivanovich**, **Sadko** and **Svyatogor**.) A few gods lived on: examples are **Mati-Syra-Zemlya (Mother Earth)** and the death-goddess **Baba Yaga**. The missionaries either went on fulminating for centuries against pagan beliefs – as late as 1618 the Jesuits cut down a sacred oak to prevent its being worshipped – or took them bodily into Christianity, for example when the ancient Slavic belief in the cleansing power of **fire**, originally denounced, was incorporated in Orthodox belief.

In early Slavic myth there were two gods, one black (Chernobog), one white (**Byelobog**) for **light and dark**, good and evil. Later, gods of individual peoples (for example **Rod**) arose, and were assisted by ancestor spirits. The Slavs believed that the soul lived on after death. They took great care of ancestral burial places, putting luxuries into the graves, leaving food there – a habit that persisted into the twentieth century – and holding feasts in honour of the dead. At a domestic level each place or activity had its own spirit: the **Domovoi**, Domania or Kikimora looked after the home, the Dvorovoi the yard, the **Bannik** the bath-house, the Ovinnik the barn, **Dugnai** bread-rising, **Pri-parchis and Kremera** pigs, Kurwaichin sheep, Walgino cattle, the **Polevik** fields, the **Russalki** and the **Vodyanoi** water. Complex cosmogenies developed, with deities for the Sun (**Dazhbog**; **Saule**), the Moon (**Meness**), Dawn and Sunset (the **Zoryas**), Sky (Rod and **Yarilo**), Earth (Mati-Syra-Zemlya), fire (**Svaro-zich** and Gabijia), water (Kupala), the home (Zemepatis), pasture (Pudnuitsa), the forests (the **Leshy**; Zuttibur), war (Pyerun, **Rugievit** and Yarovit), wind (**Stribog** and **Varpulis**), even bees (**Zosim**), blacksmiths and different kinds of fruit.

SLEIPNIR
Europe (North)

Sleipnir, in Nordic myth, was the eight-legged, flying horse sired by the stallion Svadilfari and born to **Loki** disguised as a mare. Loki gave him to **Odin**, and he became the warrior-god's charger, carrying him about the sky at the head of his hosts of the Dead. Odin used him to leap the walls of **Niflheim** and consult the prophetesses of the **Underworld** – and he once lent him to Hermod to go to Niflheim and try to rescue **Baldur**.
➤➤+ **Borak, Pegasus**

SMITHS

Most myth-systems were conceived and elaborated before metal-working was widely known. This means that smiths made late appearances in myth, and indeed were absent from many traditions. In systems where smiths did appear, they often had lower status than other supernatural beings, and were tolerated as servants rather than honoured as equals. Indeed, some human smiths whose skills earned them promotion to **Heaven** never properly lost their mortality, never achieved the status of ranking gods.

Smith-stories, whether about mortals or immortals, tended to peter out as soon as the main event – forging invincible weapons for a hero, building a golden palace, repairing a Sun-ship – was complete. Often, smiths were imagined as lame and ugly, their shoulders grotesquely over-developed from their work. They were associated with dwarfs, those secretive miners of the Earth's interior and hoarders of its gold. Sometimes they made good marriages – **Hephaestus** married **Aphrodite**, goddess of **beauty**; **Ptah** married **Sekhmet**, daughter of the Sun – but such unions were seldom happy, and the smith-god was often cuckolded by one of his own most important customers, the god of war.

In early Indian myth, the smith-god **Tvashtri** crafted the chalice which held the immortal drink *soma*, made thunderbolts for **Indra**, built cities, taught human beings arts and **crafts** – and was also moody and a buffoon. Ancient Irish myth told of three craft-gods, Goibhniu the smith, Luchta the wright and Creidhne the metal-worker. They forged unfailing weapons, Goibhniu making the blades, Luchta the shafts and Creidhne the rivets. (In Goibhniu's spare time he presided at feasts in the Otherworld, for which, like his Welsh counterpart Govannon, he brewed ale of **immortality**.) Irish myth also told of the lordly smith Culain – but only in the context that the boy-hero Setanta killed his guard-dog and was forced to work for six months as the new guard-dog,

which earned him the nickname 'Culain's hound,' **Cuculain**. In Finnish myth the smith-god **Ilmarinen** won the hand of a sorcerer's daughter by making magic presents, and then acted as a kind of supernatural Sancho Panza to the hero **Väinämöinen**. The Phoenician god Hiyon made bull-statues for **Baal**. Other smiths, from various traditions, made wind-cloaks, jewels (in Indian myth, from raindrops) and fabulous steeds (such as flying horses or saddled eagles) which senior gods then endowed with life.

Many myth-systems linked smiths with intelligence. **Fire** was a symbol of **wisdom**; the sparks from the smiths' anvils were like shafts of insight; the smiths were therefore custodians or granters of knowledge. (In the Greek myth of **Prometheus**, for example, the fire Prometheus stole to give to mortals was a spark from Hephaestus' anvil.) Sadly, smiths themselves, in myth, seem regularly to have been bypassed by the wisdom they controlled. They were often wily, but seldom wise.

➤ **(Africa): Gu, Ogun; (Celtic): Oberon, Volund; (Greece): Cyclopes; (India): Vishvakarman; (Japan): Inari; (Slavic): Kalvaitis; (Mesopotamia): Cain; (Nordic): Thor**

SNAKES

Snakes were central to most myth-systems, perhaps because of their perceived quality of being at once familiar and exotic. The look of their faces (for example their unblinking, lidless eyes), and their behaviour, seemed to imply that they were intelligent, that they lived by reason rather than instinct; and yet their thought-processes were as alien to those of humans as their ways of movement.

In some cultures (for example in Australia and among the African Bushpeople) snakes were phallic symbols. The Hopi people of North America danced an annual snake dance, to celebrate the union of Snake Youth (a **Sky** spirit) and Snake Girl (an **Underworld** spirit) and renew the **fertility** of Nature. During the dance live snakes were handled, and at its end they were released into the fields to guarantee good crops. In other cultures snakes symbolized the umbilical cord, joining all human beings to **Mother Earth**. The **Great Goddess** often had snakes as her familiars – sometimes, as in ancient Crete, twining round her sacred wand – and they were worshipped as guardians of her mysteries of birth and regeneration.

Snakes and immortality. Many cultures regarded snakes as immortal, because they appeared to be reincarnated from themselves when they sloughed their skins. In a similar way, the snake was often associated with **immortality** because when it coils it forms a spiral, and when it bites its tail – which few people in real life can have seen a snake do – it formed a circle, and spirals and circles were symbols of eternity. The circle was particularly important in Dahomeyan myth (where the snake-god Danh circled the world like a belt, corseting it and preventing it flying apart in splinters) and in ancient Egypt (where a serpent biting its tail symbolized the **sea**, the eternal ring which enclosed the world).

Snakes and creation. Snakes were a common feature of **creation** myths. Many peoples in Africa and Australia told of a **Rainbow Snake**, either Mother Earth herself who gave birth to all animals, or a water-god whose writhings made rivers, creeks and oceans. In ancient Indian myth, the drought-serpent **Ahi** swallowed the primordial ocean, and it was not until **Indra** split her stomach with a thunderbolt that all created beings were released. In another myth, **Brahma** creator of all slept on the coils of the world-serpent **Shesha** (or **Ananta**, 'endless', one part of Vishnu the child of the primordial waters); Shesha in turn was supported on **Kurma** (another part of Vishnu) – and when Kurma moved, Shesha stirred and yawned, and the gaping of its jaws caused **earthquakes**. One of the oldest Greek cosmological myths tells of Ophion, the snake which incubated the primordial egg from which all created things were born. In Egyptian myth, the state of existence before being was symbolized as Amduat, a many-coiled serpent from which **Ra** the Sun, and all creation with him, arose, returning each night and being reborn each morning.

Snakes and the Underworld. Because snakes lived in cracks and holes in the ground, they were regularly thought to be guardians of the Underworld, or **messengers** between the Upper and Lower Worlds. The **Gorgons** of Greek myth were snake-women (a common hybrid), whose gaze turned flesh to stone. In Indian myth, *nagas* and *naginis* were human-headed snakes whose kings and queens ruled

571

jewel-encrusted underground or under-water paradises and who were perpe-tually at war with **Garuda**, bird of the Sun. In Nordic myth Evil was symbo-lized as a snake, **Nidhogg** the 'Dread Biter', who coiled round one of the three roots of **Yggdrasil**, Tree of Life, and tried to choke (or in some versions, gnaw) the life from it. In Egyptian myth, similarly, **Aapep** the serpent (symbo-lizing chaos) each morning attacked the Sun-ship (symbolizing order). Aapep tried to engulf the ship, and the sky was drenched red at dawn and dusk with its blood as the Sun defeated it.

The idea of snake-people below the Earth was particularly prominent in American myth. The Aztec Under-world, **Mictlan**, was protected by py-thon-trees, a gigantic alligator and a snake, and spirits had to evade them (by physical ducking and weaving, or by cunning) before they could begin their journey towards immortality. In North America, the Brule Sioux people told of three brothers transformed into rattlesnakes which permanently helped and guided their human relatives. The Pomo people told of a woman who married a rattlesnake prince and gave birth to four snake-children who were able to pass freely between the worlds of their two parents. The Hopi people told of a young man who ventured to the Underworld and married a snake prin-cess, and the Navajo people told of Glispa, a girl who lived for two years with the Snake People by the Lake of Emergence in the Underworld, and returned with magic healing lore. Heal-ing and snakes were similarly associated in ancient Greek myth. **Aesculapius** had snake-familiars which crawled over the bodies of sick people asleep at night in his shrines, and licked them back to health.

Snakes and water. As well as with the Earth, snakes were commonly associated with water. The primordial ocean was a coiled snake – examples are Ahi in early Indian myth and **Jormungand** in Nordic myth. Sea monsters, from Greek **Scylla** with her twelve snake-necks to Koloowisi the sea-god of the Zuñi people of North America or **Leviathan**, the se-ven-headed crocodile-serpent of He-brew myth, lived in every ocean, and in some cultures eels (which spend some of their lives in fresh water before returning as adults to the sea) were regarded as magic crea-tures. Rivers and lakes often had snake-gods or snake-guardians – a typical example is Untekhi, the fear-some water-spirit of the Missouri Riv-er. Until very recently, Northern Europeans held 'well-dressing' cere-monies to appease the snake-spirits of village wells, and told legends of Saints vanquishing malevolent lake-snakes – Saint George, for example, in a story exactly paralleled among the Colombian people of Guatavita, killed a maiden-devouring serpent, and Saint Columba rebuked the Loch Ness Mon-ster, which at once gave up its taste for human flesh and became shy of hu-man visitors.

Snake gods. The anthropomorphic bias of most religions made it rare for gods to be depicted solely in the shape of snakes. (Exceptions were Ndengei, the Fijian creator-god; the dozen or so creator-snakes of the Solomon Islands, each with different responsibilities;

Coatlicue, the Aztec Mother Earth; and **Damballah**, Simbi and Petro, snake-spirits in Voodoo belief.) More commonly, snake-gods were hybrids or **shape-changers**. North American snake-spirits, for example, could shift at will between human and serpentine appearance, retaining in each form the attributes of both. The most important American snake-god of all, **Quetzal-cóatl** ('Plumed Serpent'), spirit of wind and intelligence, was balanced in Aztec myth by the Serpent of Obsidian Knives, the evil spirit of sacrifice and one of the four pillars supporting the sky – but in each case, the association with snakes seems more to do with imagery than with particularly snakish qualities. The Mayan sky-goddess I had snake-hair – a common attribute, except that in her case the snakes leaned into her ears and whispered the secrets of the universe (which is to say, the secrets of herself). **Shiva**, in Indian myth, had a cobra coiled on his head and another at rest on his right shoulder, ready to rear and strike his enemies. Egyptian myth included snake-gods of many kinds, from the two-headed **Nehebkau** who was one of the guardians of the Underworld, to 'the coiled one' Mehen, who sailed on Ra's sun-boat and helped to fight Aapep and maintain the diurnal cycle.

Snakes and wisdom. Snakes were associated with wisdom in most myth-systems – perhaps because they appear to ponder their actions as they stalk or prepare to pounce, and because of their hissing – which West African medicine men imitated as a preliminary to prophesying. Some-times their wisdom was of the ages and non-human, indeed directed against humans. But usually they were beneficent. This was particularly so in East Asia, where snake-dragons oversaw such things as the cycle of the seasons, good harvest, **rain**, weddings, **fertility** and the making of money. In ancient Greece and India, snakes were regarded as lucky, and snake-amulets and pet snakes were talismans against evil. Snakes were associated with healing in West Asia and Northern Europe, and in South Asia were – and in some places still are – considered to have aphrodisiac qualities. In Greek myth, if a snake licked your eyes or ears you acquired second sight or second hearing (this happened to Melampus); **Tiresias** acquired his insight into the supernatural world, and his dual nature as man and woman, as a result of killing a pair of snakes coupling in a wood. In Hebrew myth, a snake guarded the Tree of Knowledge in the Garden of Eden, and it is the extension of this story (the corruption of Eve) in Judaic and Christian teaching that leads to the idea now common in the Western world that snakes and humans are eternal enemies – a view shared by few other myth-cultures across the world.

⋙ (Africa): Da; (Americas): Bachue, Sisiutl, Umai-huhlya-wit, Uncegila; (Australia): Bobbi-Bobbi, Djulunggul, Jurawadbad, Kunapipi; (Egypt): Atum, Tefnut; (India): Kadru, Manasa, Muchalinda, Vasuki, Vritra; (Indonesia): Naga Pahoda; (Mesopotamia): Illuyankas; (Oceania): Honoyeta

SNOQALM AND BEAVER
Americas (North)

Snoqalm ('**moon**'), in the myths of the peoples of the Northwestern American coast, ruled the **sky**. At that time Sky was an exact reflection of **Mother Earth**, except that Sky was all-light and Earth all-dark, because Snoqalm hoarded the **Sun** in a fire-box, taking out only as much as he or his people needed. One day, curious about the dark of Earth, he told Spider to weave a rope so that he could climb down through the clouds and see what was to be seen. Unfortunately, he forgot that if he could climb down, Earth-creatures could climb up – and this is what happened. Beaver climbed up the rope, clambered into Snoqalm's village while Snoqalm was asleep, and stole not only the glowing Sun-orb from its box but also Snoqalm's fire-making tools. He climbed back down the rope, on the way hanging the Sun in the sky like a lamp, to light Mother Earth. As soon as he reached the surface he showed human beings how to use flint and tinder to make fire. Snoqalm woke up to find the Earth glowing far beneath him, and his own kingdom lit by no more than a pale reflection.

This myth is told by several Northeastern peoples. The Snoqalmie people of Washington State add details. In their version, it was Fox who climbed into Sky; he changed himself into Beaver when he clambered through the hole in Sky and found himself at the bottom of a lake, and when he went back down to Earth he carried not just fire but also trees, ancestors of the forests of the Cascade Mountains of the Northwestern US. Snoqalm pursued him down the rope, but was too heavy and crashed to Earth – and became Mount Si, not far from modern Seattle.

⇒ **light and dark**

SOIDO
Oceania

Soido, a Melanesian **fertility**-god, married a mortal wife. She was not able to sustain the love-making of a god, and died as soon as he entered her. But her womb teemed with his sperm, and when he buried her taros, yams, sweet potatoes and bananas grew from her grave – the first ever seen on Earth. Soido travelled the world looking for a new wife, masturbating endlessly to ease his frustration (and in the process clothing the Earth with plants). Eventually he found a woman, Pekai, who could tolerate love-making with a supernatural being, and settled happily with her as god of agriculture.

⇒ **farming**

SOL: *see* Helius

SOMA (DRINK)
India

Soma, in the Vedic myths of the Aryans who invaded India in the seventeenth century BCE, was the drink which guaranteed the gods' **immortality**. It was a companion to their celestial food *amrita*, and if mortals could somehow make their own supply and drink it, they would be granted not full immortality but temporary communion with the gods and the universe. **Demons**, too lazy to make *soma* of their own, were always trying to steal the gods' supply, so that they could become immortal and usurp the gods' privileges in **Heaven**.

The origin of *soma*. In some myth-stories, *soma* was pressed out for the gods through a gigantic sieve, the **sky**. The noise of the pressing was **thunder**, and the milky liquid was **rain** – the semen of the sky which guaranteed the Earth's **fertility**. In other accounts, **Indra** discovered the plant *soma* in the Himalayas and took it to Heaven; in others, *soma* was made during the churning of the **Sea** of Milk (see **amrita**), from every healing or magic herb in the universe, tossed into the primordial ocean.

In the most elaborate myth of all, *soma* existed in Heaven at a time when the gods still lived on Earth. They asked **Suparni**, goddess of poetry, to send messengers to fetch it down for them. Suparni had three children, each a four-syllable line of poetry made into a goddess. The eldest child, Jagati, turned herself into a bird and flew to Heaven. But the journey tired her so much that she lost three syllables and had to limp back, exhausted. The second daughter, Tristubh, lost only one syllable, but still came back without *soma*. The third child, Gayatari, brought back not only *soma* but also the syllables shed by her sisters. (This is why the eight-syllable line, *gayatari*, was later chosen for writing the sacred hymns, the *Vedas*.)

In later, Hindu myth, *soma* was personified as a god: see next entry.

SOMA (GOD)
India

Soma (also called Chandra, 'radiant'), in Hindu myth, was the god of the waning and waxing **Moon**. Two different myths explain his waxing and waning. In one, for half of each month, he is consumed by 36,300 gods, guaranteeing their **immortality** – this is why the Moon wanes in the sky. For the other half, he is fed by water from the celestial ocean fetched for him by **Surya** (either Surya the **Sun** or a female Surya, Soma's wife) – this is why the Moon waxes in the sky. In the second, he irritated his father-in-law **Daksha** by preferring one of his 27 wives (Daksha's daughters) above all the others, and Daksha put a withering curse on him, only to be persuaded by the entreaties of the other 26 wives to make it not inexorable but cyclical.

Soma and Tara. Tara was the beautiful wife of **Brihaspati**, teacher of the gods. Soma lusted after her and abducted her. There was war in the universe, and stalemate: the gods on one side, Soma and the **demons** of darkness on the other. At last **Brahma** forced Soma to return Tara – and Brihaspati found that she was pregnant. He refused to accept her back, until a child was born so beautiful that he claimed it as his own son. Soma made a counter-claim, and war once again seemed imminent. Brahma settled it by asking Tara who the father was, and she named Soma. Brahma gave Tara back to Brihaspati, pardoned Soma, and made the child father of all lunar dynasties – a settlement which sacrificed equity in the interests of universal harmony.

Although Soma the god is an individual personality, it is easy to see how his myths developed from those of the immortal drink soma (see separate entry). He is a favourite *god of poets: Indian religious verse is full of his praise, and tells of his powers and exploits. In art he has many forms, most of them hallucinatory and blurred: they include bird, bull, embryo, milk, plant with milky leaves and water-**giant**.*

SOMNUS: *see* Hypnus

SONG JIANG
Asia (East)

Song Jiang, in Chinese myth, was a master criminal on Earth who wangled his way into **Heaven** and procured for himself the post of patron god of thieves.

SOSOM
Oceania

Sosom, in the myths of Southern Papua New Guinea, was the **Sun**'s brother and the god of **fertility**. He whirled his penis like a bullroarer, and even its noise in the distance (the rumble of coming **rain**) was enough to stock the Earth with produce.

Needless to say, Sosom was the spirit invoked during the puberty-rites for adolescent boys. When the rituals began and the bullroarer sounded, women and girls knew that the god was present, and stayed away.
≫→ fertility

SOWN MEN
Europe (South)

When **Cadmus**, in Greek myth, killed the earth-serpent which guarded the plain on which the city of **Thebes** was to be built, he gathered its teeth

and sowed them like seed-corn. An army of soldiers instantly grew; Cadmus tossed a pebble among them, and they fell on each other and fought until all but five were dead. The five knelt and promised Cadmus obedience. Their names were Chthonius ('earthman'), Echion ('snakeman'), Hyperenor ('more than man'), Oudaeus ('born from the soil') and Pelorus ('giant snake'). Together they were called the Spartoi ('sown men'), and they were the ancestors of Thebes.

SPHINX
Europe (South)

Sphinx ('throttler'), in Greek myth, was the monstrous offspring of Echidna and **Typhon**; her siblings included **Cerberus**, **Chimaera**, **Hydra** and the **Nemean Lion**. She was woman from the waist up, dog from the waist down and had vulture's wings. **Hera** sent her to punish **Thebes** for hiding **Zeus**' bastard child **Dionysus**. Every day the Sphinx posed the same riddle – 'Four-legs morning, two-legs noon, three-legs evening, most legs weakest – what am I?' – and when the Thebans failed to answer she ate one of their children. Then **Oedipus** arrived, fresh from visiting the Delphic oracle, and realized that the inscription carved above **Apollo**'s temple there, 'Remember you are mortal', contained the answer to the riddle. Four-legs morning: crawling, as a baby; two-legs noon: walking upright, in the prime of life; three-legs evening: walking propped on a stick – the answer is a human being. When he shouted this answer, Sphinx was so startled that she flew straight up in the air, crashed down on a jagged rock (later named Sphikion after her) and broke her neck.

Apart from the name, there is no connection between Sphinx in Greek myth and the Egyptian sphinx – in fact the Egyptian sphinx was given that name in recent times, by archaeologists conversant with Greek myth. The Egyptian sphinx was male, symbolizing royal power in the form of the pharaoh's head on the body of a crouching lion (which in turn stood for the power of the rising Sun). It was unwinged, tame and (except to enemies of the state) entirely benevolent. Its Egyptian name was Harmakhis, 'Horus in the Horizon' (that is, 'Rising Sun'), and its statues were placed on guard outside temples and monuments (such as the pyramid complex at Giza), or in avenues like that which links the temples of Egyptian Thebes (modern Luxor) and Karnak, three kilometres away.

⇛→ **monsters and dragons**

sPYAN-RAS-GZIGS
Asia (Southwest)

sPyan-ras-gzigs, in Tibetan myth, was a monkey-god, one of the two first beings in the world. He mated with the other, the rock-giantess **sGrolma**, and their offspring were all created beings. In Tibetan Buddhism sPyan-ras-gzigs became identified with **Avalokiteshvara**, who still repeatedly takes human form (as the Dalai Lama) to guide his people.

⇛→ **animal-gods, creation**

SRAOSHA
Asia (West)

Sraosha ('listen'), in ancient Iranian myth, was the mediator between gods and mortals. During the day he stood by **Ahura Mazda**'s throne, listening for human prayers and relaying them to his master. At night he went down to Earth to hunt **demons**, in particular Aeshma lord of anger. In later myth Sraosha became Surush, and from there he passed into Muslim belief as the angel Jibril (**Gabriel**).

⇛→ **messengers**

STAR COUNTRY
Americas (North)

Star Country, in the myths of the Hopi people of the Southwestern US Pueblos, was the sky. It was an exact reflection of **Mother Earth**, with lakes, rivers, **mountains** and fields, and in it the star-people lived and hunted as mortals did on Earth. Their elders were the **Sun** and **Moon**, and they lived placid and uneventful lives. When they felt like travelling, Spider spun them ropes down which they climbed to explore their reflected world, the Earth. Sometimes, they became trapped in pools and lakes, and had to wait there until Spider noticed and came down to haul them home again.

STORMS: *see brighus*, Indra, Ixchel, Maruts, Rudra, Susano

STRIBOG
Europe (East)

Stribog ('wind-lord'), in Eastern Slavic myth, was the grandfather of all other winds. In some areas he was also the god of wealth, spreading it as widely and as randomly as the winds blow. In others, less poetically, he was winter-king, and his gusts distributed snow and chilled the bones of **Mother Earth**.

STYMPHALIAN BIRDS
Europe (South)

The Stymphalian Birds, in Greek myth, infested the Stymphalian Marshes in Arcadia, and **Heracles**, for his sixth **Labour**, was sent to kill them or drive them away. The birds ate human flesh; they had bronze beaks, talons and feathers, and killed their prey by dropping razor-sharp feathers from above and then tearing it to pieces with their talons. So long as Heracles wore the skin of the **Nemean Lion**, he was safe from their attacks, but he could find no way to dislodge them from their nests. He could only shoot one at a time, and there were countless thousands. In the end all his arrows were fired, and he angrily shook his empty quiver at the birds. Its bronze casing rattled against the bow, and at once the birds rose in a dense cloud, clattering their metal wings. Heracles began running up and down, shouting the terrible hunting cry taught him by **Pan** and rattling his god-given weapons (or, some say, a special bird-scarer given him by **Athene**). The birds flew off in a bronze cloud, glinting in the sun, settled on a barren island in the river which girds the world, and were never seen again by mortals, except for the **Argonauts** on their way to Colchis to steal the **Golden Fleece**.

⫸→ monsters and dragons

STYX
Europe (South)

Styx ('hate'), in Greek myth, was a river-goddess, daughter of Ocean whose waters girded all **creation**. She had four children, Force, Might, Victory and Zeal, and when the gods were fighting the **giants** for control of the universe, she sent her children to help them. In gratitude, **Hades** built her a palace in his **Underworld** kingdom, **Poseidon** gave her power over all other waters in the world, and **Zeus** allowed her authority over the gods themselves: it was in her name that they swore their oaths.

Styx lived in a rock-palace at the edge of the Underworld. From its peak gushed a river of icy water, called after her. It spread out in ten streams, **Acheron**, **Cocytus**, **Phlegethon** and others, and held the Underworld in its grip as Ocean gripped the Upper World. The last of the ten streams was called Oath of the Gods, and any god who swore an oath had to drink from it. If mortals drank Styx water, it turned their blood to ice and killed them.

⫸→ justice and universal order

SUCELLUS
Europe (North)

Sucellus ('good striker'), in Celtic myth, was the king of the gods. He wore a wolf-skin cap, traveller's boots and tunic, and carried a pot (from which he dispensed benefits to the human race) and a hammer (which he used both to strike plenty from the ground, and to hit dying people on the forehead, so granting them a quick **death** and an easy passage to the **Underworld**).

⫸→ supreme deity

578

SUDIKA-MBAMBI AND KABUNDUNGULU
Africa

Sudika-Mbambi ('thunderbolt') and Ka-bundungulu ('thunder-from-the-West'), in the myths of the Mbundu people of Angola, were miraculous **twins**. They were born fully formed, Sudika-Mbambi (the elder by an eye-blink) as a warrior armed with a knife and the tree of life, and Kabundungulu as his companion. They made war on the **demons** of darkness, killing monsters, mating with witches and pillaging the **Underworld**. Finally they quarrelled over the two daughters of the king of the Underworld. They fought, briefly, then agreed to a stand-off. Sudika-Mbambi married the elder daughter and set up his castle in the East; Kabundungulu married her sister and set up his castle in the West. The **thunder** we hear rolling round the sky is the brothers calling to each other.

SUGRIVA
India

Sugriva, in Hindu myth, was the monkey-king, a son of **Surya** the **Sun**. Dethroned by his half-brother **Balin**, he was helped back to his throne by **Rama**, and repaid him by gathering the huge army of monkeys and bears which fought the **demon**-king **Ravana** who had kidnapped Rama's wife **Sita**. Sugriva went on to become the ancestor of every ape and monkey in the world.

SUMITRA
India

Sumitra, in Hindu myth, was the third wife of King **Dasaratha**. She drank one third of the *soma* provided by **Vishnu** in answer to Dasaratha's prayer for sons, and conceived **twins**, **Lakshmana** and **Shatrughna**, each of whom possessed one quarter of the god's attributes, powers and nature.

SUN: *see* Amaterasu, Apollo, Aten, Belenus, Dazhbog, Dudugera, Hana and Ni, Helius, Horus, Hyperion, Inti, Kodoyanpe, Lug, Marduk, Mithra, Ninhursaga, Ninurta, Page Abe, Päivä, Ra, Sarasvati, Shamash, Surya, Tonatiuh, Tsohanoai, Unelanuki, Viracocha, Vivasvat, Yi

SUN BIN
Asia (East)

Sun Bin, in Chinese myth, was a mortal general who, when his toes were sliced off in a battle, invented shoes to cover them – and was promptly promoted to **Heaven** and made patron god of cobblers.
≫→ crafts

SUPREME DEITY
In some accounts, the supreme deity was the original creator of the universe, or was the universe itself, conceived either as an abstraction or as an active, sentient force. In others, the supreme deity was merely the first among gods, and reached that position either by creating all the others, by might or awesomeness, or because his or her weapons were more powerful than those of any other god. (In several traditions, those weapons were thunderbolts, and the supreme deity ruled the sky.)

A few myths said that once the supreme deity made and tenanted the universe, he or she lost interest and withdrew to some region beyond the reach of human imaginings – or, in disrespectful accounts, became so senile that retirement was imposed. This idea was particularly common in areas where one group of myths had superseded another: the chief god or gods of the older system, displaced by newer powers, abandoned the bustle of ordinary existence, most of them forever, others to await the coming of some dire emergency such as the imminent destruction of **creation**. Most myths, however, imagined the supreme deity as an active absolute ruler, emperor of the supernatural world, head of an enormous hierarchy, final arbiter, patriarch of a large (and usually quarrelsome) extended family, and in some cases not only grand but tetchy, lecherous and cunning. These imperial deities were almost always light-gods or sky-gods (some *were* the sky), and were locked in conflict with their eternal enemy, the ruler of darkness. (In Western myth, this was a straightforward conflict; in Eastern myth, **light and dark** were aspects of *yin* and *yang*, and their harmonious co-existence was essential if the universe was not to collapse into chaos.)

≫→ (Africa): Akongo, Katonda, Leza and Honeybird, Mulungu, Ngewowa; (Americas): Aiomum Kondi, Kitshi Manito, Ometecuhtli, Wakonda; (Arctic): Torngarsak; (Celtic): Sucellus; (China): Shang Di, Yu Huang; (Egypt): Amun, Aten, Ra; (Finnish): Ukko; (Greece): Zeus; (India): Amitabha, Brahma, Vishnu; (Mesopotamia): Adad, Ashur, El, Yahweh; (Nordic): Odin; (Rome): Jupiter; (Slavic): Svandovit, Svarog

SURMA
Europe (North)

Surma, in Finnish myth, was the monster which guarded the gate to the realm of **Kalma**, goddess of **death** in the **Underworld**. Surma was a bodiless pair of jaws with rows of fangs like swords and an endless, hungry gullet. It allowed the Dead to pass unharmed, but any living being which tried to enter the Underworld was snatched by the jaws, torn to pieces by the teeth and dispatched down the gullet into oblivion.
≫→ **demons**

SURT
Europe (North)

Surt ('soot') was the **giant** ruler of **Muspell**, the fire-world which existed before the **creation** of the universe. At **Ragnarök**, he will erupt in volcanic frenzy, hurling fire until all creation is destroyed.

SURYA (DAUGHTER OF SAVITRI)
India

Surya ('shiner'), in the Vedic myths of the Aryans who invaded India in the seventeenth century BCE, was the daughter of **Savitri**, a portion of the **Sun**'s radiance turned into a serene, beautiful goddess. She was the shared wife of the **Ashvins**, the horse-lord healers who were also her cousins.
≫→ **beauty**

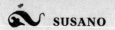

SURYA (THE SUN)
India

Surya (also called Savitar, 'shiner'), in the Vedic myths of the Aryans who invaded India in the seventeenth century BCE, was the god of the **Sun**'s disc. In Vedic myth he was one of **Dyaus**' sons, and formed a heavenly triad with **Indra** and **Agni**. He upheld the universe during the day, handing it over to **Varuna** at night. He knew all, saw all, and gave mortals disease, healing and the glow of intelligence.

Surya in Hindu myth. In Hindu myth Surya was the son either of **Brahma**, or of **Aditi** and **Kasyapa**. His symbol was the swastika, sign of plenty. The best-known story about him is a variant of the Vedic myth of **Vivasvat** and **Saranyu**. He married Sanjna, daughter of the smith-god **Vishvakarman**, and their children included Vaivasvata, **Manu**, **Yama** and Yami. But Sanjna found his radiance insupportable, left her servant Shaya ('Shadow') in her place and hid in the woods as a mare. Surya found her, changed to a stallion and fathered the **Ashvins** on her. For a time he and Sanjna lived as horses, but then they returned to their palace. Surya agreed that Vishvakarman should reduce his radiance by one eighth, shaving him down on the smith-god's lathe. So he and Sanjna lived happily ever after – and from the shavings Vishvakarman made weapons for the gods.

In art based on Vedic myth, Surya the Sun is shown as a dwarfish warrior with a body of polished copper, riding a golden, one-wheeled chariot drawn by seven mares (or one seven-headed mare) representing the days of the week. In Hindu art he is shown as a prince with dark red skin, three eyes and four arms. Two of his hands hold water-lilies, the third beckons and the fourth blesses. Sometimes he rides the Sun-chariot, sometimes he sits on a red lotus, smiling seraphically, light-beams radiating from his body.

SUSANO
Asia (East)

Susano, the storm-god in Japanese myth, was born from the water-drops when **Izanagi** washed his nose to rid himself of the pollution of the **Underworld**. (In some accounts he was created when Izanagi blew his nose.) Izanagi gave rule of the **Sun** to Susano's sister **Amaterasu** and rule of the **Moon** to his brother **Tsukuyomi**. Susano was given rule of the sea, or some say of Earth, and refused to accept it. He roared and raged about **creation**, constantly harassing Amaterasu. In the end he went too far, causing the death of her sister Wakahirume (Dawn), and Amaterasu retreated from the world to a cave, taking her light with her. The gods eventually enticed her into coming out again, and punished Susano by cutting off his beard, fingernails and toenails, fining him and banishing him from **Heaven** forever.

This punishment chastened Susano. He retreated to Earth, and began using his powers for good, not bad. In particular, he sucked up **water** from the **sea** and carried it to land in the form of **rain**, which brought the world its first **fertility**. When he shaved or cut his hair he planted the strands on mountain-slopes to grow as trees. At this time water-**snakes** and other **monsters** sent from the Underworld by **Izanami** were terrorizing human beings, mortal children of Susano's father Izanagi. (Although Izanagi created 1500 new humans each day, Izanami killed 1000.) Susano harnessed his storms to fight the monsters.

In Izumo province, where the gods met once every year to discuss human affairs, Susano rescued a beautiful girl, Kushinada, from the fiercest of all Izanami's water-monsters. It had already eaten her seven sisters; it had fire for eyes, eight heads and eight tails, and was so vast that its body covered eight valleys and eight mountain-peaks and trees grew on its back. Susano saved Kushinada by turning her into an ornamental comb which he stuck in his hair. He told her parents to fill eight barrels with *sake* (rice-wine), and offered one of the barrels to each of the monster's eight heads. As soon as the beast was drunk – this was the first alcohol it had ever tasted – he cut off its heads and chopped its body into tiny pieces. Then he turned Kushinada back into a woman, made her his consort, and settled down to rule the world.

*The Shinto priests who retold this myth added a detail with vital religio-political importance. When Susano chopped up the monster's tails, buried in one of them he found the magic sword Kusanaginotsurugi ('harvests enemies like grass'), and presented it to his sister Amaterasu. She later gave the sword to her grandson **Ninigi** when she sent him from Heaven to rule the Earth, and from him it descended from generation to generation of the royal*

house, one of the most sacred objects in the Imperial regalia.

≫→ Okuninushi, Izanami and Izanagi

SUTTUNG
Europe (North)

Suttung, in Nordic myth, was a **giant**. His father **Gilling** was murdered by two dwarfs, Fjalar and Galar, who had previously brewed the mead of inspiration from the blood of another of their murder-victims, **Kvasir**. Suttung forced them to give him the mead, and stored it in a cave in the heart of a mountain, guarded by his daughter **Gunnlod** – from whom **Odin** rescued it for the gods.

SVANDOVIT
Europe (East)

Svandovit, or Svetovid, in Baltic myth, was the father of all gods, in particular **Sun** and Fire. He controlled the world's **fertility** and was lord of **prophecy** and **war**.

Svandovit's prophecies were given in two ways. His statues held drinking-horns, and at the end of each year priests saw how much liquor was left and foretold from it the size of the following year's harvest. In his temple in Arcona lived a sacred white war-horse. Each year, it was driven through an obstacle course of spears – and the fewer 'hits', the better the future. Svandovit's statues had four faces (one for each cardinal compass point), and the inner shrines of his temples were so sacred that they were guarded by armed soldiers day and night, and the high priests (the only people ever admitted) had to hold their breath while cleaning them.

≫→ Dazhbog, Radigast, Rod, Rugievit, supreme deity

SVAROG
Europe (East)

Svarog ('very hot'), in Slavic myth, was **Sky**, father of all other gods. When his sons **Dazhbog** (the **Sun**) and **Svarozich** (Fire) became more powerful, he surrendered his powers to them, remaining a benevolent but remote presence in the universe.

*The name Svarog is close to the Sanskrit word svar ('bright'), and suggests to some mythographers that Svarog came originally from North India. Other scholars trace a succession in chief Slavic gods, from the original **Byelobog** to Svarog, and from Svarog to Dazhbog. In Baltic myth, Svarog's equivalent was **Svandovit**.*

≫→ Pyerun, supreme deity

SVAROZICH
Europe (East)

Svarozich (from *svarog*, 'very hot'), son of **Svarog** and brother of **Dazhbog** in Slavic myth, was the god of **fire** and of **prophecy** – the glow of inspiration allowing glimpses into non-mortal time and space.

SVYATOGOR
Europe (East)

Svyatogor, a **giant** in Slavic myth, boasted that he could lift the whole weight of **Mother Earth**. One day, riding along, he saw a bag on the ground. He tried to lift it with his stick, and failed. He leaned down to pick it up, and it was too heavy. He dismounted and used both hands; he thought he'd raised the bag to his knees, then realized that it had stayed where it was while his legs had sunk knee-deep into the ground. He tried to climb out of the hole, straining until he wept tears of blood; but he was stuck, and starved.

In later stories, Svyatogor was identified as **Ilya Muromets**, one of the *bogatiri*.

SZEUKHA
Americas (North)

Szeukha, Earth-maker's son in the myths of the Pima people of the Southwestern US desert, lived on Earth with the humans his father had created from balls of mud and sweat. Great Eagle, lord of water, had no time for humans. He began by preying on them, snatching them to his mountain-eyrie and eating them alive. Then he sent a **flood** to engulf **creation** and end them. Only Szeukha survived, floating among the flotsam and jetsam on a lump of pine resin. As soon as the waters began to recede, he stepped out on the top of a mountain – by chance, right into Great Eagle's eyrie. A magic duel ensued, and Szeukha won only by enlisting the spirits of rock and mud, **Mother Earth**'s own children, to fight for him. As soon as Great Eagle was dead, Szeukha gathered bones and skin-scraps from the debris round the eyrie, laid them on the ground and breathed life into them. So humankind was reconstituted: not the first creation, imbued with existence by Earth-maker himself, but a degenerate version made from its own remains.

The Wooden Horse (*P. Lombault, 18th century*)

TA'AROA
Oceania

Ta'aroa, in some Polynesian **creation-myths**, was the first and only being. At the beginning of creation, he hatched from an egg which floated in chaos. Finding that the time was not right to be born, he formed a second egg and waited inside it until the time again came to be hatched. Then he made the shell of the first egg into **Atea**, **Sky**, and the shell of the second into Fa'ahotu, Earth. To complete creation, he used his own body, turning his flesh into soil, his internal organs into clouds, his bones into mountains, his feathers into plants, his intestines into eels and his blood into birds. Thus, when creation was finished he was simultaneously nowhere and everywhere, part of all that was.

*In some accounts, Ta'aroa later reconstituted himself as **Tangaroa** or **Tangaloa**, god of the **sea**. The sea was his own sweat, caused by the exertions of creation. He was therefore both the sea and lord of it.*

TAGARO
Oceania

Tagaro, in the myths of the people of Vanuatu, modelled the first human beings from mud. There were ten of them, all images of himself, and he stood them in a row and played skittles with them, throwing fruit at them. One fruit stuck to the penis of one of the mud-men, and when Tagaro pulled it away, the penis came with it. So the first woman was created, and she married one of the men and had children of her own.

⟫⟶ **creation, Chinigchinich, Enki, Esaugetuh Emissee, Humanmaker,**

Hurukan, Na'pi, Prometheus, Woyengi

TALIESIN
Europe (North)

Taliesin ('shining brow'), in Celtic myth, was a powerful wizard and bard. He was born as Gwion, a humble farm-boy, without inspiration. But Caridwen, a witch who had borne an unbelievably ugly son, determined to compensate the child by giving him all the knowledge in the world, filled a pot with magic herbs and set it to boil for a year and a day. This boiling would reduce it to three drops, which would contain all-knowledge. Caridwen asked Gwion to watch the mixture, and one day as he was stirring it a drop of the liquid fell on his finger and he licked it off. At once he was given one third of all the world's knowledge, including the fact that Caridwen meant to kill him as soon as the boiling was finished.

Caridwen chased Gwion to kill him. Among the skills he'd learned was that of shape-changing, and he made himself a hare, a fish, a bird and a grain of corn. Caridwen pursued him as greyhound, otter, hawk – and finally as a hen, eating the corn-grain. Nine months later, having resumed her normal shape, she gave birth to another child – Gwion, reborn – and this time tried to kill him by sewing him in a bag and throwing him into the river. River-currents carried the bag downstream to the salmon-leap owned by Prince Elphin, who opened it and was dazzled by the radiance streaming from Gwion's face, a glow like golden corn. 'Taliesin!' he exclaimed – and took the child to his own palace, where Taliesin/Gwion grew up to be the seer, prophet and chief entertainer of his people.

This tale seems to have been told in honour of a real bard called Taliesin, who lived at the Welsh court in the sixth century CE, and is said to be buried at the village still called after him. No surviving poems are known actually to be by him, though a large fourteenth-century collection of poetry in Welsh, by miscellaneous hands, was named The Book of Taliesin *after him. (This includes a set of 'Taliesin's riddles', and an account of his shape-changing and of such miraculous exploits as visiting* **Noah** *in his ark, Jonah in his whale, God on his throne,* **Satan** *in his kitchen and* **Romulus and Remus** *building the walls of Rome.) Some French accounts of the* **Arthur** *myth attribute the story of his encounter with Caridwen to the young* **Merlin**, *but Welsh sources insist that they were two quite different people, and that the only occasion when Taliesin came into contact with Arthur was when he guided him to* **Annwn**, *the Underworld, to recover stolen treasure.*

⋙→ prophecy, shape-changers

TAMENDONARE: *see* Ariconte and Tamendonare

TAMULU: *see* Tamusi and Tamulu

TAMUSI AND TAMULU
Americas (South)

Tamusi and Tamulu, in the myths of the Caliña people of South America, were sons of **Amana** the creator, sent from her sea-kingdom in the Milky Way to protect Earth against the fire-serpents of her enemy the **Sun**. Tamusi, Light, was born in the morning before the day's heat began; Tamulu, Dark, was born in the evening when it was done. The brothers hated each other, but were inextricably linked, since Light and Darkness cannot exist without one another. They divided their responsibilities rigorously: Tamusi slept while Tamulu ruled, and although Tamulu sometimes lingered for a while in the sky when his brother rose in the morning, he very soon gave way.

The Sun attacked the Earth with **fire-serpents**, sending them snaking up through vents in the surface. During the day, Tamusi sliced them to pieces with his **lightning**-sword and tossed the fragments into the sky, where they made shooting-stars and comets. Tamulu smothered them in his cloak of darkness.

As soon as the Earth was safe from the Sun, Amana told Tamusi and Tamulu to people it. Tamusi's creations, children of light, were animals, insects and human beings. Tamulu's creations, children of darkness, were **monsters**, dreams and phantoms.

≫→ creation, light and dark

TANE
Oceania

Tane, or Kane, in Polynesian myth, was the son of **Rangi** (Father Sky) and **Papa** (**Mother Earth**). At the beginning of the universe, **Sky** and Earth were united in such a close sexual embrace that all **creation** was trapped in Papa's womb. Tane, god of forests, planted his feet in Papa, lifted his arms to Rangi and grew until he had separated them. He clothed Sky in a cloak of darkness studded with jewels (the stars, the Milky Way) and lined with red (Dawn); he clothed Earth with shrubs and trees – at first planting them upside down (mangroves), but then right way up. He taught Earth's people, the human race, all knowledge, in two branches: the Upper Jaw (information about the gods, space and time, the order of the universe) and the Lower Jaw (everything needed for life on Earth, from **farming** methods to **music**, from law to myth).

Tane favoured human beings so much that he decided to live with them. He tried to find a mate. Because no human woman could have **sex** with a god and live, he was forced to mate with trees, plants, stones and pools, fathering all kinds of creatures including **snakes** and dragons. He asked his mother Papa what to do, and she told him, first, that he should mould himself a wife from sand (or, in some accounts, carve her from sandstone), and second, that the union would bring disaster. Ignoring the warning, Tane made himself a wife, Hine Ahu One ('Earth-girl') and breathed life into her. The result of their first, botched mating was an egg – which hatched to produce the ancestor of all birds on Earth. At their second attempt Hine Ahu One was transformed into her own daughter, Hine Titama ('Dawn-girl') or Tikikapakapa. When this child grew up, Tane married her, and they had another daughter, Hine Titamauri. But then Hine Titama asked Tane who her father was, and when he answered by pointing to his penis, she was so ashamed to have committed incest with her own father that she fled to the **Underworld**. She became Hine Nui Te Po, goddess of death, and dragged all members of Tane's human race down to her kingdom when their time on Earth was done.

In some accounts, the coming of **death** into the world made Tane abandon his attempts to live with humans. He became aloof, as his father Rangi had done before him, and left mortals to live their own (now foreshortened) lives and make their own mistakes. In other accounts, he remained on Earth, but retreated to the high hills, where he married a new wife (Hine Tu A Muana, 'mountain-girl'), born of the dew which was his father Rangi's tears; their offspring were mountain springs, streams and the water-**monsters** that live in them.

≫→ **Atea, civilization, crafts, creation, farming**

TANGALOA
Oceania

Tangaloa, in Samoan myth, was the first god in existence. He saw a stone floating in the primordial ocean, carried it into space and carved a wife from it. He threw the remains of the stone into the sea, where they formed the Polynesian islands. Tangaloa told his daughter Tuli ('snipe') to fly down and plant a vine on the largest island. The vine divided itself into plants and vegetation of every kind. Grubs scrabbled round its roots, and Tangaloa transformed them into animals, birds, fish, and finally human beings, to complete **creation**.

≫→ **Ta'aroa**

TANGAROA
Oceania

Tangaroa the sea-god. Tangaroa, in Polynesian myth, was the eldest son of **Papa** (**Mother Earth**) and Vatea (that is **Rangi**, Father Sky). In some accounts he took part in the council of gods which tried to separate Papa and Rangi from their stifling, incessant sexual embrace, and later quarrelled with **Tane**, god of trees, forever attacking dry land (in tides), biting holes in the shoreline and snatching people and animals into the **sea**-kingdom. His wives were Faumea, who loved him enough to magic a nest of male-swallowing **monsters** out of her vagina and allow him intercourse, and Hina A Rauriki, whom he rescued from the octopus-**demon** Rogo Tumu Here.

Tangaroa and Rongo. In one Mangaian myth – a story so biased towards red-haired people that one wonders who invented it – Tangaroa and Rongo were **twins**, the eldest children of Papa and Vatea. Tangaroa was the elder, but generously allowed Rongo to be born first, and himself arrived later from a boil on his mother's arm. He knew all the secrets of the universe, and taught Rongo (who was less intelligent as well as junior) how to look after growing plants. As elder, he should have been sole ruler, but Vatea said that his saltiness would kill all life on land, and ordered that Rongo be given it instead to rule. Tangaroa agreed, asking only that he be allowed rule of everything red in creation: red birds, red fish, red-leaved trees, red vegetables and fruit, red-haired people. Rongo agreed, and the result was that, although red creatures and produce are the minority in creation, they are also the choicest.

Tangaroa appears in many different traditions, and his name is sometimes spelled Ta'aroa, Tagaro or Tagaroa.
≫→ sea

TANTALUS
Europe (South)

Tantalus (Tantalos, 'all wretched'), in Greek myth, was the son of **Zeus** and the **Titan** Pluto (not the same person as the king of the **Underworld**). Although he chose to live with mortals on Earth, his immortal parentage guaranteed him regular access to **Olympus**, and he was a frequent visitor at banquets of the gods. He married **Atlas**' daughter Dione, and their children were **Niobe** and **Pelops**.

Tantalus either cared nothing for right and wrong, or was a fool. He did what he wanted, regardless of the consequences – and suffered for it. On one occasion, he stole **ambrosia** and **nectar**, the gods' food and drink of **immortality**, and would have shared them with his mortal friends if the gods had not snatched them back in time. On another, he gave a banquet for the gods – and fed them a stew made from his own son Pelops. His third crime was smaller than either of these, but still the last straw for the gods. Tantalus' friend Pandareus stole a golden guard-dog made long before to protect the infant Zeus – and Tantalus hid it, suspecting (rightly) that no one would question a son of Zeus. No one, that is, but Zeus himself, who soon found out what had happened. He punished Pandareus by turning him to stone, and hurled him at Tantalus – a boulder which toppled Tantalus from **Heaven** to the Underworld.

In the Underworld, Tantalus was tied fast and surrounded by luscious fruit and a pool of clear water. As the centuries passed he became ever more hungry and thirsty – but whenever he tried to eat or drink the food and the pool slipped out of reach, leaving him forever tantalized. The boulder which had dashed him to the Underworld hung overhead, half-slipping and threatening to crush him to even lower depths – and he was condemned to endure these not-quite-punishments throughout eternity.

TAPIO
Europe (North)

Tapio, in Finnish myth, was the god of forests. He was himself without shape or substance, but his beard and clothes were made entirely of trees, and he had bottomless lakes for eyes. He lay sleeping across the countryside of Finland (which some called Tapiola after him); occasionally he stirred uneasily as he dreamed, sending storms rippling through his tree-cloak. Mortals sometimes settled among his trees, as ticks live in a sheep's fleece – and gradually, over time, as they listened to the rustling and whispering of the branches, they heard tiny echoes of Tapio's secrets, the knowledge of the gods.
≫→ farming

TARA
Asia (Southwest); India

Tara in Hindu myth. Tara was the beautiful wife of **Brihaspati** who was abducted and made pregnant by **Soma**.

Tara in Buddhist myth. Tara was a **sea**-goddess, and her mood changed in the same way as the sea: sometimes she was calm and serene, sometimes stormy and destructive. Like a squid or an octopus, she revealed her mood by the way her colour changed: when she was angry she turned blue, red or yellow, and when she was calm she turned green or white. She led a company of sea-**nymphs** who rescued sailors in danger.

Tara in Tibetan myth. In Tibetan myth the sea-aspect of Tara's character was, of necessity, turned into metaphor. Born from the Sea of Wisdom, she was Perfect Understanding, and ferried worshippers over the River of Experience to the Shore of Enlightenment. She was the wife of **Avalokiteshvara**, and the mother of all human beings on Earth.

Images of Tara are often painted on or pinned to boats. They show her as a serene, smiling woman, sometimes carrying a lotus and usually sitting on a lion (symbolizing the stormy water she has tamed).

TARAKA
India

Taraka ('star'), in Hindu myth, was a **demon**-queen who used to bite off mountain-tops with her teeth and hurl them at people she disliked. While **Rama** and his brothers were growing up, the sage **Vishvamitra** asked them to kill her. At first Rama was reluctant to fight a female, but he finally agreed. He and **Lakshmana** fought Taraka. Lakshmana cut off her nose and her ears to stop her sniffing them out or hearing

their approach, and Rama cut off her arms to stop her hurling rocks. But she went on biting mountains and spitting boulders until Rama fired an unerring arrow and shot her dead.

TARANIS
Europe (North)

Taranis, in Celtic myth, was the god of **thunder**. Its rumblings were caused by the wheels of Taranis' war-chariot rolling across the **sky**, and **lightning** was the sparks from his horses' hooves. Taranis was savage and destructive, but if he was appeased (by human sacrifice, the victims being drowned or burned), he sent prosperity to the earth in the form of **rain**.

TAWERET
Africa (North)

Taweret ('great one', Greek Thoueris), **Set**'s wife in Egyptian myth, was as benign as her husband was savage. She helped mortal women in **childbirth**, frightening off evil spirits at the instant the child entered the world of light – and she did this not by actual ferocity but by her appearance, as she had a hippo's head, the body of a pregnant lioness (but with human breasts), standing upright, and a crocodile's tail.

Taweret was popular with ordinary people. Women wore Taweret-bracelets and pendants, and put her statuettes beside their beds. There were Taweret jugs, hollowed out so that the goddess' pregnant belly held the liquid, her tail was the handle, and one breast was pierced to make the spout. Her popularity persuaded the priests to incorporate her in the **Underworld** pantheon, and she was married off to **Horus** (who won her from Set, in a newly-invented myth, during their cosmic duel) and placed at one of the gates of the Underworld, where she eased the passage not of souls coming in but of those going out, on their way to be reborn.

»→ animal-gods

TAWISKARA: *see* Ioskeha

TAWISKARON
Americas (North)

Tawiskaron, in the myths of the Mohawk people of the Northeastern US woodlands, was a **demon** who shepherded wild beasts as ordinary people kept goats or chickens. He and his pets lived in a corner of the **sky**, and from time to time he let down a bridge of cloud and sent his animals to Earth to prey on mortals.

TEFNUT
Africa (North)

Tefnut (or Tefenet, 'wetness'), in Egyptian myth, was the daughter of **Atum** and sister of **Shu**. She was either born from semen after her father masturbated, or (as the sound of her name suggests) from his spittle when he spat. She mated with Shu to engender **Geb** (Earth) and **Nut** (Air), but thereafter played little part in myth. In some accounts she quarrelled with **Ra**, left Egypt for Nubia and had to be enticed back by **Thoth**; in others, morning dew is her vaginal fluid.

In art, Tefnut was shown sometimes as a pair of spitting lips, and occasionally – perhaps because the Nubia story led her to be confused with **Sekhmet** or **Hathor** – as a lioness. She was also shown as a snake coiling round the pharaoh's sceptre: a guarantee that so long as pharaoh ruled and Tefnut supported him, there would be no drought.

TELCHINES
Europe (South)

The Telchines ('enchanters'), in Greek myth, were nine of the earliest and most elusive sea-**monsters** of all. They were the children of Sea, the first creatures ever able to breathe both on land and in water. They had dogs' heads, and flippered, stumpy arms like sealions; if they were angered, poisonous mist flashed from their eyes and killed any animal or mortal who came within range. They were craftsmen who made (some said) the sickle used by **Cronus** to attack Uranus (see **Ouranos**), and who invented the art of sculpture.

At first the Telchines settled in Rhodes (or some say Crete). But like many of the older gods, they cared nothing for the **Olympians**. They were not powerful enough to cause real trouble, but loved playing practical jokes and pranks. They interfered with the weather, to **Zeus**' irritation. They insulted **Aphrodite** so much, on one of her visits to Rhodes, that she lost her temper and sent them mad, so that they rioted across the island, fouling and breaking everything in sight. In the end **Poseidon** decided to rid his kingdom of them forever. He sent a **flood** to swallow them, but they scattered and escaped. Ever afterwards, they appeared briefly and unexpectedly all over the world, and every time they did they caused havoc. Sailors often claimed to have been attacked by them, in the shape of sea-**demons** surging on the wings of the East Wind. On land, like all supernatural sea-beings, they could assume any form they chose – and on one occasion they disguised themselves as hunting-dogs, and led the pack which tore Actaeon to pieces.

»→ crafts, shape-changers, tricksters

TELEMACHUS
Europe (South)

Telemachus ('late-battle'), son of **Odysseus** and **Penelope**, in Greek myth, was born just before Odysseus sailed to take part in the **Trojan War**, and grew up during the twenty years of his father's absence. When Odysseus came home, Telemachus helped him to kill the suitors who were pestering Penelope. But an oracle told Odysseus that his own son would one day murder him, and – not knowing of the existence of any sons except Telemachus – he banished the boy from Ithaca forever. Telemachus went first to Sparta (which he had visited some years earlier, to ask **Helen** and **Menelaus** if they had news of Odysseus' adventures after the Trojan War), and then to the floating island of Aeaea, where he married **Circe**, or in some accounts her daughter Cassiphone, and founded a royal dynasty.

Soon after this, Telemachus left Aeaea. Some say that he accidentally killed Circe and was banished, others that he inherited his father's wanderlust, and that he and Circe joined Penelope and Telegonus (who had married Penelope after Odysseus' death) and sailed South to a country previously unknown to Greeks. They called it Italy after Telegonus' and Penelope's son Italus, and Telemachus' and Circe's son **Latinus** later founded a dynasty, becoming the ancestor of the Latin people.

TELEPINU
Asia (West)

Telepinu, god of **farming** in ancient Syrian myth, was temperamental, liable to take offence at small slights (such as a frown from his father Taru, the weather-god) and to hold back or blight the crops. On one occasion he lost his temper altogether, threw on his clothes so quickly that he put his boots on the wrong feet, and disappeared. All over the world plants died, crops failed, human beings began to starve and the gods were denied their sacrifices. **Demons** swarmed from the **Underworld** to feast on corpses. The gods quartered the universe to find Telepinu and persuade him back. The **Sun** smashed down the gate of his palace and ran through the corridors and courtyards looking for him, but they were empty.

Then Hannahanna, Mother of All, sent a bee to find Telepinu's hiding place and sting him into reappearing. Instead of looking in palaces and cities, the bee went where bees go, and found Telepinu hiding among the flowers of a meadow. It stung him on the nose, knees and elbows, but instead of bringing him to his senses the pain made him even angrier, and he began jumping up and down and roaring at the gods.

Hannahanna sent Kamrusepas, goddess of magic healing, to poultice his stings with the herb of **immortality** and soothe the pain. Reluctantly Telepinu let himself be wooed back to work and the order of the universe was saved.

Gods of agriculture are often comic in myth, particularly in traditions where city-dwelling story-tellers have reworked stories from more ancient times. (Agriculture-gods in animist traditions seldom undergo such revisionism.) In Telepinu's case, another cause of mirth seems to have been that he was not the first god in his family to indulge in frets and sulks: a similar myth (now surviving only in fragments) seems to have been told of his father Taru. Other myths, however, suggest that Telepinu was not entirely a buffoon: in one, when the dragon Illuyankas stole the gods' eyes and hearts, it was Telepinu who seduced the dragon's daughter and persuaded her to get them back.

TEMAZCALTECI
Americas (Central)

Temazcalteci ('grandmother of the sweat-bath'), in Aztec myth, was the goddess of cleanness and patron of bath-houses. She protected people inside while they made themselves vulnerable to **demons** by stripping and washing. In some accounts, she was one aspect of **Cihua-cóatl**, the **Great Goddess**.
≫→ water

TEN CORN MAIDENS
Americas (North)

The Ten Corn Maidens, in the myths of the Zuñi people of the Southwestern US Pueblos, were beautiful dancers who came to the Upper World with the human race. They themselves were invisible, but their presence could be seen as they danced with corn-plants in the breeze. Witches transformed them into human girls, and imprisoned them, causing famine all over Zuñi lands. Then the harvest-god **Payatamu**, who was in love with Yellow Corn Maiden, rescued them and took them back to the Zuñi, where they danced and restored the harvest.
≫→ beauty, farming

TENGRI
Asia (Central)

Tengri ('power'), also known as Od and Odlek, in Mongolian myth, created the universe by wresting order from chaos. He gathered **fire**, wind and **water** and moulded them to make human beings. He himself, universal power, galloped in a disembodied form through the world on the horses of the storm to right wrongs and punish evil-doers. His wife was Itugen, **Mother Earth**, or Umai, Mother of All, and their children (also called Tengri) went to live on Earth as the spirits of everything in existence, both of visible entities such as trees, rivers, **mountains** and flames, and of such abstract notions as order, law and virtue.
≫→ civilization, creation

TEN YAMA KINGS, THE
Asia (East)

The Ten Yama Kings, in Chinese myth, were judges of the Dead. Each presided over a different court. The first King weighed each soul to see if it was heavy with guilt and should go to another court for judgement, or was light enough to pass straight to the Wheel of Transmigration and return to the mortal world in a new body. The second King judged greedy business-men and incompetent doctors, the third liars and politicians, the fourth blasphemers and misers, the fifth mur-derers and rapists, the sixth atheists, the seventh cannibals and slave-tra-ders, the eighth those who failed to honour their parents and the ninth arsonists and people killed in acci-dents. In all these courts, the Yama Kings had at their disposal an arsenal of punishments ranging from pillory and stocks to impaling, roasting, boil-ing in oil and throwing to wild beasts. Finally, the souls reached the tenth court, where appropriate new lives were settled before they passed at last to the Wheel of Transmigration and their new lives as aristocrats, paupers or animals.

≫→ **Underworld**

TEREUS
Europe (South)

Tereus ('on guard'), son of **Ares** in Greek myth, was a king of Thrace who helped King Pandion of Athens in a war against **Thebes** (or, some say, Megara). In gratitude, Pandion let Tereus marry his daughter Procne. Procne pined for her sister Philomela, and Tereus went South to bring Philo-mela to Thrace. As soon as he saw her, however, he was filled with lust, raped her, cut out her tongue to prevent her telling anyone, shut her in a remote castle and went home to tell Procne that she was dead.

Unfortunately for Tereus, the gods were so outraged that they helped Phi-lomela and Procne to take vengeance. Philomela embroidered the story of her rape on a tapestry and sent it to Procne, and Procne rescued her and took her to Thrace, with the gods' help, before Tereus arrived home. They butchered Tereus' infant son Itys, and when Ter-eus arrived Philomela served him the child's flesh in a stew of welcome. At the end of the meal Philomela appeared from behind a curtain, gibbering, and threw Itys' severed head on the table in front of Tereus. He drew his sword to kill the sisters – and the gods intervened for the last time, turning all four hu-mans into birds. Tereus became a hoo-poe (or, in some accounts, an owl – forever watchful), Philomela a nightin-gale (sweetly singing forever in recom-pense for her severed mortal tongue), Itys a pheasant (or, some say, a sand-piper) and Procne a swallow.

This gory myth gave rise to some of the most beautiful of all Greek lyric poetry. Ignoring the rape and child-murder, poets concentrated on the transformation, and on the way in which the nightingale and swallow have mourned for Itys ever since, the sweetness of their singing only enhan-cing the heartbreak which inspires it. The 'Lament for Itys' was a favourite subject for lyric poets, and was often set for competitions; the phrase 'Itys, Itys' ('ee-tun, eetun') became a kind of vocalization of grief, similar to English 'Alas', and features in poems otherwise unconnected with the myth. Sophocles wrote a tragedy about the original myth (now lost), and

Aristophanes' Birds parodies parts of it, introducing Tereus as a tattered bird-king, full of regret for his glorious past and of a mock-tragic, seedy arrogance.

TERRA: *see* Gaia

TESHUB
Asia (West)

Teshub, the ancient Syrian storm-lord, was the son of two male gods. When Kumarbi and **An** fought for the throne of **Heaven**, Kumarbi bit off An's penis, was fertilized by it and gave birth to three full-grown offspring, **Rain**, **Lightning** and **Thunder**, of which Teshub, Thunder, was the most fearsome. He rode the sky on a bull, brandishing an axe in one hand and a thunderbolt in the other, and was surrounded by a group of admiring goddesses, all of them so concerned with the **fertility** of the universe that they were determined to mate with him.

As soon as Teshub and his brothers were born, they dethroned their parent Kumarbi. He retaliated by masturbating over a stone and engendering a **giant**, Ullikummi. Ullikummi was made of green quartz, and never stopped growing. His weight gradually made **Mother Earth** sink into the primordial ocean, and he began to push the sky-arch ever higher, threatening to smash the gods' palaces and spill the stars into the gulf of space. Teshub and his brothers attacked him with rain, lightning and thunder, but he was impervious. **Ishtar**, Teshub's sister, tried to seduce him, but he had no sexual organs and ignored her. At the last possible moment, just as Ullikummi was about to break open the sky, blotting out the gods, Teshub dived deep into Ocean, found where the giant's feet were planted in Mother Earth and hacked them off at the ankles. Ullikummi toppled into Ocean, Mother Earth and Heaven were restored to their proper places, and the universe continued as if he had never existed.

*This myth survives only in fragments, and the account is incomplete – for example, what happened to Kumarbi is not recorded. An interesting feature is the proliferation of storm-gods. In the **mountains** where the story originated, storms were thought to be caused not by single deities but by whole armies racketing across the sky. It was only in later myth that the various attributes of Teshub, his brothers and his followers were gathered and given to a single deity, usually known just as **Baal** ('lord').*

TEUTATIS
Europe (North)

Teutatis or Toutatis ('people') was the Gallic war god – and as his name suggests, he also symbolized the strength of the entire Gallic nation. With his companions **Taranis** and the mysterious Esus (about whom nothing else is known) he was worshipped with human sacrifice, the victims being ceremonially drowned or burned.

TEZCATLIPOCA
Americas (Central)

Tezcatlipoca ('smoking mirror'), in Aztec myth, was the original **Sun**-god, but was toppled from the sky (in some accounts, by **Quetzalcóatl**) and became the god of darkness and sorcery, afraid of daylight. His other names included Telpochtli ('young man'), Yaotl ('warrior') and Yoalli Ehecatl ('wind of the night'). He was one of the gods who existed before **creation**, and he plunged into the primordial ocean to wrestle with **Coatlicue** (in her guise as Cipactli the crocodile), tearing off her lower jaw to make the Earth. (In some accounts, she bit off one of his feet, and he replaced it with a mirror of polished flint, which reflected not just the present but the past and future. In others, he lost his foot by trapping it in one of the doors of the **Underworld**). When he was first hurled from the sky he had neither form nor shape, but was the all-present 'wind of the night', the invisible presence which terrifies human beings alone at night. Then he put his shape-changing powers to work, and became a black jaguar on Earth and in the sky the star-constellation the Great Bear. He also retained his invisible nature, gazing with four unseen faces in each of the four cardinal compass directions. His servants were wizards, **demons** and soothsayers, and he had power over wind and stillness, darkness and silence.

Tezcatlipoca took other forms as well. As consort of Tlazoltéotl, goddess of lust, he often appeared as a nude young man and set girls' hearts racing. To armies in the field he appeared as a warrior in full armour, recognizable as himself by his mirror-foot and a diagonal black stripe across his face. Another favoured form was that of a skeleton, gibbering in lonely woods, with a heart throbbing inside ribs which flapped open and shut like the doors of a cage. To conquer him, you thrust your arm between the ribs and tore out the heart – and at once he offered you riches to put it back. (He usually lied.) These depredations weakened him, and once every year he died and had to be revived at a bloody ceremony in which the heart of a living man was torn out and offered, still pulsing, at his altar.

Tezcatlipoca's mirror worked both ways. It showed the future to those of his worshippers who could read its secrets, and it gave him all-knowledge of human wishes and intentions. However, and perhaps unexpectedly in view of his unceasing thirst for human blood, he used his knowledge to help mortals, not harm them. He rewarded the good and punished the wicked, taking particular care of slaves, widows and orphans. His malevolence was chiefly directed towards the gods who had dethroned him as lord of creation, and he especially hated Quetzalcóatl. In the end he tricked Quetzalcóatl into self-disgust and self-immolation; light left the world, the Golden Age came to an end, and in the darkness and cruelty which filled human hearts thereafter, Tezcatlipoca once more ruled supreme.

*The Tezcatlipoca cult gave the invading Spaniards their chief defence for exterminating the Aztecs. Claiming that his dark secrets and bloodthirsty rituals were typical of the whole people, they set about butchering an entire nation in the name of their own redemptive God. It was as if visitors from Mars were to exterminate a nation of fundamentalist Christians on the grounds that they believed in **Satan**.*

>>→ light and dark, prophecy, shape-changers, twins

THANATOS
Europe (South)

Thanatos ('**death**'), in Greek myth, was the child of Night and the brother of Sleep. He was a warrior whose task was to collect mortals whose time on Earth was over and take them to the gates of the **Underworld**, after which **Hermes** led them below for judgement. Thanatos is the same person as the (female) Roman **Mors**.

THEBES
Europe (South)

Thebes, in Greek myth, a city on the banks of the river Ismenus on the Boeotian plain, was one of the most beautiful places in the world. The gods chose it as the site of their earthly paradise, and sent Prince **Cadmus** of Phoenicia to build a city there. But Cadmus killed the sacred guardian of the place, **Mother Earth**'s own serpent-offspring, and polluted the ground by spilling its blood. Mother Earth took her revenge by demanding the blood of each generation of the royal line of Thebes, and ever afterwards, while the city lasted, Theban kings and queens duly slaughtered one another and gave the ground their blood. **Agave**, Cadmus' daughter, tore her own son **Pentheus** to pieces. Zethus' (see **Amphion and Zethus**) wife, creeping into the nursery to murder the children of her sister-in-law **Niobe**, killed her own child by mistake in the darkness. **Laius** tried to kill his infant son **Oedipus**, to prevent an oracle that the child would grow up to murder him – and failed. Oedipus killed Laius. Oedipus' sons **Eteocles** and **Polynices** killed each other, fighting for the throne. **Creon** executed **Antigone**, and caused the death of his own son Haemon.

After seven generations of slaughter, the rest of Greece at last rose up to put an end to Thebes. They sacked the city, smashed the walls, ploughed the rubble and sowed salt. The soil, already rank with blood, was poisoned: nothing ever grew there again, and the gods' dream of making Thebes an earthly paradise was frustrated forever.

>>→ Heaven, Seven Against Thebes

THEMIS
Europe (South)

Themis ('justice'), in Greek myth, was a **Titan**. **Zeus** mated with her, and their offspring were the **Fates** and the Seasons. In some accounts, it was she and not Clymene who mated with her fellow-Titan Iapetus and gave birth to **Prometheus**. She was always depicted as a beautiful woman with bandaged eyes, or blind, and holding a sword in one hand and a pair of scales in the other.

>>→ justice and universal order

THESEUS
Europe (South)

Theseus and Athens. Theseus ('layer-down'), in Greek myth, was the son of King **Aegeus** of Athens and Princess Aethra of Troezen. Aegeus, visiting Troezen, got drunk, slept with Aethra and left in a hurry. He left a golden sword and a pair of sandals under a rock, and told Aethra that if she bore a son, and the son grew up, she should tell him what had happened, and then if the gods gave the boy strength to lift the rock and find the sword, he should come to Athens as Aegeus' heir.

In due course Theseus was born, grew up, recovered the sword and sandals and set out for Athens. In the meantime, however, **Medea** had settled there, having fled to Aegeus after killing her children by **Jason**. Black magic told her who Theseus was, and she tried to poison him before Aegeus recognized him and made him his heir instead of Medea's own son Medus. But Aegeus recognized his sword and sandals from years before, and dashed the poison-cup from Theseus' hand. (Medea fled to the **Underworld**, where **Hades** welcomed her; Medus fled to Asia Minor.) Theseus next killed the fifty sons of Aegeus' brother Pallas, who were besieging Athens, and tamed a miraculous white bull (in some accounts the bull that fathered the Cretan **Minotaur**), which had swum ashore at Marathon not far from Athens; the Athenians hailed him as saviour and king-in-waiting.

Theseus and the Minotaur. Every year, as tribute to King Minos, the Athenians sent seven young men and seven young women to Crete. They became bull-leapers, and at the end of the season were sent into the Labyrinth where the Minotaur devoured them. Determined to end this custom, Theseus sailed to Crete in place of one of the young men, and began training as a bull-leaper. Minos' daughter **Ariadne** promised to help him kill the Minotaur if he took her away from Crete afterwards. She gave him a spindle wound with wool, and led him through the corridors and chambers of the Labyrinth, while he unwound the wool to mark his way. They came to the den where the Minotaur slept, and Theseus killed it with his golden sword. They retraced their steps, winding up the wool, and freed the other Athenians from their cells. It was night, and there were no guards – for Crete was an island, and who but **Daedalus** had ever escaped from it? The Athenians scuttled the ships of the Cretan fleet, jumped into their own ship and rowed for home.

Theseus, Ariadne and Dionysus. Theseus planned to marry Ariadne as soon as they reached Athens. But on the way they landed on the island of Naxos for water, and while the Athenians went to the stream, Ariadne fell asleep on the beach – and **Dionysus** caught sight of her and lusted after her. He blurred the minds of Theseus and his companions with forgetfulness, so that they sailed away without Ariadne. She woke up alone on a deserted shore. Then Dionysus appeared, dancing over the sand-dunes with his maenads and **satyrs**; he spoke gently to her, charmed all memory of Theseus from her mind, and made her his consort.

Dionysus' forgetfulness-spell still clouded Theseus' mind. Before he sailed for Crete, he had promised Aegeus he would hoist a purple-red sail (or some say a white sail) to show success, and to tell his men to hoist a black sail for failure. He now forgot to change the sails, and when Aegeus, watching anxiously for news, saw a black sail on the horizon, he jumped from the Acropolis wall and killed himself.

Theseus, Antiope and Phaedra. After Aegeus' death the Athenians made Theseus king. He began to join other **heroes** on their expeditions and adventures. He was invited to the wedding of **Pirithous**, king of the Lapiths, and helped him in the battle which followed against the **Centaurs**. He and Pirithous became close friends, and had many adventures together. They went with **Heracles** to steal the belt of **Hippolyta**, queen of the **Amazons**. On the way they besieged the Amazon town of Themiscyra, and Princess **Antiope**, watching from the battlements, fell in love with Theseus and opened the gates for him. He took her to Athens as his mistress, and fought off a huge force of Amazons which tried to win her back. They lived happily for several years, and had a son, **Hippolytus**. But then King Minos died in Crete, and Theseus planned to make an alliance with the new king, Catreus, and to celebrate it by marrying **Phaedra**, **Ariadne**'s sister. Antiope burst in on the wedding ceremony with a band of Amazons to stop it, and in the battle which followed Theseus killed her.

Antiope's father, **Ares** god of war, and her patron, **Artemis**, waited to punish Theseus until his son Hippolytus was grown-up. Then they made Phaedra fall in love with the young man – and when he refused to have anything to do with her, they made her send a letter to Theseus claiming that Hippolytus had raped her, and then hang herself. Theseus sent soldiers to arrest Hippolytus, and Hippolytus jumped in a chariot and

fled down the road beside the shore. In his fury, Theseus prayed to the gods to kill his son, and Poseidon sent a tidal wave which terrified Hippolytus' horses and made them rear; the chariot crashed and Hippolytus broke his neck.

Theseus' madness and death. The deaths of Phaedra and Hippolytus drove Theseus mad. He and Pirithous planned to kidnap and marry two daughters of **Zeus**, one for each of them. They stole twelve-year-old **Helen** from Sparta, then made their way into the **Underworld** and demanded no less a person than Queen **Persephone** herself. **Hades** pretended to welcome them and invited them to sit at a banquet. But the seats he offered were the Thrones of **Lethe**, which fused with the flesh of whoever sat on them, holding them in the Underworld forever. Theseus and Pirithous would have sat until they were totally engulfed in stone, if Heracles, on his quest to steal **Cerberus**, had not seen his old friends' torment. He tore Theseus from his throne, ripping all the flesh from Theseus' legs. Then he turned to help Pirithous – too late, for the ground gaped open and swallowed Pirithous to the lowest depths of Hell.

Theseus hobbled back to the Upper World on his rags and bones of legs. He had been four years in the Underworld, and during that time Castor and Pollux (see **Dioscuri**), Helen's brothers, had rescued her, conquered Athens and set up a new king there. None of Theseus' former people recognized him, and he limped away, a discarded beggar. A captain bound for Crete took pity on him, and gave him free passage. But on the way they landed on the island of Scyros, and Artemis whispered to

Lycomedes, king of the island, who Theseus really was and told him to kill him for murdering her servant Antiope. Lycomedes threw Theseus over a precipice and drowned him.

In ancient Athens, Theseus was regarded as not mythical but real. At the battle of Marathon, fought by the Greeks against the Persians in 490 BCE, Athenian soldiers reported that his ghost had come fully armed to help them, and had scattered a whole wing of the invading army. The Athenians asked the Delphic oracle what this meant, and the oracle advised them to collect Theseus' bones from Scyros and bury them. In an ancient burial-mound on Scyros they found a gigantic human skeleton and an ornate golden sword, carried them back to Athens and placed them in the temple called the Theseum, where they were thought to protect the city ever afterwards.

*In myth, Theseus lacks the psychological complexity and emblematic force of such other **heroes** as **Odysseus** or **Orestes**. He is a reactive figure, at the mercy of events rather than controlling them – and his story seems to tell us little, to have no point except the interest of the adventures themselves. No creative artist in ancient times – and none later until Mary Renault in her novels* The Bull from the Sea *and* The King Must Die *– treated his story as a unified whole and made coherent sense of it. Instead, single episodes were given individual treatment, ranging from the Minotaur story (which was a favourite of ancient Greek vase-painters, and became a standard hero-kills-monster tale in later children's literature) to events in which Theseus' own part is peripheral, for example the abandonment of Ariadne – Monteverdi's* Ariadne's Lament, *to take just one treatment, was one of the best-known of all Renaissance compositions based on ancient Greek stories – or Phaedra's passion for Hippolytus, which inspired playwrights from Euripides (who described it from Hippolytus' point of view) to Racine (whose* Phèdre *became a pinnacle of the French tragic repertoire). Twentieth-century fine artists and sculptors, notably Ayrton, Lipchitz and Picasso, have been especially fascinated by the Minotaur – and once again Theseus has been marginalized.*

THETIS
Europe (South)

Thetis ('disposer'), daughter of **Nereus** in Greek myth, was a beautiful **sea-nymph** whom both **Zeus** and **Poseidon** wanted to make their consort. But **Prometheus** revealed a secret told him by the **Fates**, that she would bear a son greater than his father, and the gods hastily found other consorts and married Thetis instead to a mortal, **Peleus**.

Thetis was determined to make her children immortal. Accordingly, when each child was born, she burned it in fire to remove its mortal flesh and then sprinkled the ashes into the sea. When her last child, **Achilles**, was born, Peleus rushed in and stopped her, so she took the child instead to the **Underworld** and dipped him in the River **Styx**. This made him immortal – except for the heel by which she'd held him, and into which **Paris** was later to fire the arrow which killed him.

When the **Trojan War** began, Thetis (who, like all sea-creatures, had second sight) knew that Achilles was fated to die in it. She tried to stop him going by dressing him as a woman and hiding him in the harem of King Lycomedes – but the plan failed when he heard the trumpet-call of the recruiting party and ran out shouting his war-cry. At the end of the Trojan War, after Paris killed him, she gathered his ashes in a golden urn and scattered them on the sea, as unlucky with her last child as she'd been with all the others.

THIAZI
Europe (Northern)

Thiazi, in Nordic myth, was a **giant shape-changer** who spent much of his time as an enormous black eagle. He tricked **Loki** into bringing him **Idun**, goddess of youth, guardian of the golden apples of **immortality**, and the gods would have aged and died if Loki hadn't found another trick to fetch her back again. (*see* Idun.) Thiazi's daughter **Skadi** married the **sea**-god **Njörd**.

THOR
Europe (North)

Thor ('thunder') or Thunor or Donner, in Nordic myth, in some accounts was the son of **Odin** and Fjörgyn; in others, he derived his identity from the older **thunder**-god Donar. He was the god of the **sky**, generally a sunny, chuckling **giant** (in which case the weather was fine), but uncontrollable when angry. His weapon was the stubby-handled hammer Mjöllnir ('crusher'), made for him by dwarfs. Nothing withstood its blows, and it returned to his hand like a boomerang every time he threw it. Often, it glowed red-hot, and he wore a pair of iron gloves to hold it. He also owned a magic belt, which doubled his strength every time he put it on.

Thor and Thrym. Thor was the gods' champion against the **giants**, and hunted them mercilessly. On one occasion giant Thrym stole Mjöllnir, and refused to give it back unless the gods let him marry **Freyja**, goddess of desire. When Freyja refused, **Heimdall** suggested that Thor himself dress as a bride. Reluctantly, Thor did so, and he and **Loki** went to Thrym's feast-hall for the wedding-reception. Here Thor astonished the giants by eating a whole ox, eight salmon and the cakes and sweets made for the entire female group of giants, washed down with three barrels of mead. (Loki explained that the bride had been so eager for the wedding that she'd not eaten for a week.) Thrym bent to kiss his bride and was astonished to see eyes glowing red like coals: Loki explained that the bride had been so excited that she hadn't slept for weeks. Finally Thrym laid the phallic Mjöllnir in Thor's lap to symbolize the wedding, and Thor threw off his headdress and began hurling Mjöllnir round the room until Thrym and all the other giants were dead.

Thor and Hrungnir. At a banquet in **Asgard** (to which he had been invited without Thor knowing), the giant Hrungnir got drunk on mead and boasted that he would destroy Asgard, topple the gods and steal both Freyja and Thor's own wife **Sif**. He challenged Thor to a duel. Thor's weapon was Mjöllnir, Hrungnir's an enormous whetstone. They hurled them at the same moment, and Mjöllnir smashed the whetstone to pieces in midair.

Some of the fragments killed Hrungnir, but one embedded itself in Thor's own forehead. The witch Groa tried to say a spell to pull it out, but Thor distracted her by boasting how he'd once rescued her husband from the giants' kingdom, and she was so enthralled that she lost the thread of her magic. Ever afterwards, the lump of stone stayed embedded in Thor's head.

Thor and Skrymir. Thor and Loki were travelling, as they often did, in **Jotunheim**, land of the giants, when they stopped to shelter in a building so huge in the darkness that the gulf of eternity itself seemed to stretch between its entrance and the nearest wall. It was not until daylight that they discovered that it was the thumb of one glove of the giant Skrymir, who walked off with their provisions, taking such enormous strides that he was out of sight before they even noticed he'd been there. They hurried after him, and caught up with him at nightfall, only to find him sleeping. Thor hit him on the head three times with Mjöllnir: the first time Skrymir took it for a falling leaf, the second for an acorn, the third for bird-droppings. He told the gods to hurry to **Utgard**, where even bigger and fiercer giants were waiting.

In Utgard, the giants challenged Thor and Loki to trials of strength. Loki and the giant Logi held an eating contest – and Logi won by eating not just the meat of the cattle but their bones, the wooden trenchers they lay on, and even the table. Thor tried to drain a drinking-horn – but it was filled with water from the primordial ocean, and welled full each time he drank from it. He wrestled the pet cat of Utgard-Loki, lord of Utgard, and succeeded only in lifting one of its paws from the ground. Finally he wrestled Utgard-Loki's foster-mother **Elli**, an aged, bent crone who nevertheless made him sink to his knees and would have finished him if Utgard-Loki had not ordered the contest to stop. Utgard-Loki now claimed that the contests had proved giants superior to gods – and this was hardly surprising, since Logi was not really a giant at all but Fire, the cat was **Jormungand** the world-serpent in disguise, and the crone was Old Age (against whom not even gods could defend themselves once they left Asgard and the Golden Apples of **immortality**). Thor snatched up Mjöllnir to kill Utgard-Loki – and the entire kingdom and everyone in it disappeared before his eyes. Everything, from Skrymir and his glove to the feast-hall and the wrestling-opponents had been illusions, conjured up by the giants who were too terrified to face the gods in person.

Thor and Jormungand. Thor had no particular dislike of Jormungand, but the Fates decreed that they were to meet and fight throughout this cycle of the universe. When Thor challenged the giant **Hymir** to a fishing-competition, it was Jormungand he hauled up from the depths. In fantasy-Utgard he wrestled the world-serpent Jormungand, disguised as a cat. And at **Ragnarök** he and Jormungand will fight to the death. Thor's weapon will be Mjöllnir, and Jormungand will use his coils and his venom. They will kill each other, Thor smashing the world-serpent's skull only to drown in the poison that pours out of it.

Thor was one of the most popular of the Nordic gods, and his worship survived well into Christian times: as late as the eleventh century CE he was Christ's main rival in Northern Europe, displacing even **Odin**. In Scandinavia his sacred tree was the rowan (because of its flame-red berries); in Germany it was the oak, and lightning-blasted oaks were regarded as particularly holy. In art he was shown as a burly, flame-bearded warrior, riding a chariot hung with pots and pans (whose rattling made **thunder**) and pulled by two winged goats, Tanngrisn ('tooth-grinder') and Tanngniort ('tooth-gnasher'). When he was hungry he ate the goats, then hammered their bones back to life with Mjöllnir.

Thor's hammer, shaped like a letter T with a cross-bar at the bottom, was a common symbol, in rock-carvings, paintings and above all in metalwork: hammer-amulets, rings and pendants range from simple everyday wear to the finest ancient Nordic craftsmanship. People made the 'sign of the hammer' as they prayed to Thor, for example over a baby's head at its naming-ceremony – an action readily converted by conquering Christians into the sign of the cross. Another symbol, the swastika (perhaps representing a ring of flickering flames) was also associated with Thor-worship, and may have reached Europe originally from India. Hitler's Baltic brigade took it to Germany, where it was adopted as the Nazi emblem and acquired connotations quite different from any it had before.

Thor is Thursday's name-god.

≫→ **Geirröd (giant)**

THOTH
Africa (North)

Thoth (or Djeheuty, 'he of Djehut'), god of wisdom in Egyptian myth, was in some accounts born from **Set**'s forehead after Set (a god who enjoyed fellatio) swallowed some of **Horus**' semen. Having no form of his own, he entered the body of the baboon god Hedjwer, and was given the task of supporting the Moon-disc in the sky. In other accounts Thoth was the son – or perhaps the heart or tongue – of **Ra** the Sun, and was himself the Moon. He had a portion of his father's all-knowledge, understanding time and truth; in some versions this knowledge was intuitive, in others it was contained in books from his father's library which only he knew how to read. He invented every intellectual skill which required organization: astronomy, fine art, geometry, law, magic, medicine, music, and especially writing. In later times he was even credited with creating the world by naming it (a skill which had once belonged to **Ptah**).

Thoth was the patron of one of the ancient world's main **mysteries**, that of Trismegistus, 'the Thrice-Greatest' whom Greeks identified with **Hermes**. Cult members believed that Thoth's magic books, or portions of them, were owned by his priests, and that devotees could learn to read them and decipher in them the secrets of the universe.

In less hermetic worship, Thoth was the patron god of scribes and doctors. His temple at Ashmunen (Greek Hermopolis, 'Hermes-city') was a healing-shrine for three millennia. In art he is shown either as a baboon (or baboon-headed man) dictating to a scribe who sits cross-legged before him, or as an ibis-headed warrior trampling his enemies. This image arose partly because the curved beak of the ibis represented the crescent moon, and partly

because of a pun – more apparent in Egyptian than in English – between hib ('ibis') and hab ('tread on').
≫→ animal-gods, creation, disease and healing, Underworld

THREE DOOR GODS, THE
Asia (East)

The Three Door Gods, in Chinese myth, were Qin Shupo, Hu Jingte and We Jeng. Many other gods and spirits protected doors and those who passed in or out through them, but these three were the main deities, and their pictures were often painted or hung on doors, and were replaced each year. The gods were originally mortals, ministers of Emperor Tai Song of the seventh century CE. He fell ill, dreaming that he was being tormented by **demons**, and the ministers took turns to stay awake at his bedroom doors each night until he recovered. He was so impressed that he had their pictures hung on doors throughout the kingdom, and the gods also rewarded them by granting them **immortality**.
≫→ guardians

THREE GODS OF HAPPINESS, THE
Asia (East)

The Three Gods of Happiness, in Chinese myth, all began as mortals but were promoted to **immortality** for their extreme goodness while on Earth. They lived in the Palace of Immortality in the Happy Isles, but often sailed from there in their ceremonial barge to bring good luck to mortals. They were Fu Xing god of happiness, Lu Xing god of salaries and Shou Lao god of long life.

THREE LAVATORY LADIES, THE
Asia (East)

The Three Lavatory Ladies, in Chinese myth, were goddesses of **childbirth**. They were originally mortal princesses, and won their name and **immortality** by using a privy-bucket and its contents as a weapon during a supernatural battle. In later times, a red privy-bucket, known as the 'golden bushel of troubled origins', was given to each married couple as a wedding-present, and was used not only as a privy but during childbirth – hence the Lavatory Ladies' main prerogative.

THREE SOVEREIGNS, THE
Asia (East)

The Three Sovereigns, in Chinese myth, inaugurated civilized life on Earth. In order, they were **Fu Xi**, **Shen Nong** and Yen Ti.
≫→ civilization, crafts

THUNDER
Thunder-gods. Thunder, one of the most awesome forces of Nature, was treated with appropriate respect by most peoples – but not by all. One Melanesian tale said that Thunder, as a foetus, racketed round his mother's womb so noisily that the gods were appalled and gave him the power of instant growth. But although he leapt to physical maturity as soon as he entered the light of day, his mind

remained that of an irritable baby, and he has been howling and squalling round the world ever since. Similarly, **Ajisukitakahikone**, the Japanese thunder god, was so rowdy that the gods set him sailing in a boat sent eternally round Japan – which is why the sound of thunder still advances and recedes. The North American Wyandot thunder-god, Heng, was a butterfingers, so destructive that his relatives threw him out and forced him to live eternally on his own.

The Cherokee people of North America depicted Thunder as **Lightning**'s twin brother. They called him Tame Boy, and said that he played rumbling games of ball across the sky with his brother, Wild Boy. For the Chibcha people of Colombia, Thunder's fury was caused by pain when the Sun God kicked him in the testicles, rendering him impotent; he has raged round the world, smarting, ever since. Kadaklan, the thunder-god of the Tinguian people of the Philippines, lived in a tree with his dog Kimat, lightning, and sent him to bite people he disliked. **Enumclaw**, the thunder-god of several peoples of Washington State, US, was a mortal who grew so skilled at hurling fireballs that the sky-spirit, afraid for his own position, promoted him to **immortality** and found him celestial work to do.

Most thunder-myths, however, avoided such knockabout. Unlike the Tame Boy and Enumclaw stories, for example, most thunder-myths from North America – in common with those of ancient Siberia – imagined the god as a powerful, eagle-like bird which was both creator and destroyer.

The Japanese pantheon included not only the buffoon Ajisukitakahikone, but also a gigantic, rook-like **thunderbird** which guarded the gates of **Heaven**. The Sumerian storm-bird Zu had a lion's head (its roars were thunder) and was the servant of **Ninurta** the war god. The Sioux thunder-gods were five fierce brothers who, when mortal, refused to give up cannibalism and who ever afterwards craved human flesh. Other thunder-gods were equally implacable to humans. The Maori thunder-spirit Taohirimatea defended his father **Rangi** (the sky-spirit) against his brothers and sisters who were set to dethrone him, and killed them all save Tumataunega, spirit of human aggression – since when thunder and humans have always been enemies. **Lei Gong**, the Chinese thunder-god, carried a drum for noise, and a chisel to hurl at evil-doers. Pillan, thunder-god of the Araucanian people of Chile, had a hatred for humans as unexplained as it was implacable, and employed an army of human-headed snakes to blight their crops. The thunder-god of ancient Peru was summoned to help mortals – and appeased from harming them – by an annual festival culminating in the sacrifice of white llamas (symbolizing fleecy clouds).

Other thunder-gods were beneficial to humans. The roaring and teeth-gnashing of the Mayan **Chac** heralded his tears, which watered the Earth with **fertility**; the same god among the Inca, **Tlaloc**, took dead souls to the earthly paradise Tlalocan. Hinun, the Iroquois thunder-god, used his invincible bow and fire-arrows to destroy evil – not least, at the beginning of time, the giant water-snake which preyed on humans. **Vajrasattva**, the Tibetan ur-**Buddha**, origin of the other six Buddhas and known as 'adamantine' and 'thunder-hurler', protected devotees seeking enlightenment by sending thunder, lightning, rain and snow to fight the **demons** which might distract them.

Thunder as a weapon. Thunder was often imagined as a weapon, a visible sign of a god's power and anger, and as something which could be handed on or stolen. When **Athene**, in **Greek myth**, wanted to borrow one of **Zeus'** thunderbolts, she begged him to unlock the cupboard where they were kept, and had to convince him that she had a legitimate need for it, and would not use it in a revolt against him. **Teshub**, the ancient Babylonian storm-god, used thunder and lightning first to fight his brother and sister (who were seeking to dethrone their father **Anu** the **Sky**), then turned his weapons on Anu himself. (Teshub was the same person as the Sumerian storm-god **Baal**, who however was beneficial to mortals, using thunder and lightning to vanquish Mot, god of desert dryness, and to bring water to growing crops.) The youthful Polynesian god Tuamoto, on growing up, borrowed the long-forgotten weapon of his ancient ancestors, thunder, and used it to dethrone his father **Atea**, Sky. In Indian myth, **Shiva** (known as Rudra, 'thunderer'), shot lightning-flashes of anger to consume his enemies. Adad, the Sumerian thunder-bringer, and **Jumala**, the original Finnish sky-god, wielded thunderbolts in the shape of jagged lightning-spears. **Thor**, the Norse blacksmith-god, carried the hammer which was the

thunderbolt; he inherited it from his predecessor **Donar**, and it was the gods' sole protection against the **giants**. He honed his skills with it by hunting trolls, and hurled it in epic battles against all who would unseat the gods.

Thunder and creation. Thunder played a central part in three creation-myths. The Pawnee people told how **Tirawa** the creator sent his servant Lightning to hang constellations in the sky. Lightning carried a bag of stars and constellations, fragments of his own body – and also filled with their opposing medium, darkness. While he was busy hanging stars, **Coyote** the **trickster** prevailed on Wolf to rummage in the sack – and light and darkness spilled out, tussling for supremacy, and filled the sky. So thunder was born, and with it plague, blight and death arrived on Earth. In a more genial myth, part of the ancient Indian tradition, Vritra (or Ahi), serpent of drought, drank the primordial oceans and everything they contained, and **Indra**, lord of thunder, sent a thunderbolt to split its belly and so release all life. And in the Greek creation-myth, when the gods tried to unseat the **Titans**, civil war lasted for forty seasons of the world. The immortal combatants were unharmed; the chief victim was **Mother Earth**, who from being placid and beautiful became a ragged no-god's-land. In the end she whispered to Zeus a way to end the war. He crept to the inner recesses of the **Underworld**, where Mother Earth's giant-children the blacksmith-**Cyclopes** had long been imprisoned. He gave them **nectar** to drink, and it filled them with godlike intelligence. At once they set to work to forge weapons for him: thunder, trapped and stored in thunderbolts. Thereafter Zeus used thunderbolts to control the universe, and the Cyclopes, working in forges under Mount Etna, constantly renewed the supply.

In a pendant to thunder-stories, the Chinese for centuries revered Li T'ien, a real person of the eleventh century CE who was the first ever to use firecrackers to scare evil spirits from processions and festivals – a miniature version of thunder which quickly became a standard part of all religious celebrations.

⟫⟩ (Africa): Sudika-Mbambi and Kabundungulu; (Americas): Catequil, Hinu, Ilyap'a, Pillan, Tupan, Valedjád; (Celtic): Taranis; (Finnish): Ilmarinen; (Mesopotamia): Ada, Imdugud; (Rome): Jupiter; (Slavic): Pyerun, Varpulis; (general): creation, rain, war

THUNDERBIRDS

Thunderbirds were an entire species of supernatural beings. They were known in Siberia (as ducks whose sneezing brings rain), but were otherwise virtually exclusive to the peoples of Northern America. They controlled **thunder**, **lightning**, **rain**, **fire** and truth – if you lied or broke your word, they sent a lightning bolt to punish you. They were ruled by the Great Thunderbird. He was the most senior of four elders; the others were the Red Thunderbird of the North, the Yellow Thunderbird of the East and the White (or some say Blue) Thunderbird of the South. Between them they guarded the nest of bones in which a giant egg was incubated – the egg from which all small

thunderbirds, storms and parching winds, were hatched.

The appearance of thunderbirds. Thunderbirds were often shown in statues and on totem-poles as eagle-headed human beings with wings for arms and talons instead of toes. In some cases, they had second, human heads in their bellies and enormous penises in the shape of forked lightning. The Crow people said that they wore eagle-feather cloaks, and Pacific-coast peoples said that the Great Thunderbird carried a lake on his back and ate whole whales. But all such depictions differ from the most widely-accepted myth. In this, thunderbirds had no form. Their bodies billowed like clouds. They had claws but no feet, fanged beaks but no heads, wings but no shoulders. The flapping of their wings made storms, and they created lightning by tearing trees open with their beaks or by opening and shutting their eyes (or what would have been their eyes if they'd had eyes).

In contrast to the rest of the world, which had a clockwise rotation and moved forwards in time, Thunderbirds existed in an anti-clockwise dimension and communicated in backwards-speech. These powers gave them their authority. Entranced mortals could enter their dimension briefly, listen to their speech and learn some of their secrets; but to stay too long was dangerous.

Thunderbirds and creation. The Algonquian people of the Northeastern US believed that thunderbirds were the supernatural ancestors of the human race, 'our grandparents'. Others connected them with the **creation** of the universe or the coming of **justice and universal order**. In many myths, thunderbirds were the enemies of **snakes** (which symbolized evil and anarchy.) In one Sioux creation myth, for example (from the US Great Plains), the Great Thunderbird Wakan Tanka was the grandson of the Sky-spirit who made the world. The Sky-spirit created human beings and put them on the fertile Earth, where they scurried about like ants. Unktehi, the water-spirit of the Missouri River, a gigantic, horned water-snake with a horde of smaller offspring, took them for lice. She and her followers spouted water from their horns to flood the countryside and drown human beings.

In the flood which followed, most of our ancestors perished; the survivors scrambled to a mountain-top as the waters continued to rise, and prayed for survival. Wakan Tanka and his thunderbird followers set out to save them. For many ages of the world they battled Unktehi and her wriggling spawn. Each creature picked an enemy of its own rank and size. Fire fought water, and though fearful wounds were dealt, neither side won. Then Wakan Tanka soared with his followers high in the sky, out of reach of the water-monsters. They concentrated their lightning and sent it crashing down. The water-monsters cowered in the crevices of Earth – and the thunderbirds' lightning began to sear and scorch **Mother Earth** herself. The ground baked hard and cracked open, and the monsters' water-flesh dripped from their bones and drained away. At last nothing was left but parched bones – and they can still be seen in the regions humans call the Badlands.

This battle, the story ends, gave the thunderbirds power over water as well as fire. It originated the first Age of the World, and ever afterwards the thunderbirds have used their powers to help human beings, and humans have responded by honouring them, and the Great Thunderbird especially, as rulers of the universe.

≫→ **animal-gods, creators**

THYESTES
Europe (South)

Thyestes ('beater' or 'sacrificer'), in Greek myth, was one of the sixteen sons of **Pelops** and Hippodamia. Jointly with his brother **Atreus**, he ruled the small town of Midea near Mycenae. When King **Eurystheus** of Mycenae died, the gods told his people to let Atreus and Thyestes decide among themselves which of them should rule. Atreus owned the fleece of a golden ram which he had stolen from **Artemis** and hidden in a box. But unknown to him, Thyestes had been having an affair with Atreus' wife Aerope, and she had given him the fleece as a love-token. He now suggested that whichever brother owned the fleece should rule – and when Atreus agreed, triumphantly produced it and took the throne.

At once the gods sent omens. The **Sun** and stars reversed their courses and the Earth shrieked. Terrified, Thyestes admitted what he'd done, and Atreus took power and banished him. But his revenge was not finished.

He invited Thyestes to a banquet of reconciliation – and served him his own children, cooked in a stew. Thyestes cursed his brother and fled to Sicyon, where his daughter Pelopia was a priestess of **Athene**.

In Sicyon, Thyestes asked the gods how his dead children might be avenged, and the oracle told him to father a child on Pelopia: the fruit of incest would avenge the murder. Thyestes hid beside Athene's temple, and when Pelopia came out to wash her dress (which she'd stained in the blood of a sacrifice) he jumped out, masking his face in his cloak, raped her and fled. Pelopia had no clue about her attacker except for his sword, which fell from his belt in the struggle.

Pelopia's baby was born, and she gave him to goatherds to bring up. But the child's uncle Atreus discovered him and took him to Mycenae to grow to manhood with the royal princes **Agamemnon** and **Menelaus**. Not knowing who he really was, they called him **Aegisthus** ('strength of goats'). While the boys were growing up, Thyestes spent his life in exile, begging. But then the gods sent plague on Mycenae, and said that only the death of a 'son of Pelops' would end it. Agamemnon and Menelaus arrested Thyestes and took him to Mycenae, thinking that he was the man they meant.

To avoid the taint of killing a blood-relative, Atreus ordered Aegisthus, the son of unknown parents, to butcher Thyestes. Aegisthus raised his sword – and Thyestes recognized it as the one he had dropped years before in Sicyon. He embraced Aegisthus as his son, told him how Atreus had butchered his brothers and sisters, and begged him to take revenge. Aegisthus murdered Atreus, and Thyestes seized power and banished Agamemnon and Menelaus. They, however, went straight to King **Tyndareus** of Sparta, and Agamemnon raised an army, captured Mycenae and sent Thyestes once more into beggary, in which condition the old man died.

TIAMAT
Asia (West)

Tiamat, in Mesopotamian myth, was salt **water**, one half of the chaos which existed before **creation**. The other half was Apsu, fresh water. When Tiamat mingled with Apsu, gods were created, generation after generation. At first they all shared the universe in harmony. But then **Ea**, the young gods' waterlord, challenged the power of Apsu and killed him. Tiamat, his consort, formed herself into a dragon with an eagle's head, and led an army of **monsters** to take revenge. But Ea's son **Marduk** puffed her up with wind and shot her dead, then split her in two and used her carcass to build the universe.

≫→ **creation, sea**

TIAN
Asia (East)

Tian, in Chinese myth, was the **sky**. In some myths, dating from most ancient times, it was worshipped as a god, consort of **Di** (**Mother Earth**), but generally it was imagined as a dome (*pi*) with a hole in the centre through which **rain** and **lightning** fell to Earth.

The pi disc was a favourite good luck charm, and hundreds of thousands have been found from earliest times to the present: those carved from jade or other precious stones are commonest.

TIBER
Europe (South)

The river Tiber, in Roman myth, was originally called Albula ('white') after the brightness of its waters. But when King Tiberinus of Alba drowned in the floodwaters, and **Jupiter** made him a god and guardian spirit of the river, it was renamed Tiber after him. (It was also called Volturnus, 'rolling water', and this name was sometimes also applied to Tiberinus.)

This myth explains why the Tiber was always shown as a virile, reclining prince, with streams of water flowing from his hair and beard – a favourite sculptural theme in ancient Rome, and one which influenced river-god statues, and images of river-gods in fountains, ever afterwards.

≫→ **water**

TIDE JEWELS, THE
Asia (East)

The Tide Jewels, in Japanese myth, were carved by the jewel-workers of Ryujin, Emperor of the **sea**. The Low Tide Jewel sucked up the entire ocean, leaving the bottom exposed; the High Tide Jewel returned the waters to their former height. Ryujin gave the jewels to his young son, the beach-god Isora, and Isora played with them, sending tides surging up and down the shores of the world's oceans. When a Japanese fleet attacked Korea, Isora lent the jewels to the Empress Jingo, who used them first to drain the sea in front of the Korean navy, then to drown the ships as they floundered on the sea-bottom. In some accounts, Isora next presented the jewels to Jingo's son Ojin (later deified as the **war**-god **Hachiman**); in others he went back to his seashore games with them.

TIME: *see* Ages of Brahma, Estsanatlehi, Five Ages of Mortals, immortality, Janus, Ushas, Zurvan Akarana

TIRAWA
Americas (North)

Tirawa, or Tirawahat ('arch of Heaven' or 'this expanse'), in the myths of the Pawnee people of the US Great Plains, created the world in the shape of a bowl floating in space. He gave the stars the tasks of supporting the world and protecting it. Four of them churned the surface of the primordial ocean to make land, and Tirawa stocked it with plants and creatures. Then he ordered the **Moon** and **Sun** to mate and produce a son, and the Evening and Morning Stars to mate and produce a daughter: parents of the human race.

When the Earth was finished, Tirawa sent **Lightning** to inspect it. On his back Lightning carried a sack full of minor stars and constellations, and as he crossed the Earth he hung them one by one in the sky to light his path. Wolf (or, in some accounts, **Coyote**) snatched the sack and turned it out, not only scattering a Milky Way of stars in the sky but dropping crumbs and fragments of light on the Earth, where they took the form of storms, diseases and death. So Paradise was polluted, and Tirawa and the other gods disdained it, leaving it for mortals and never visiting it personally but sending only **messengers**. They taught humans **hunting**, **farming**, religious rituals and the arts of **civilization** – but what comfort were those to humans, if **immortality** was denied them? **»+** creation

TIRESIAS
Europe (South)

How Tiresias became a prophet. Tiresias (Teiresias, 'delighter in omens') of **Thebes**, son of Everus and Chariclo in Greek myth, was an ordinary man blessed – or cursed – with prophetic powers by a chain of bizarre events. One day when he was hunting he found two **snakes** coupling in a clearing. He hit them with a stick and killed the female. At once, **Gaia** (**Mother Earth**, protector of snakes) changed him into a woman, and he remained female for seven years. Then, by chance, in the same clearing, he found another pair of snakes. This time he killed the male, and immediately changed back into a man.

While Tiresias was a woman, he had several lovers; as a man, he made love with several women. This made him the ideal person to settle an argument between **Zeus** and **Hera** about whether sex gives more pleasure to the female or the male. (Zeus said that the male gives more pleasure than he gets; Hera said the opposite.) They asked Tiresias, and from personal experience he agreed with Zeus, saying that the male gives

nine times more pleasure than he gets. Hera was so angry that she blinded Tiresias; but Zeus rewarded him with the prophet's gifts of second hearing and second sight, and a life-span of seven mortal generations.

Tiresias, Aphrodite and Athene. Other accounts give completely different explanations. Some say that Tiresias' change of sex was caused by **Aphrodite**. She was arguing with the three **Graces** about which of them was most beautiful, and asked Tiresias to judge. He chose the Grace Kale, and Aphrodite punished him by changing him into an old woman. Even after he turned back into a man (thanks to Zeus' help after the argument with Hera), he still kept wrinkled, old-woman's breasts.

In still another account, the argument between Zeus and Hera never happened. Tiresias lost his sight because one day on Mount Helicon he saw **Athene** bathing in the spring called Hippocrene. The punishment for any mortal who saw a goddess naked was blindness, and could not be avoided. But Chariclo, Tiresias' mother, was one of Athene's servant-**nymphs**, and pleaded so eloquently for her son that Athene compensated Tiresias for his lost sight by giving him prophetic powers, and a cornel-wood stick which guided his steps as clearly as if he could see.

Tiresias' life and death. Tiresias spent most of his long life in Thebes, where his prophecies helped the townspeople steer a path between their own wishes and the edicts of the gods. (This sometimes brought him into conflict with those who thought that they understood oracles and omens better than he did: an example is **Oedipus**, whose blindness to the truth made him accuse Tiresias of taking bribes to bring about his downfall.) He had two special skills: he understood the language of birds, and he could talk without fear to the ghosts of the **Underworld**. In the last days of Thebes, after the Epigoni besieged the city (see **Seven Against Thebes**), he warned the people of the coming destruction and helped them escape from the city under cover of darkness.

After the fall of Thebes, Tiresias wandered, led by his daughter Manto, looking not for a home on Earth but for death. In the afternoon heat he felt thirsty, and drank a handful of water from a spring. The spring was Tilphussa, which drew its icy waters directly from the river **Styx** in the Underworld. The chill froze Tiresias' blood, and he died and passed to the Underworld. Even there, the gods still favoured him: he kept his knowledge of the future, and any person bold enough to consult his ghost was rewarded with accurate prophecies. (For example, he told **Odysseus** every detail of his coming adventures on the journey home from Troy to Ithaca.) Even after death, he still appeared and gave prophecies at two shrines on earth: on Mount Tilphussa beside the icy spring, and at Orchomenus near Thebes.

⋙→ prophecy

TIRKANTHARAS
India

Tirkantharas ('those who make the crossing', or 'teachers'), in Jain religious teaching, were beings who practised physical and mental austerities to the point where they freed themselves from all passions and distractions from true knowledge. Because they possessed all the knowledge in the universe, including the secrets of the gods, they were superior to or equal to gods, but they chose to take human form and teach the way which had made them Jaina ('conquerors'). Since this age of the world began, there have been twenty-four tirkantharas, the best-known of which are **Rishabha** (of unknowable date), the first, **Parshva** (eighth century BCE), the twenty-third, and **Mahavira** (sixth century BCE), the twenty-fourth.

TITANS
Europe (South)

The Titans ('lords'), in Greek myth, were the twelve original gods, offspring of **Ouranos** (Father Sky) and **Gaia (Mother Earth)**. The six females were Mnemosyne (Memory), Phoebe (Phoibe, 'brightness'), **Rhea** (Earth), Thia (Theia, 'divine'), **Themis** (Right) and Tethys (Settler). The six males were Coeus (Koios, 'intelligent'), Crius (Krios, 'ram'), **Cronus** (Kronos, 'crow'), **Hyperion** ('dweller-on-high'), Iapetus ('racer') and Oceanus ('swift'). Like their parents, the Titans were living beings but had no fixed shape. Sometimes they took on human form; sometimes they patterned themselves after water, rocks or fire; sometimes they abandoned shape altogether and spread their essence invisibly across the universe.

When Cronus' children the gods were born, they began a cosmic war with the Titans for control of the universe. **Prometheus**, son of Tethys, went to them with the secret of intelligence, a sure way to win the war, but they ignored him and he took it to the gods instead. In due course the gods won the war. In some accounts, the Titans were banished to the depths of space or the **Underworld**, or abandoned shape altogether and survived as entities with no location, brooding endlessly on their own folly and the power it had lost them. In others, they were pardoned, and given a beautiful home in the Far West of the universe, the Islands of the Blessed – on condition that they never troubled the gods, or the universe, again.

➤➤→ shape-changers

TIWAZ
Europe (North)

Tiwaz (also known as Tiw, from which we get 'Tuesday'), in Nordic myth, was an ancient sky-god: one-armed, stern but just, oath-guarder and battle-lord. In some accounts he was a pillar of wood, an enormous totem-pole or a tree which supported the universe. In prehistoric times, his functions were taken over by **Odin** and **Thor**, and he retired from myth except as a memory – and, here and there, as a spirit of darkness who lurked in dark woods and could be appeased only by human sacrifice.

➤➤→ justice and universal order

TJINIMIN AND PILIRIN
Australia

Tjinimin ('bat'), in the myths of the Murinbata people of the Northern Territory, was a **trickster** of the Dream Time. Like all other spirits, he teemed with creative energy – but instead of its being productive (as theirs was) it took the form of endless, insatiable lust. His particular obsessions were the Green Parrot Girls, consorts of the **Great Rainbow Snake**, and nothing deterred him from trying to rape them. They drove him off with bees, sent a river to wash him out to sea, and finally dropped him over a cliff on to jagged rocks. Summoning up all his magic, he regenerated himself (testing the spell by cutting off his own nose and recreating it) – but then turned his magic into a spear and used it to stab the Rainbow Snake itself. The Snake writhed in agony across the land, gouging rivers and waterholes, and finally gathered up all the fire in the world and dived with it to the bottom of the sea. Only one charred stick was left, and neither Tjinimin nor anyone else knew what to do to bring back **fire**, light and heat.

It was at this point that Pilirin ('kestrel') came to the rescue. He showed human beings how to use fire-sticks to call up the spark-spirits which slept in wood. So the world, and the human race, were saved. But Tjinimin ever afterwards stayed well away from the world of light, coming out only at night; he also foreswore **sex**, even roosting upside-down so that he could see only the barren sky above and not the world and its teeming life below. His magic waned, and as it did so his recreated nose fell off – which is why bats are still snub-nosed.

This story is one of the few to treat the spirits of the Dream Time with knockabout humour – and Tjinimin's wooing of the Green Parrot Girls is ribaldly embroidered at each new telling. As recorded here, it is more rounded and self-contained than most Australian myth-stories; some (white) scholars suggest that it may have this 'literary' form because it was one of the first tales to be retold by Westerners.

≫→ animal-gods, tricksters

TLÁLOC
Americas (Central)

Tláloc ('growth-maker'), the Aztec **rain-god**, was responsible for the **fertility** of **Mother Earth**. His tools, **lightning** and **thunder**, were the divine equivalents of a mortal ploughshare and axe, and he kept four brimming water-tubs in each of his mountain-top palaces: the nourishing morning rain, blighting mid-day showers, frost-bringing evening drizzle and – for when he really lost his temper – storms. His consorts were Chalcitlicue, goddess of fresh water, and Uixtocijuatl, goddess of salt water, and when he mated with them, morning and evening, their sexual juices replenished the water-bowls. Rain itself was delivered to the Earth by Tláloc's cloud-servants, the Tlaloques, and if they missed your farm or fields you could attract Tláloc's attention by burning rubber, whose pungent smell he savoured as other gods enjoyed the meat-scents of sacrifice.

Tláloc's garden, Tlálocan, was a hill-top paradise in the far South. It was filled with plants and birds, and its orchards and pastures were fed by the unceasing marriage of sun and rain. Tláloc welcomed there the spirits of mortals dead from disease (especially leprosy and smallpox), drowning and the fury of his own lightning-strikes.

*Despite Tláloc's apparent gentleness, he became the centre of a particularly blood-thirsty practice: in dry seasons, the priests killed and ate babies, whose tears – if they cried before dying – meant that rain was sure to follow. Some scholars suggest that there was no distinction in Aztec minds between the gods' two aspects, that human sacrifice and cruelty were necessary components of Aztec worship, without moral overtones. Others, more prosaically, suggest that two ancient gods, a savage thunderer (possibly one of the gods of the Toltecs whose culture the Aztecs overwhelmed) and a mild bringer of **fertility** (from a different native tradition), were run together and given Tláloc's name.*

TLAZOLTÉOTL
Americas (Central)

Tlazoltéotl ('dirty woman'), in Aztec myth, was the goddess of all kinds of uncleanness, and especially of lust (which the Aztecs thought created a moral miasma, a stench which only gods could smell). She was also known as Tlaelquarni ('cleanser'), because, as goddess of confession and absolution, she could eradicate filth as well as cause it.

*The cult of Tlazoltéotl roused the Christian Spaniards' disgust more than any other save that of **Tezcatlipoca**. They claimed that her temples were centres of prostitution, where young girls, torn from their families, were taught every kind of sexual perversion before being sent into the barracks of young army recruits and then, when they* were 'used up', sacrificed to their grim mistress. Once a year, at each of her temples, a chosen young man was flayed alive, and his skin was used to clothe the goddess' statue. For the rest of the year she was naked, and was – at least in the Spaniards' accounts – a witch-hag who rode a broomstick and carried a sacrificial knife, a severed snake's head and a pulsing human heart. All this fits oddly with her other attributes: she was the goddess of **beauty** (wearing a mask because her face was so beautiful that no human could see it and survive), the patron of fidelity in marriage and of demure femininity (symbolized by her holding a distaff and spindle), and the goddess of the Aztec equivalent of the sauna.

≫→ sex

TOBADZISTSINI: *see* Nayenezgani and Tobadzistsini

TOCHOPA AND HOKOMATA
Americas (Central)

Tochopa and Hokomata, in the myths of the Walapai people of Mexico, were twin sons of **Mother Earth**. When the human race was formed, Tochopa played with them as a child plays with dolls, teaching them the arts of **civilization**. Hokomata was jealous, and tried to destroy them. First he taught them to fight, and when they failed to exterminate each other he sent a **flood** to wash them from the Earth. Just in time, Tochopa saved his daughter Pukeheh by hiding her in a hollow tree (or some say, a dugout canoe). When the water receded, Tochopa sent two other gods, Sunshaft and Waterfall, to mate with her, and she became pregnant with a second human race. However, even

though we are the descendants of gods, we are still at the mercy of the heavenly **twins**' rivalry, forever torn between Tochopa's urgings towards good and Hokomata's attempts either to kill us or to make us destroy ourselves.

TO KABINANA AND TO KARVUVU
Oceania

To Kabinana and To Karvuvu, in the myths of the Tolai people of Vanuatu, were twin brothers created from sand at the beginning of time. To Kabinana, the Sun, was sensible; To Karvuvu, the Moon, was a fool. To Kabinana made a woman by breathing life into a coconut; To Karvuvu tried to do the same, but picked a bad nut so that the woman was dead. (This is why human beings die.) To Kabinana carved fish to feed his children, and when To Karvuvu tried to do the same, he made sharks. To Kabinana said that the brothers should take it in turns to 'look after' the first woman when she grew too old for child-bearing. When To Karvuvu's turn came, the only way he could think of 'looking after' her was killing her and eating her – the origin of cannibalism.

≫→ creation, twins

TO KARVUVU: *see* To Kabinana and To Karvuvu

TONATIUH
Americas (Central)

Tonatiuh, in Aztec myth, also known as Pilzintecuhtli ('majesty'), was the latest of four **Sun**-gods to light the sky down the ages. Supporting the universe exhausted his strength, and he died each evening. To bring him to life each morning, it was necessary to offer him human hearts still pumping blood. He owned a paradise, Tollan, where the souls of those victims whose blood he had drunk, of dead warriors, and of women dead in **childbirth**, feasted throughout eternity.

TONENILI
Americas (Northern)

Tonenili ('waterer'), in the myths of the Navajo people of the Southwestern US desert, was the god who brought **rain**. He was a jester, fond of dancing and capering – and the Navajo rain-dance, intended to catch his attention, used similar movements.

TORNGARSAK
Arctic

Torngarsak ('good one'), the supreme being in Eskimo myth, was a remarkable collection of cancelling opposites. He had no shape, or was a bear, a one-armed warrior or a finger-sized midget. He was all-**creation**, but created nothing. He was immortal, but could be killed by the **Thunder**-god. Later mythographers have had a fine time psychologizing him as (for example) 'What Is' or 'The Human Condition'; the Eskimo peoples, more pragmatically, simply paid him respect.
≫→ supreme deity

TOTOIMA
Oceania

Totoima, in the myths of the Orokaiva people of Papua New Guinea, was a monster who married a mortal woman. While they had intercourse he took human shape, but every time she bore children he changed into a wild boar and ate them. Eventually she bore **twins**, a boy and a girl, and hid them. Totoima rooted after them, found them and ate the boy. He was just about to kill the girl when his wife ran up with a shaman who brought the son to life in his father's belly. The boy grew to adulthood in an instant, burst his father's belly and was reborn. The shaman married the daughter, and Totoima's wife divided the boar's huge body among all the people for the marriage-feast.

This story was re-enacted annually, on the occasion of a huge pig-feast. The Orokaiva people believed that boars were universal power in animal shape, and that if you ate them, you shared in it.
≫→ animal-gods

TRICKSTERS

In many stories, both myths and folktales, tricksters were morally neutral: their quick-wittedness was simply an attribute like physical strength or artistic ability, and other people expected and accepted it without overmuch admiration or condemnation. The victims of **Odysseus**, arch-trickster of Greek myth, for example, complained about what he did to them, but everyone else treated him as hero, king and lord – at least until he turned his trickery on them. Many tricksters helped in the process of creating mortals – and if their cleverness got in the way and 'changed' things (for example when they nicked the groins of the mud-doll humans and so accidentally created sexual organs), this was no more blameworthy than if a clumsy god had dropped them or an artistic god given them extra hands to play lyres and flutes. Trickster-gods were often put in charge of asking humans whether they wanted to be mortal or immortal – and curiosity distracted them on the journey from **Heaven** to Earth, with the result that we are mortal. (Often, the trickster repaid us for this by teaching us **civilization**.) Even the most destructive trickster of all, **Loki** who constantly threatened universal balance in Nordic myth and who will one day bring about **Ragnarök**, universal cataclysm, was told about in a matter-of-fact manner, without overtones of regret or blame.

The coming of the great monotheistic religions, however, changed perception. In systems where truth was an absolute, the possession only of God and those who surrendered themselves to God, trickery and deception became undesirable qualities, and in some cases were even associated with God's enemies, the **demons** and devils of darkness. This led on the one hand to some highly suspect readings of ancient stories – Christian mythographers in medieval Scandinavia, for example, identified Loki with **Satan** – and on the other to a general downgrading of tricksters, to become the pixies and other supernatural pranksters of children's stories. **Anansi**, **Gluskap** and **Maui** are examples: originally spirits who helped to set the entire universe in order, they became the heroes of thousands of jokes and anecdotes, surviving not because of

their importance in myth but because they were almost entirely divorced from it.

➤➤+ (Africa): Dubiaku; (Americas): Annency, Coyote, Gluskap, Ictinike, Ogoun; (Australia): Tjinimin and Pilirin; (Finnish): Lemminkäinen; (Greece): Autolycus, Hermes, Odysseus, Sisyphus; (India): Hanuman; (Mesopotamia): Enki; (Oceania): Olifat

TRINAVARTA
India

Trinavarta, in Hindu myth, was a **demon** who tried to kill the baby **Krishna** by turning himself into a whirlwind and snatching him from his mother's arms. Just as he caught hold of the child, however, Krishna gave him a god-sized kick which sent him spiralling into a cliff and killed him.

TRIPITAKA
Asia (East)

Tripitaka, in Chinese Buddhism, was a real person: the monk Hsuan-Tsang who travelled from China to India and back in 629-640 CE, bringing back accurate copies of the holy scriptures. His journey was later used by the sixteenth-century writer Wu Cheng-en as the basis for a rip-roaring picaresque narrative, *Pilgrimage to the West,* part novel part folktale-collection, in which Tripitaka and his companions **Hanuman** (or 'Monkey') the **trickster**, Chu Pa Chieh ('Pig') the lecherous glutton and the priest Sha Ho-shang outwitted **demons** of all kinds, sometimes by magic or martial arts but more often by a combination of slyness and intellectual sleight-of-hand which was totally beyond the demons' slower wits.

Pilgrimage to the West remains one of the most popular books in Chinese literature, the source of a thousand films, TV series and comic strips. Many Chinese artists have produced sets of paintings either illustrating Wu's stories or inventing new adventures, and the saga grows by accretion, so that Tripitaka's (or, equally often, Monkey's) adventures are known to millions who have never heard either of the original book or of Hsuan-Tsang's Buddhist pilgrimage which inspired it.

TRISTAN AND ISOLDE: *see* Tristram and Yseult

TRISTRAM AND YSEULT
Europe (North)

Tristram ('sad soul'), in Celtic myth, was the son of Queen Elizabeth of Lyonesse, and was named because his mother died when she bore him. He was brought up by his uncle, King Mark of Cornwall, and defended the kingdom against a band of Irish raiders who came to demand tribute, led by the **giant** Morholt. Tristram killed Morholt, half-brother of the king of Ireland. Soon afterwards, Mark sent him to Ireland to fetch Yseult the Beautiful back to Cornwall to be Mark's queen. On the voyage home, on a particularly hot day, Tristram and Yseult quenched their thirst with the nearest drink they could find – a love-potion made by Yseult's sorceress-mother for her daughter to give to Mark. They fell passionately and hopelessly in love.

Back in Cornwall, Yseult and Mark were married. On the wedding night, Yseult's maid Brangen took her place in the marriage-bed – and Mark suspected nothing. But in the days that followed, when he saw Tristram and Yseult together, he did grow suspicious, and his courtiers, jealous of Tristram, told him that they were having an affair. He prepared to burn them alive, but they escaped and hid in the woods. Pursuing them, Mark found them asleep together, but with a drawn sword between them. This convinced him that their love was innocent, and he agreed to take Yseult back so long as Tristram left Cornwall forever.

Tristram went to France and married another Yseult, Yseult White-hands. But he pined for his real love, and never consummated the marriage. Yseult White-hands planned revenge. Her chance came when Tristram was wounded by a poisoned spear. On his deathbed he sent Brangen to fetch Yseult the Beautiful from Cornwall, so that he could see her for the last time. If Yseult agreed to come, Brangen was to return in a white-sailed ship; if she refused, Brangen was to hoist black sails. Brangen did as she was asked – but when she and Yseult the Beautiful returned, Yseult White-hands treacherously told Tristram that the sails were black. He died, and when Yseult the Beautiful found his body she, too, died of grief. Recognizing the strength of their love at last, Mark selflessly took their bodies back to Cornwall and buried them in the same grave. He planted two trees above the grave, and as time went on – the myth ends – the trunks leaned together and the branches intertwined.

The bones of this story are references in the Arthurian myth-cycle and the **Mabinogion** – both of which concentrate on Tristram's early giant-killing exploits. The tale of his and Yseult's doomed love was first told by the medieval German poet Gottfried of Strassburg, and his Tristan is the basis for Wagner's Tristan and Isolde, in which the passion and romantic coincidences of the plot are transfigured by the headiness of the music.

➤ Adonis, beauty, Brynhild

TROILUS
Europe (South)

Troilus (Troilos, 'Trojan from Ilium'), son of King **Priam** and Queen **Hecuba** in Greek myth, was an adolescent when the **Trojan War** began, and the gods decreed that if he reached the age of twenty safely, Troy would never fall. But **Achilles** came up against him in single combat, and, overcome with lust, offered to spare his life if Troilus made love with him. Some accounts say that Troilus indignantly refused, whereupon Achilles cut off his head; others that Achilles raped him, still in full armour, and crushed him to death even as he penetrated him.

In medieval Europe, this story was embroidered in ways which had no foundation whatever in ancient times. Troilus fell in love with Cressida (that is, with Chryseis the beautiful daughter of Chryses; she was called Cressida in these versions because the medieval Latin for 'Once Troilus loved Chryseis' is Olim Troilus Cressida amavit). Cressida's uncle Pandarus offered to arrange assignations between them. But Cressida's father Chryses (or in Shakespeare's version, confusingly, **Calchas**) meanwhile arranged an exchange: Cressida was to be taken to the Greek camp and married to **Diomedes**, and the captured Trojan prince Antenor was to be returned to Troy. Troilus raged out across the plain, trying to find Diomedes and kill him – and it was then that he met Achilles, with fatal results. (Shakespeare's Troilus and Cressida, whose subtext concerns the mind-numbing futility of war, breaks off before this dénouement, taking Achilles to fight **Hector** and leaving Troilus raging at the injustice of the world.)

TROJAN WAR
Europe (South)

Heroes. In Greek myth, at the end of the heroic age of the world, the human race was thriving, but for the first time in its existence it was also beginning to squabble and argue. A main cause – as the name 'heroic age' suggests – was the gods' own children, the **heroes**, whom they had fathered or mothered with human partners. The heroes swaggered and lorded it over lesser beings, strong, fearless, always in search of challenges (such as fighting the **Erymanthian Boar** or sailing as **Argonauts** to steal the **Golden Fleece**) – and happy, if no other excitement could be found, to invent causes and fight wars just for the sake of it. **Zeus** decided to cut down the heroes' numbers by setting up the fiercest war mortals had ever seen. It would be fought by princes from every state – and when it was all over and the most arrogant heroes were dead and gone, the world would return to its former peace.

Troy and Greece. Zeus chose as battle-ground the city of Troy, beside the Bosphorus on the westernmost edge of the continent of Asia. He sent a Trojan raiding-party to Sparta in Greece; their leader was Prince **Paris** of Troy, and they stole half the treasure in Sparta – and Queen **Helen**, Zeus' daughter, the most beautiful woman in the world. The Greeks assembled a war-fleet to win her back. Heroes gathered from every Greek state, each bringing ships and soldiers. They waited at Aulis until their leader **Agamemnon** won favourable winds from the gods by sacrificing his own daughter **Iphigenia**, then sailed for Troy.

The two sides were equally matched. The Trojan defenders were led by Prince **Hector**, eldest of **Priam**'s fifty sons, and their city was protected by walls built long ago by two gods, **Apollo** and **Poseidon** – walls which could not be breached by mortals except in one place, a narrow section built by the mortal king **Laomedon**. The Greeks, led by Agamemnon and his brother, Helen's husband **Menelaus**, included such heroes as **Achilles**, **Ajax**, **Diomedes** and **Odysseus**, the most cunning man in the world. (Another Greek hero, **Philoctetes**, owned the bow and unerring arrows which had once belonged to **Heracles** himself. But because he had offended the goddess **Artemis**, he was kept in exile on the island of Lemnos until the very last days of the war.) Gods themselves took sides. Some, including **Aphrodite** and **Poseidon**, favoured the Trojans throughout the war. Others, including **Apollo**, **Athene** and **Hera**, favoured the Greeks. Others again, notably **Ares** the war god himself, changed sides many times as the war went on. Only Zeus remained impartial.

Achilles and Hector. The fighting lasted for ten years. Every skirmish ended in a small victory for one side or the other, but there was no overall advantage, and no sign that the fighting would ever end. At last Zeus brought matters to a head by organizing a quarrel between the Greek heroes Achilles and Agamemnon. Achilles had given a beautiful girl, Chryseis, to Agamemnon, a prisoner-of-war. But she was the daughter of a priest, and Zeus sent plague into the Greek camp and refused to lift it until Agamemnon sent Chryseis back to her father. Agamemnon immediately found himself another mistress, Achilles' own concubine Briseis – and Achilles retreated to his camp and sulked, refusing to have anything more to do with the battle. At once, with Achilles out of the fighting, the Trojans began to win the war – and Achilles' friend and squire **Patroclus** put on Achilles' armour, went out to lead the Greeks against the Trojans, and was killed by Hector. Achilles, enraged, surged back into the fighting, killed Hector and dragged his body three times round the walls of Troy.

End of the war. At this point the gods moved decisively for Greece and against Troy. They told the Greeks to fetch Philoctetes from Lemnos: his bow and arrows were essential if the city was to be captured. They told them to steal the **Palladium**: the statue of Athene which was worshipped in a shrine at the heart of Troy and symbolized the city's luck. And Athene suggested to Odysseus the trick of the **Wooden Horse**. Philoctetes fought and killed Paris; Odysseus and Diomedes stole the Palladium; the Wooden Horse was built, manned with soldiers and left on the beach while the rest of the Greeks pretended to sail away. Thinking that the war was over, the Trojans dragged the Horse into the city and set it up in Athene's temple – and that night the soldiers hidden inside let themselves down on ropes, opened the gates and sent a signal to their companions to sail back to Troy and capture the city.

The aftermath. After the sack of Troy, the victorious Greeks divided up the spoils and the prisoners and set out for home. They had been ten years away, and many had made enemies of particular gods, who now took delight in delaying their return still longer. Many came back to find that their wives had taken lovers, or that enemies had seized their thrones. The **Underworld** was thronged with the ghosts of heroes killed in the fighting, squabbling or brooding as if the war had never ended. As for the Trojans, their city was destroyed, their wealth was stolen and their people were dead or slaves. A small band of refugees, led by **Aeneas**, took the statues of the city's gods and sailed South to find a new homeland, a new Troy, first in Africa and then in Italy.

TROPHONIUS
Europe (South)

Trophonius and Agamedes. Trophonius (Trophoneios, 'nurturer'), son of the **Argonaut** Erginus in Greek myth, was one of the stonemasons who built **Apollo**'s first temple at Delphi. His collaborator was his brother Agamedes ('much praise'). There are two accounts of how they died. In one, instead of paying them the wages they asked for, Apollo invited them to a week of wining and dining in **Olympus**, at the end of which they were found dead in bed. This, however, was not a trick: it was not until after death that they could receive his reward, the gift of **prophecy**. In another, King Hyrieus of Boeotia commissioned them to build a treasury, and they made it totally secure apart from one removable stone in the wall. Every night thereafter they crept in and stole as much gold as they could carry. One night Agamedes took too much and stuck fast. To keep their secret Trophonius cut off his head, and was immediately punished when **Gaia** (**Mother Earth**) gaped open at his feet and swallowed him.

Trophonius' oracle. Soon after Trophonius disappeared from the world, the people of Boeotia asked the Delphic oracle how they could end a drought that was threatening their lives. Apollo told them to follow the road from Delphi to **Thebes** until they found a forest cave overhung with bees. There, Trophonius' spirit would tell them what to do. They found the cave and the oracle told them how to channel an underwater stream to irrigate their parched land. Ever afterwards, Trophonius was honoured as a god, Apollo's adopted son, and his oracle was renowned for its reliability.

As the oracle of Trophonius lay on the road between Thebes and Delphi, it built up a thriving trade as a kind of antechamber to the Delphic oracle, offering to tell pilgrims whether their questions to Apollo would be answered or not. The priests made the consultation process as elaborate and impressive as they could. At most oracles, all you had to do was ask your question and wait for the answer. But if you wanted Trophonius' advice you had to spend several days at the shrine, fasting and sacrificing. Then, on the day of the consultation, you bathed, rubbed yourself with oil, put on sackcloth and drank from two ice-cold fountains, the Spring of Memory and the Spring of Forgetfulness (said to be tributaries of the river **Lethe** in the **Underworld**). Then two boys took you to the cave of the oracle, an eight-metre-deep hole in the forest floor. In the centre of the floor was another hole, just wide enough to admit one person at a time. You wriggled into this and lay waiting in the pitch-black cavern beyond until the oracle spoke to you, then squeezed back through the hole and up to the surface, where priests were waiting on the Throne of Memory to explain what the oracle's words meant. People who went through this ordeal believed that they'd visited the Underworld and spoken with Trophonius' ghost. Despite all this apparent charlatanry, the oracle was famous for its accuracy, and for centuries people visited it from all over Greece.

TSAI SHEN
Asia (East)

Tsai Shen, god of wealth in Chinese myth, began as a mortal hermit and magician called Jao Gong Ming. He tamed a black tiger, and rode it into battle, hurling diamonds and pearls like bombs to scatter the enemy. The enemy general made a statue of Jao Gong Ming and shot it in the eyes and heart – and at that moment Jao died and was taken into **Heaven**. Because of his easy way with precious stones, he was made Heavenly Treasurer-in-Chief and god of wealth. He was shown in art as a fat-bellied, cheerful man, sometimes riding his tiger, and was particularly worshipped by merchants.

TSAO JUN
Asia (East)

Tsao Jun ('kitchen god'), in Chinese myth, began as a mortal called Jang who divorced his wife and married his mistress. The gods stole his sight and his money, and his mistress left him. He wandered the streets as a blind beggar, and one day came by chance to the house of his first wife, who gave him a plate of his favourite dish, noodles. As soon as he tasted them he realized where he was, and was so ashamed that he jumped into the stove and was burnt to ash – all except for one leg, by which his ex-wife tried to pull him out. (Stove-rakes have been called 'Jang's legs' ever since.)

At this point the gods took pity on Jang, carrying him into **Heaven**, giving him **immortality** and appointing him god of the kitchen. Because of his past life, they made him overseer of the morals of each household, and once a year he had to report to the celestial court on the behaviour of each family member. To sweeten his accounts, people made him offerings of honey or honey-cakes – and if they were unsure that this would work, another way was to leave gifts of drink, enough to make him tipsy.

TSOHANOAI
Americas (North)

Tsohanoai ('Sun-bearer') the Sun-god, in the myths of the Navajo people of the

Southwestern US desert, was no grand ruler but a humble porter. Every day he struggled across the sky, with the **Sun** in a bundle on his back; every night when he went home, he hung it thankfully on a peg and went to bed. In some accounts, he mated with **Estsanatlehi** and their children were **Nayanezgani** and **Tobadzistsini**.

TSUKUYOMI
Asia (East)

Tsukuyomi ('moon-counter') or Tsukiyomi ('moon-bow'), in Japanese myth, was created from the **water**-drops which fell from **Izanagi**'s right eye when he washed himself after visiting **Yomi**, the **Underworld**. Izanagi made Tsukuyomi god of the **Moon**, consort of **Amaterasu** the **Sun**-god. For a time they lived peaceably together, but when Tsukuyomi killed **Ukemochi** the rice-goddess, Amaterasu refused to have anything more to do with him – which is why night and day are forever separate.

*Tsukuyomi's connection with rice is explained by a pun in Japanese: the symbols for 'Moon' and 'rice-pounding' are similar. The association, coupled with the identification of hares and rabbits with the Moon, common in many cultures from China to North America, leads to his symbolic image in Japanese ritual painting: a hare pounding rice – a reference which no surviving myth explains. The Moon's regular waxing and waning led to Tsukuyomi being regarded as a god of **prophecy**, and his priests foretold the future by examining and measuring the Moon's reflection in huge mirrors. (Looking at it directly was dangerous, for although Tsukuyomi never blinded those who stared him in the face, as Amaterasu the Sun did, he filled their minds with delusion and sent them mad.)*

TUONELA
Europe (North)

Tuonela ('Tuoni's realm'), in Finnish myth, was the **Underworld**. It was an exact mirror-image of the Upper World. Its inhabitants were dead, not living – instead of moving from birth to death their lives progressed from adulthood to infancy and thence to non-existence. Instead of light they had darkness, instead of hope despair, instead of conversation silence, instead of presence absence.

Only **demons** and diseases, children of **Tuoni** and **Tuonetar**, were ever allowed out of Tuonela. And only the Dead were allowed to enter it. Living mortals who tried to reach it had to travel for a week through thorn-thickets, a week through empty woods and a week through forests, swim an icy river of darkness on whose surface a black swan sang binding-spells of **death**, and finally face **Surma**, the flesh-tearing monster that guarded **Kalma**, goddess of decay. Any visitors who survived were then welcomed by Tuonetar, who offered them beer of oblivion to make them forget their former lives – and while they drank, her children threw iron nets across the river to stop them ever returning to the world of life.

TUONETAR
Europe (North)

Tuonetar ('Tuoni's wife'), in Finnish myth, was the consort of **Tuoni**. She

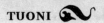
was queen of the **Underworld**, matriarch of an enormous family of **demons**, plagues and diseases.

TUONI
Europe (North)

Tuoni, in Finnish myth, was darkness personified, not a visible being but the quintessence of nothing. He ruled **Tuonela**, the **Underworld**, and fathered an enormous population of **monsters**, plagues and diseases.

TUPAN
Americas (South)

Tupan ('his holiness'), in the myths of the Guarañi people of Argentina, was the son of the sky-goddess. When a flood swamped the universe, he escaped by climbing a tree. Every day thereafter, he set out in his canoe to visit his mother, and what mortals took to be **thunder** was in fact the splashing of his paddles in the ocean of space.

TURNUS
Europe (South)

Turnus, in Roman myth, was the son of King Daunus and the **nymph** Venilia. He was a favourite of the goddess **Juno**, who granted him invulnerability in battle so long as he was pure, honourable and steadfast. In the war between Turnus' people, the Rutulians, and the Trojan settlers led by **Aeneas**, Turnus showed all these qualities, leading his troops with as much dignity and honour as Aeneas himself. But he let his guard slip for an instant, killing the young prince **Pallas** who had rashly challenged him to single combat, and wearing his belt as a trophy. At once Juno withdrew her protection, and when Aeneas and Turnus faced each other in hand-to-hand combat, and Aeneas saw the belt, Turnus' death was certain.
≫→ **heroes**

TVASHTRI
India

Tvashtri (originally Tvashtar, 'shaper'), in the Vedic myths of the Aryans who invaded India in the seventeenth century BCE, was the craftsman-god. In the earliest myths of all he was thought to contain the seeds or embryos of everything in **creation**, and to grant them existence as he chose: he was thus the universal creator, the single principle from which all arose. This idea survived only partially in later times: Tvashtri was regarded as the god of human **fertility**. He gave human beings embryos, and supervised the birth of healthy children. Only creatures with testicles were allowed to approach him: male priests, male offerings (which were not sacrificed, but set free when the ritual was done), no plants or flowers.

Tvashtri as craftsman-god. In his diminished role in later myth, Tvashtri was a kind of supernatural handyman. For the gods' supply of *soma*, he made a cup which replenished the drink even as they drank it. He made weapons and chariots for the war-gods, most notably **Vishnu**'s discus, **Indra**'s thunderbolts and **Shiva**'s trident. (The trident and thunderbolts were made from shavings from the Sun-god **Surya**, whom

Tvashtri turned on his lathe to reduce his dazzle.) He built palaces for Indra and for **Varuna**: Varuna's underwater, a dazzling white building studded with jewels and golden flowers, Indra's on Mount **Meru**, a cloud-palace where the spirits of **heroes** dead in battle were welcomed, and which had the power to vanish and resite itself at will.

In some later accounts, Tvashtri was identified with **Vishvakarman**, architect of the gods.

Tvashtri figures in poetry less as a being than a principle: the matrix, all-power, the generator. He is rarely shown in art: in painting sometimes as a swirl, a kind of soup of all matter, and in carvings as a disembodied hand.
≫+ crafts

TWINS

Twins offered an excellent way to embody the pairs of balancing opposites of which the myth-universe and its beings were made: good and bad, **light and dark**, male and female and so on. In several stories, after the Earth was first created, twins were sent to stock it, and rivalry between them was why both bad and good later existed in the world, and why it was sometimes hard to tell them apart. Twins often featured in the myth-cycles of important cities and states, as founders – and after their work was done many were promoted to the sky, either as full gods or as pairs of stars.

≫+ **(Americas): Ariconte and Tamendonare, Enumclaw and Kapoonis, Gluskap, Hahgwehdiyu and Hahgwehdaetgah, Ioskeha, Kuat and Iae, Malsum, Nayanezgani and Tobadzistsini, Quetzalcóatl, Tezcatlipoca; (Australia): Kurukadi and Mumba; (Egypt): Geb, Nut, Set; (Greece): Amphion and Zethus, Clytemnestra, Dioscuri, Helen; (Iranian): Ahriman, Ahura Mazda; (Rome): Romulus and Remus; (Oceania): To Kabinana and To Karvuvu**

TYCHE: *see* Fortuna

TYNDAREUS
Europe (South)

Tyndareus ('pounder'), King of Sparta in Greek myth, was noted more for his devotion to the women of his family than for his common sense. His wife **Leda** was seduced by **Zeus** in the form of a swan, and Tyndareus showed no irritation when she gave birth to bird's eggs instead of children. He forgave her adultery and brought up the four offspring (the **Dioscuri** Castor and Pollux; **Clytemnestra** and **Helen**) as if they were his own. (In some accounts two of them actually were his own: each pair of **twins** included one immortal child, descended from Zeus, and one mortal, descended from Tyndareus. His son was Pollux and his daughter was Clytemnestra.)

When suitors from all over Greece came asking for the hand of Tyndareus' daughter Helen, he refused to choose one of them – a father's prerogative and duty – and instead did something as unheard-of as it was indulgent: let her select her own husband. (She chose **Menelaus**, the handsomest man there.) Soon after the wedding, Tyndareus, whose other daughter had married

Agamemnon and gone to Mycenae (and whose wife and sons had been taken to **Heaven** by the gods long ago), let Helen wheedle him into handing his throne over to Menelaus and living a lonely, pensioned-off existence in a corner of the royal estates.

TYPHON
Europe (South)

Typhon ('smoke' or 'hurricane', also known as Typhoeus), in Greek myth, was a **monster**, the offspring of **Gaia** (**Mother Earth**) and Tartarus (the fathomless gulf below the **Underworld**). When he stretched himself out fully he covered the whole of Greece like a cloak of darkness. His body was formless smoke, out of which sprouted a hundred dragons' heads; his countless arms and legs were snakes; his eyes flashed flame and his mouths spat molten rock.

Gaia bore Typhon to punish the gods for defeating the **Earthborn Giants** in the battle for power in the Universe. As soon as Typhon was created, he surged up and began battering the ramparts of **Olympus**. The gods, terrified, fled to Egypt, where they disguised themselves as animals and cowered: **Apollo** pretended to be a crow, **Aphrodite** a fish, **Artemis** a cat, **Dionysus** a goat, **Hermes** an ibis, and **Zeus** a ram. Only **Athene** stayed in Olympus, and she jeered at Zeus until she shamed him into flying back to fight. He sent Typhon reeling with a thunderbolt, and ran to finish him off with the diamond-sickle **Cronus** had used to mutilate **Ouranos**. But Typhon, even weakened by a thunderbolt, was more than a match for

Zeus. He entwined him in his serpent-hands and flew to a cave on Mount Casius in Syria. There he took the sickle and hacked out the sinews of Zeus' hands and feet. Zeus' immortal flesh soon healed, but without the sinews he lay helpless, unable to move. Typhon gave the sinews to a she-monster, Delphyne, to guard, and flew off to deal with the other gods.

In the meantime, however, Athene had persuaded Hermes and **Pan** to leave Egypt and come and fight. They crept to Delphyne's cave. Pan sent his terrible cry echoing across the countryside, and while Delphyne shrank back in panic, Hermes replaced the sinews in Zeus' arms and legs. Zeus snatched up his thunderbolts and raged after Typhon. Typhon had gone to Mount Nysa in Greece (where Dionysus had once invented wine) and demanded food and drink. The three **Fates** were waiting there; they enticed him and flattered him, but instead of giving him immortal food they fuddled him with wine and gave him a fruit called 'for a day' – mortal nourishment which would weaken him and sap his strength. Satisfied, he flew out across Mount Haemus in Thrace, and the battle with Zeus began.

Even weakened by mortal food, Typhon still had the strength of a thousand gods. His weapons were **mountains**, ripped up and hurled at Zeus. There was no defeating him by force: the only weapon was cleverness. So, instead of aiming his thunderbolts at Typhon, Zeus hurled them at the rocks he threw. The blast turned the rocks in mid-air, sending them crashing back on Typhon. Jagged splinters tore the monster's flesh; his blood dyed the mountain red (and gave it its name: 'Mount Blood'); roaring in agony, he picked up his ragged body and fluttered to Sicily. Now Zeus used strength. He picked up Mount Etna and flung it at Typhon. In some versions of the myth, the weight of the mountain pushed Typhon through the Earth's crust, through the Underworld, down to the dark chasms of his father Tartarus where he lay, Zeus' prisoner forever. In others, the fight was beaten out of him, and he either went to live peaceably in Olympus (where he fathered a number of destructive winds, called typhoons after him), or lay for all eternity under Mount Etna, where his gasps of pain provided **fire** for the furnaces of Zeus' blacksmith-**Cyclopes**.

TYR
Europe (North)

Tyr ('dayshine' or 'god'), in Nordic myths, was in some accounts the original **sky**-god, precursor of **Odin**; in others he was the son of Odin and **Frigg**, or Frigg and the **giant Hymir**; in others again he was the same person as **Tiwaz**. He presided over the gods' councils of war, and was their commander in battle.

Tyr was fearless. When **Loki**'s wolf-offspring Fenrir was brought to **Asgard**, he looked after it, feeding it haunches of meat and exercising it as if it were a tame puppy. Fenrir kept growing, and soon terrified all Asgard. The gods decided that it must be bound before it destroyed the universe. They begged from the dwarfs a magic rope (made from cat's stealth, woman's beard, mountain-root, bear-sinews, fish's breath and bird-spittle), and challenged Fenrir to break it. Fenrir agreed to be bound, so long as he could hold one of the gods' arms in his jaws to guard against treachery. Tyr volunteered, and when the wolf found that the rope was as unbreakable as it was invisible, it bit off Tyr's arm. So Fenrir was bound for this cycle of the universe, safe until **Ragnarök** – and Tyr fought one-handed from that day on.

Venus (*Roman bronze statue, 2nd-century* BC)

UAICA
Americas (South)

Uaica, in the myths of the Juruña people of the Xingu river, was given healing powers by **Sinaa** the creator, and used them to help his people. He brewed potions, made poultices from herbs and insects, set bones and sang spells to keep mortality at bay. But his powers depended on sexual abstinence, and they waned, first when his people gave him a wife and then when the wife took a lover. Finally the lover tried to kill Uaica, and Uaica disappeared into the ground forever, taking his healing powers with him. Before he went, he offered his people one last chance, if they followed him to the shadow-world; but they refused, and from that day on, human beings have been plagued by disease and **death**.

≫→ **disease and healing**

UGRASENA
India

Ugrasena, in Hindu myth, ruled the Yadava people of northern India. When his wife **Pavanarekha** was raped by the **demon Drumalika**, and gave birth to **Kansa**, Ugrasena brought the young demon up as his own son, only to be dethroned as soon as Kansa was old enough to rule. Later, **Krishna** led the Yadava people against Kansa, killed him and restored Ugrasena to his throne. But Ugrasena's remaining time on Earth was short: when Krishna was killed, he was so distraught that he threw himself on the god's funeral pyre and was carried with him into **Heaven**.

UGRASURA
India

Ugrasura, in Hindu myth, was a snake-demon who tried to kill the boy **Krishna** by swallowing him as a cobra swallows a frog. Krishna rescued himself by growing to full god-size inside the demon's gullet and bursting it apart.

UKEMOCHI
Asia (Southeast)

Ukemochi, in Japanese myth, was a **fertility** goddess, married to the blacksmith-spirit **Inari**. Tsukuyomi, god of the **Moon**, paid them a visit, and Ukemochi laid a feast before him: meat, fish and piles of rice. However, Tsukuyomi had glimpsed her preparing the dishes, apparently by vomiting up the food, and he was so disgusted that he killed her. Because what she'd made could not be unmade, he filled a sack with the rice, gave the animals and fish back their lives, stocked the Earth with animals and the sea with fish, and put Inari in charge of all of them.

There is enormous confusion over both Ukemochi and Inari. Sometimes they are treated as husband and wife, sometimes as the same person – so that Inari, the partner most usually shown in art, can be male or female – and sometimes as forms of a third deity, Ugonomitama goddess of agriculture. Ukemochi is also sometimes shown as a fox, bringer of good luck. Possibly she was a shape-changer, and what Tsukuyomi saw was not her vomiting but turning herself into the food she then offered him – but the cults of Ukemochi are among the most ancient in Japan, the myths which survive are fragmentary, and none takes this line.

UKKO
Europe (North)

Ukko ('old one'), in Finnish myth, was king of the gods, successor to the first sky-god **Jumala**. He was an elder of the universe, and his existence kept it in being and guaranteed its survival. He stayed aloof: the only signs of his presence mortals ever saw were rain-clouds. He was the supreme authority, to be invoked only when all other prayers had failed.

⟫→ **supreme deity**

ULGAN
Europe (North)

Ulgan, or Yryn-ai-tojon, the Siberian and Lapp **sky**-god, created the Earth by setting a vast saucer of land on the backs of three fish frisking on the surface of the primordial ocean. The leaping of the fish caused **earthquakes**, and pieces of the Earth-disc broke off and floated free, until Ulgan anchored them as continents and islands. He was startled when one of the smallest specks suddenly spoke, announcing that it had no intention of letting plants grow on it – and he took it at its word and instead of making it into land he turned it into **Erlik**, the first created being.

⟫→ **creation**

ULL
Europe (North)

Ull ('dazzler'), also known as Holler, Oller, Uller and Vulder, in Nordic myth, was the god of frost-glitter. **Thor**'s wife **Sif** bore him to a frost-giant, and he later married the giantess **Skadi**. (In some accounts he was promiscuous, and had **sex** with his own mother and with **Frigg**). A powerful archer, Ull was able to track down his prey and escape his enemies by skiing: he invented the skill, and refused to share it with any other god. He was a show-off, streaking the whole Northern sky with firework-displays of his own radiance – the lights mortals called the Aurora Borealis.

In some accounts, Ull was **Odin**'s rival (not least for the favours of Frigg), and they challenged each other for universal power. In the end **Forseti** persuaded them to accept a standoff: for six months of each year, Ull and Odin would share rule of **Midgard** and **Asgard**, and there would be winter; for the rest of the year Ull would live with **Hel** in **Niflheim**, leaving Odin to fill the upper worlds with summer.

≫→ archers

ULURU
Australia

Uluru, in the myths of the Pitjandjara people of the Gibson Desert in West Central Australia, is the area centred on what white Australians now call Ayers Rock. Originally the Rock was a sandhill beside a waterhole. In the Dream Time, a group of harmless snake-people, the Woma and Kunia, settled there, and lived peacefully until they were attacked by the venomous-snake Liru people. There was an enormous battle, the Woma and Kunia males were all killed and the females were raped and murdered. Their bodies made rocks and boulders, and their pubic hair made brush and shrubs. The sandhill heaved itself from the ground and solidified, becoming the Rock which is there today.

ULYSSES: *see* Odysseus

UMA
India

Uma, in Hindu myth, was a mysterious mother-goddess who had no form of her own, but slipped into the bodies of other goddesses whenever she wanted to enjoy a few hours' material existence. Her 'hosts' included **Ambika**, **Devi**, **Durga**, **Rudrani** and above all **Parvati**, in whose body she seduced **Shiva** from meditation. In some accounts she was the daughter of the Himalayan **mountains**, and saved human beings from starvation after a long drought by miraculously producing fruits and vegetables from her body after it was fertilized by the **rain**.

≫→ fertility

UMAI-HULHLYA-WIT
Americas (North)

Umai-hulhlya-wit ('big **snake**'), in the myths of the Diegueño people of Southern California, was a water-monster which existed before **creation**. Then two creator-spirits, Chacopá and Chacomát, made and peopled the universe, and Umai-hulhlya-wit went from his den in the gulf of space to see what it was like. He was so enormous that he threatened to swallow all creation. But guided by Chacopá and Chacomát, the people welcomed him and invited him to sleep in a sacred enclosure made of brushwood. He coiled himself small enough to get inside – it took three mortal days – and as soon as he was in, the people set the wood on fire. The heat turned Umai-hulhlya-wit's water-blood to steam, and he gradually swelled and exploded. The force of the blast sent pieces of his skin and flesh flying everywhere in creation – and they were languages, songs, religious rituals, laws, customs and stories of the gods.

UMASHIASHIKABIHIKOJI
Asia (Southeast)

Umashiashikabihikoji ('pleasant reed sprout prince elder'), in Japanese myth, was the fourth of the five primordial deities to come into existence at the beginning of **creation** (see **Kotoamatsukami**). When it appeared, the Earth floated in the primeval ocean like a medusa jellyfish, the changing colours, like oil on its iridescent surface, showing where future continents and islands would exist. As time passed, one part of the substance of Earth began to sprout and grow like a stalagmite of molten glass. As it hardened, it turned into a reed, Umashiashikabihikoji, and grew six branches. Each branch in turn produced a pair of gods, one male and one female: the invisible Kuninotokotati and Toyokumono (spirits of majesty and awe which remained eternally aloof from universal concerns), Upidini ('lord mud') and Supidini ('lady mud'), Tunogupi ('seed coordinator') and Ikugupi ('life coordinator'), Opotonodi ('great place elder') and Opotonobe ('lady great place elder'), Omodaru ('perfect face') and Ayakasikone ('awesome lady'), and last of all **Izanami and Izanagi**, who acted on the instructions of all the others to complete creation.

UNCEGILA
Americas (North)

Uncegila, or Unktehi, in the myths of the Sioux people of the US Great Plains, was a giant water-**snake**. In the days when **Mother Earth** was young, the plains of Nebraska and Dakota were marshy, crossed by rivers and covered with jungle. They would have been a paradise for the humans who lived there – if it hadn't been for Uncegila. She spent most of her time swimming through the oceans of the world, but once or twice each year she swam up into the Nebraska swamplands, polluting them with salt water and making the level rise so that it flooded and poisoned the land. Her eyes were fire, her scales were flint and her heart was crystal.

Two boys, **twins**, went to hunt Uncegila, armed both by magic and by information that there was only one vulnerable place in her flint hide: the seventh spot down from her head. As soon as she reared out of the swamp to attack them, one fired an arrow while the other said a magic word of guidance. The arrow struck Uncegila's seventh spot and killed her. With her dying spasms she wriggled out of the water and spread her huge body across the plain – and the Sun, grateful that his old enemy was dead at last, seared all the flesh from her, sucked up all the water from horizon to horizon and burned off the vegetation, so that nothing was left but Uncegila's enormous bones, bleaching in a desert.

Meanwhile, the twins had taken Uncegila's heart back to their village, where they placed it in an underground chamber. The place became holy and they became its guardians; the heart granted them powers of **prophecy** and healing. But one day they rashly allowed ordinary people to see the heart, and it screamed like a living thing, exploded and burned to ash.

This is one of many similar myths explaining the bleached rock-formations of the Nebraska and Dakota Badlands.

UNDERWATER PANTHERS
Americas (North)

Underwater Panthers, in the myths of many peoples of the Eastern US woodlands, were creatures of destruction. Some were the mirror-images of creatures from the Upper World, like reflections seen in water. Others were **snakes**, bison, toads – or panthers with snakes', bisons' or toads' horns. They lived in the Underwater World, and sought either to drag Upper World beings into it, or to drown the entire Upper World by sending **floods**, usually in conjunction with the **Great Thunderbird** and his storm-birds.
➤➤ animal-gods, monsters and dragons

UNDERWORLD, THE

The universe existed as a balance of equal and opposite forces, and one of the most important was that between 'our' world and the 'other' world. Our world was one of light and clarity, overseen by gods and spirits who shared it with us; the other world was dark and mysterious, and its creatures were hostile and predatory. In the human view of them – theirs of us is not imagined or recorded – they were jealous of our main possession, life, and endlessly surged from their darkness to prey on us and snatch it. In many traditions the Underworld – the name was common, even though many 'underworlds' were not 'under' our own at all, and others had no physical location whatever – was filled with dead humans, expiating their lives in the Upper World before being allowed to return there or to pass on to some other future existence. It was also a kind of dumping-ground for **giants**, **monsters** and **demons** who had opposed the gods and been punished for it, and who spent their time spawning creatures even more hideous and deadly (to humans) than themselves.

Baroque ideas of this kind were prevalent in most myths – and led to a shoal of stories in which Upper-World **heroes** visited the Underworld or Underworld creatures came to the Upper World, and spectacular battles took place. A few myths, however, explored the idea of another world in more philosophical, objective ways. Their Underworlds were mirror-images of ours: places of non-being, non-consciousness, non-emotion, non-striving. Some traditions also made them cold instead of warm, inert instead of energetic, blank instead of multiform. In one Chinese myth, the Underworld was the 'real' world, and our existence was merely a dream in its inhabitants' minds; in Egyptian and Indian myth the Underworld was a way-station through which souls pass on their way to a new existence; in one Mayan myth (surviving tantalizingly in fragments), the Underworld was a place of peace and rest, and lack was viewed not (as elsewhere) as something negative, but as positive, blessed and to be wished-for.

»→ (Arctic): Sedna; Yambe-Akka; **(Celtic):** Annwn; **(China):** Di Kang Wang, Ten Yama Kings, Yen Lo; **(Egypt):** Anubis, Osiris, Serapis, Thoth; **(Finnish):** Tuonela; **(Greece):** Acheron, Cerberus, Cocytus, Furies, Hades, Hermes, Lethe, Orpheus, Persephone, Phlegethon, Rhadamanthus, Styx; **(India):** Yama; **(Japan):** Yomi; **(Mesopotamia):** Inanna, Sheol; **(Nordic):** Hel

UNELANUKI
Americas (North)

Unelanuki ('appointer'), the **Sun**-goddess in the myths of the Cherokee people of the Southeastern US, seduced her brother the **Moon**. He had no idea who he was sleeping with, but when he went to wash later he discovered that his face was smeared with sun-ash, and realized what had happened. Ever since then he has avoided her, shrinking out of the way every time she approaches – and he has never entirely removed the ash, which is why his light is less than hers.

UNKULUNKULU
Africa

Unkulunkulu ('ancient of days'), in the myths of the Amazulu people of South Africa; and known to the Ndebele people of Zimbabwe as Nkulnkulu, was the first power in existence. He had no shape, but was the immanent power of **creation**. He made the first human beings by plucking two reeds from a swamp, and gave them the Earth to live on. He sent Chameleon to tell them that they would live forever, but unfortunately Lizard darted to them first and mischievously told them that they would certainly die. Unkulunkulu could not change the message, but gave mortals the gift of **sex**, so that they could achieve a kind of **immortality** through their offspring. He showered them with other gifts – control of fire, farming, hunting, medical skills, music – hoping that these would compensate for the loss of eternity. When they or their children died he sent them to the Land of the Dead, **Heaven**, from where they still look down on their descendants with shining eyes – the stars.

Since Unkulunkulu was all-present and all-controlling, he was also the god of war, expressing his rage in thunder and lightning. His many honorific titles included uGobungquonqo ('dethroner'), uGuqabadele ('all-conquering') uKqili ('all-wise'), uMabongakutukiziwezonke ('terror-roarer') and uZivelele ('all-that-is, in one').

URANUS: *see* Ouranos

URVASHI
India

Urvashi, in the Vedic myths of the Aryans who invaded India in the seventeenth century BCE, was an *apsara*, or heavenly dancing-girl, so beautiful that none could resist her. Once, she danced for **Varuna** and **Mitra** (or, some say, **Surya**), and they were so aroused that they had orgasms on the spot. Their sperm, collected in a jar, grew into a sage: in some accounts **Agastya**, in others **Vishvamitra**.

➤ beauty

USHAS
India

Ushas, in the Vedic myths of the Aryans who invaded India in the seventeenth century BCE, was the dawn-goddess, the daughter either of **Aditi** or of **Dyaus** (Father **Sky**) and **Privithi** (**Mother Earth**). Every day she opened the doors of **Heaven**, showing off her carmine clothes and bringing light and wealth to mortals. She bustled about the world, waking all good creatures to their daily activity, but leaving the wicked to sleep forever. There was just one dark aspect to her generosity: among her gifts to mortals was time, and with time came old age and **death**.

UTGARD
Europe (North)

Utgard ('out-castle'), in Nordic myth, was a stronghold of the **giants**, visited by **Thor** and **Loki**. It seemed to be a vast castle, deep in the giant kingdom of **Jotunheim**, a Kafkaesque edifice in which every room led into another, every wall towered higher the more your eyes reached the top of it, every horizon merged into the next as you approached. In fact both Utgard and its ruler Utgard-Loki were illusions, conjured out of air by the giants who were too terrified of Thor and Loki to face them in person.

UTHER PENDRAGON
Europe (North)

Uther Pendragon ('cruel dragon-chief'), in Celtic myth, was a Welsh (or in some versions, French) prince ambitious to rule all Britain. He asked **Merlin** for supernatural help, only to be told that he would fail and that his ambition would destroy his entire dynasty. Dismissing this prophecy, Uther demanded shape-shifting powers, and Merlin briefly granted them. Taking the form of his rival King Gorlois of Cornwall, Uther slept with Ygern, Gorlois' queen, making her pregnant with the child that was to become King **Arthur**.

At this point, Uther largely disappears from myth. In some accounts, he was killed in battle, or assassinated, and was buried in the centre of Stonehenge. In others, he stuck a sword in a boulder, and announced that the man who pulled it out would rule all Britain; Merlin took charge of the education of Arthur, the 'once and future king', and when Arthur was fifteen he pulled the sword from the stone and assumed his father's throne. Other, sketchier, accounts identify Uther with the willow-tree god Bel, saying that he came into the mortal world specifically to father Arthur, and left it soon after the child was born.

➤ shape-changers

UTNAPISHTIM
Asia (West)

Utnapishtim or Utanapishtim, in Babylonian myth, was one of **Gilgamesh**'s ancestors who survived the great **flood** sent by the gods to wipe out the human race. Warned by **Enki**, he filled a

635

cube-shaped boat with treasure and with plants and creatures of every kind, then as the waters rose set sail in it with his wife and family. After seven days he sent out a dove to look for dry land, and it came back exhausted. On the eighth day he sent a swallow, with the same result. On the ninth day he sent a raven, and when it failed to come back he beached his boat, released the animals and planted the plants. The gods, seeing his simple goodness, rewarded him and his wife by granting them **immortality** and making them ancestors of the reborn human race.

In Tablet Eleven of The Epic of Gilgamesh Utnapishtim tells this story when Gilgamesh asks him how to achieve immortality.
≫→ Atrahis, Deucalion and Pyrrha, Doquebuth, Manu, Noah, Nu'u

UTSET
Americas (North)

Utset, in the myths of the Cherokee Indians, peopled the world. When the Lower World was drowned in the primordial **flood**, she led people and animals to safety up a hollow reed, and gave them the Upper World to live on. She carried the stars in a sack, but gave it to Beetle for safe-keeping, and he opened it, spilling the stars across the sky. Utset ran to pick them up, but had rescued only a few (the planets) when she realized that her people, back on Earth, were starving because she'd never taught them how or what to eat. She left the rest of the stars where they were, hurried back to Earth and

planted pieces of her own heart to make crops for her people: the first corn.
≫→ farming

UTU
Asia (West)

Utu, in Sumerian myth, was the brother of **Inanna** and god of justice. He went with the **Sun** on his journey round the heavens, judging the living during the day and the Dead at night – and his decisions were sunshafts, hurled like spears: unerring, irrevocable and impossible to argue away.
≫→ justice and universal order

UZUME
Asia (East)

Uzume ('twirling'), in Japanese myth, was the goddess of happiness expressed in dance. When **Amaterasu** barricaded herself into a cave because she was disgusted with **Susano**, Uzume danced to entice her out. As she performed, she began whirling faster and faster, and her clothes fell off one by one – causing such whoops and howls from the male deities that Amaterasu, wondering how it was possible to have such a good time while she was still in hiding, stuck her head out of the cave and was caught and dragged back to the light. The deities rewarded Uzume by making her guardian of the spring of pure water which lies at the foot of the Floating Bridge between Earth and **Heaven** (in some accounts, the Milky Way, in others, a rainbow). Ever afterwards, she let favoured mortals drink its waters, which gave them a brief taste of **immortality**. Her priests on Earth brewed potions to imitate this water, and the herb-lore they learned led to Ùzume being worshipped as goddess of good health, and her temples becoming healing-shrines.

The myths give various accounts of who exactly Uzume was. In some, she was Amaterasu's daughter, sister of Wakahirume the Dawn-goddess whose death made Amaterasu retreat from the world in the first place. In others Uzume herself was Dawn, and in still others she was the sister and/or consort of **Ninigi**, and travelled with him to Earth when he went to rule and found the Imperial dynasty.

⇒ disease and healing

Valkyries gathering dead heroes (*German engraving, 19th century*)

VAHAGN
Europe (Southeast)

Vahagn, the warrior-god in Armenian myth, was born accidentally at the beginning of **creation**. Sky and Earth were copulating, trying vainly to find ways of engendering life, and their writhings caused a reed which had been floating on the surface of the primordial ocean to fly up into the gulf of space. The reed was red, and as it whirled through space its redness concentrated at one end like a comet-tail, and formed itself into a fire-being: Vahagn. Vahagn went on to fill Sky with stars – in some accounts, the Milky Way was wisps of straw dropped from the bale he gathered to feed his chariot-horses – and to cover Earth with plants, animals and human beings.

*Vahagn is a somewhat shadowy figure in myth, but he is identified in Iranian folk-stories with the **giant**-killer and **demon**-smiter Rustem, and in Zoroastrian belief was merged with no less a deity than **Ahura Mazda** himself. His wives were Astlik, star-maker, and the **fertility**-goddess Anahit.*
⇛ creation

VAIMATSE
Americas (South)

Vaimatse ('beast-lord'), in the myths of the Tukaño people of the upper Amazon, was the spirit of forest **fertility**. He was present at every act of **sex** between humans, animals or plants, and usually took part, guaranteeing offspring. If mating took place while he was somewhere else, he blighted it, making the union infertile or giving the female involved an uncomfortable and sometimes fatal pregnancy.

VÄINÄMÖINEN
Europe (North)

Väinämöinen's birth. Väinämöinen, in Finnish myth, was the son of the fertilizing sea and the **creation**-goddess **Luonnotar**. He spent 700 years reaching maturity in Luonnotar's womb, and a further 30 years as a grown man sitting there, becoming ever more bored and shouting vainly to the **Sun** and stars to help him out. But the Sun and stars could not hear him, and Luonnotar, utterly innocent in the ways of **sex** and **childbirth**, had no idea even that she was pregnant. Finally, in desperation, Väinämöinen began hauling himself hand over hand out of her womb and up the tunnel of her vagina. He hammered on the vast membrane of her virginity, tore a hole with his left big toe, and clambered out as a man emerges from a pothole.

Väinämöinen and Joukahainen. Väinämöinen swam ashore in the country that was to become Finland. He began felling trees and clearing land for farming. Lacking tools and draught-animals, he used magic spells and songs – and these attracted the attention of the frost-**giant Joukahainen**, who sledged over the ice from the far North to challenge the intruder. Joukahainen's magic made the Earth shake, the sky cower and the mountains shudder. But he was no match for Väinämöinen, who changed his sledge into a lake, his horse to a boulder, his bow to a rainbow, his arrows to hawks, and his clothes into cloud, then planted him up to his armpits in a swamp. Joukahainen hastily offered a truce, and agreed to let Väinämöinen married his sister Aino if

Väinämöinen first set him free. Unfortunately for Väinämöinen, as soon as Aino saw him, she shrieked that he was too old and decrepit for a husband, threw herself into the sea and drowned.

Väinämöinen in Pohjola. Aino's rejection made Väinämöinen all the more eager to marry and sow children before it was too late. He set out for **Pohjola**, the Northland, to see if any of the frost-giantesses would have him, but Joukahainen ambushed him and threw him into the freezing sea. He swam for eight days, growing ever weaker, until an eagle scooped him up like a fish and took him to shore. Here Princess **Louhi** offered him her daughter in exchange for a *sampo*, a magic mill able to churn out endless supplies of salt from one side, flour from the second and gold from the third. When Väinämöinen said that no one had ever made a *sampo*, Louhi answered 'Only the one who does so will have my daughter.'

Louhi sent Väinämöinen home to Finland to make the *sampo*, telling him that he would have an untroubled journey if he neither stopped nor looked up on his journey. But Väinämöinen forgot these conditions. He heard singing, looked up and saw Louhi's daughter sitting on a rainbow spinning gold. He begged her to marry him without the *sampo*, and she agreed providing that he first split a hair with a blunt knife, knotted an egg, peeled a stone, broke a lump of ice without making splinters and carved a boat from her shuttle. Väinämöinen had no problems with the first four tasks, but when he was shaping the boat with a magic axe, three evil spirits (sent by Louhi) made him lose concentration, drive the axe into his own knee and sever the ligaments. None of his own magic was strong enough to heal this wound, and by the time he'd found a magician who knew the appropriate spell, the shaped part of the boat was lost and he had to start again.

Väinämöinen in Tuonela. This time, instead of using an axe Väinämöinen made the boat by magic. He remembered the chopping-spells and smoothing-spells for the wood, the weaving-spells for the sail and the bubbling-spell for the pitch to caulk the timbers – every piece of magic except the binding-spells needed to make the boat leap together and become complete. He searched the Upper World, listening to songs and rejecting them, and finally went to look for magic in **Tuonela**, the **Underworld**. He walked for a week through thickets, a week through woods and a week through forests, and persuaded the daughters of **Tuoni**, king of the Underworld, to ferry him across the River of Weeping to Manala, land of the Dead. Here Queen **Tuonetar** offered the beer of oblivion, and he refused it just in time. Her son dropped an iron net into the river to stop him swimming for safety – and Väinämöinen escaped only by turning himself into an eel and wriggling through the grid.

Väinämöinen and Antero Vipunen. A shepherd told Väinämöinen that the only being who knew the binding-spell was **Antero Vipunen**, a **giant** who slept underground with the earth as his blanket. He had been asleep so long that trees had grown from his face and body. Väinämöinen hacked them down, and woke Antero Vipunen by sticking his iron staff down his throat. The giant

yawned, swallowed Väinämöinen and went back to sleep. Inside his belly, Väinämöinen made his shirt into a forge, his coat into bellows, his knee into an anvil and his elbow into a hammer, and began hammering and banging until Antero Vipunen woke up, growling with heartburn, and spewed out of his mouth not only Väinämöinen but every spell and binding-song he knew.

Väinämöinen and Ilmarinen. Väinämöinen set to work to finish his ship, and in the meantime asked his brother, the **smith Ilmarinen**, to forge a *sampo* for Princess Louhi. Ilmarinen threw into his furnace swansdown, milk from a barren cow, sheep's wool and barley, blew up the flames and waited to see what would happen. On the first day a golden bowl was forged, on the second a copper ship, on the third a cow with golden horns, on the fourth a plough of gold, silver and bronze. Ilmarinen threw them all back into the flames, and on the fifth day the *sampo* appeared. He took it to Princess Louhi – and at once the promise came true, the promise Väinämöinen had forgotten: Louhi's daughter would marry whoever forged the *sampo*.

Väinämöinen and Louhi. Unfortunately for Ilmarinen, Louhi's daughter died soon after the marriage, torn to pieces by her own cattle for ill-treating the magic-working hero **Kullervo**. Ilmarinen asked Louhi for her other daughter's hand, and Louhi refused. Ilmarinen went back to Finland, made his peace with Väinämöinen, and asked him to go with him to Pohjola and steal the *sampo* – if there were no wives for the gods in Pohjola, at least prosperity could be found there for the people of

Finland. They took as companion the jester **Lemminkäinen**, and sailed to Pohjola in Väinämöinen's magic boat. On the way Väinämöinen caught a pike and made from its backbone a zither whose music had the power to charm rocks, stones, trees, rivers, and living beings into a magic sleep. With this he lulled Louhi and her people and stole the *sampo*. Just as they sailed away, however, Lemminkäinen started singing a triumph-song, and Louhi woke up and sent storm-winds and icebergs to sink the gods' ship and destroy them.

The storm washed Väinämöinen's zither to the bottom of the sea (where its melancholy music can still sometimes be heard). It smashed the *sampo*, but Väinämöinen was able to collect enough fragments to guarantee prosperity to the people of Finland forever. He also bequeathed to them his magic, breathing it into the lakes and forests, so that however often Louhi attacked the country from Pohjola with frost and ice, they were safe in the knowledge that spring would come again. Väinämöinen then sailed from the mortal world in a bronze boat, gliding up the sunshafts to settle in the no-man's-land between Earth and Heaven. There he still lives, the myth ends, ready whenever his people need him to sail on the shafts of the morning sun and help them.

*In the **Kalevala**, Elias Lönnrot stitched together the story of Väinämöinen from thousands of poems, songs, ballads, proverbs and other items of folk culture. The character is both unique and elusive, an amalgam of god, shaman and folk-hero. Some parts of the story suggest familiarity with non-Finnish traditions – the beer of oblivion, for example, is reminiscent of the water of **Lethe** in Greek myth, the magic zither recalls **Orpheus'** lute, the tests are like those given to **Gilgamesh**, the spell-bound boat has Amerindian and Polynesian parallels, and the end of the story is similar to accounts of **Arthur** and his knights sleeping 'under the mountain'. Whether these similarities are coincidence, the result of Lönnrot's own wide reading or a remarkable example of the widespread cross-fertilization of folk cultures in pre-literate times, scholars have never determined. The fact that Väinämöinen is so often a loser also makes him rare in myth and legend; some scholars have suggested that he and Ilmarinen were originally not separate individuals but two aspects of the same god.*
⇒ heroes, shape-changers, tricksters

VAJRASATTVA
Asia (Southwest)

Vajrasattva, in Tibetan Buddhist myth, was the primordial **Buddha** from whom all others came. He was fiery-tempered, and his anger sent thunderstorms and **earthquakes**. But he was also amorous, and his loving embraces of his wife both symbolized and guaranteed **justice and universal order**.

VALEDJÁD
Americas (South)

Valedjád, in the myths of the Tupari people of Brazil, was the first human being, born when a vagina-shaped rock on the surface of **Mother Earth** suddenly split apart. As soon as he was born he tried to kill his own mother and all her creatures by opening the flood-gates of the sea. Earth cried out to the **Sun**, who dried up the waters and sent a wizard called Arkoayó to make Valedjád harmless. Arkoayó waited until the **giant** was asleep, then blocked his eyes, ears and nose with beeswax and stuck his fingers together to stop him unblocking them. Then he bound him with holly (whose magic no stone-giant can break) and called the birds to carry him to the Mountains of the North and leave him there. Valedjád has lain there ever since, writhing and trying to free himself. His rage flickers in a red cloud above his head – the Aurora Borealis – and his roars and groans fill the sky with **thunder**.

VALHALLA
Europe (North)

Valhalla ('hall of the slain'), in Nordic and Germanic myth, was **Odin**'s feast-hall in **Asgard**. Its roof was of shields, supported on rafters made from spears. It had 450 doors, each of which was wide enough to admit a column of 800 marching men. Here the **Valkyries** took all mortal **heroes** killed in battle (and, some say, all wives or mistresses sacrificed on their menfolk's funeral pyres). Their wounds healed magically, and they spent their days exercising martial arts and their nights feasting. When **Ragnarök** comes, the myth ends, they will march out to battle on the side of the gods.

VALKYRIES
Europe (North)

The Valkyries ('gatherers of the slain'), in Nordic and Germanic myth, were warrior-women, servants of **Odin**. In some accounts there were three of them, all immortal; in others there were three times nine, and some were mortal. White-skinned and golden-haired, they rode above the battlefield in full armour, singing war-songs, and gathered the souls of dead **heroes** to take them to **Valhalla**. There, dressed in pure white robes, they looked after the heroes as they feasted: serving food and drink, singing and dancing, and – unless they were sworn virgins – providing **sex**.

VAMANA
India

Vamana ('dwarf'), in Hindu myth, was the fifth avatar of **Vishnu**. King **Bali**, great-grandson of **Hiranyakashipu**, shared his great-grandfather's ambition to rule the entire universe. Having conquered Earth and Middle Air, he began gathering his powers to attack **Heaven** itself. Vishnu made himself into a dwarf, crept into Bali's court and begged a tiny strip of territory to live on – as much as he could cover in three steps. In some accounts, when Bali agreed to this, Vishnu soared to god-height and in three steps traversed the entire universe, before treading on Bali's head and trampling him down to the **Underworld**. In others, Vishnu traversed the universe in two steps, and then gave up his right to a third step, allowing Bali to keep dominion over the world below.

This avatar of Vishnu is a favourite subject for statuettes, making the contrast between Bali, enthroned in royal splendour, and the misshapen, cringing figure of Vishnu-Vamana. The story is also popular as a subject for dance-drama, the scene where Vishnu dances his enemy down to the Underworld making an imposing effect.

VAMPIRES
Europe (Central; East)

Vampires (from an ancient Slavic word *vampir*, related to the Turkish *ubir*, 'undead'), in European myth, were corpses which refused to surrender their lives. Their origin may be in ancient Black Sea myths about ghosts, who could be persuaded to come from the **Underworld** by feasts of warm blood poured on the ground. Vampires, similarly, required fresh blood to keep them from the corruption of death, and found it by rising from their graves and sucking it from sleeping human victims. In sixteenth-century Central and Eastern Europe, vampires were held to be the spirits of suicides, and they could be killed only by being exposed to full daylight or stabbed through the heart with a sharpened crucifix – after both of which treatments they crumbled in seconds from living beings to heaps of dust. In the witch-hungry atmosphere of the times, they were also thought to be as sexually voracious as any other emissary of **Satan**, and to rape their virgin victims even as they drank their blood. Suspected victims were executed just as often as suspected vampires.

The vampire myth lay dormant in the European imagination until the end of the nineteenth century, when it was given huge new impetus by Bram Stoker's novel Dracula, based in part on the story of the fourteenth-century Transylvanian warlord Vlad 'the Impaler'. Stoker added the idea that vampires were half bat, half human, and his creation has more or less taken over the entire vampire industry, a staple of horror comics, novels and films ever since. In particular, his depiction of the typical vampire as a devilishly handsome, witty and tormented aristocrat completely ousted the former view of vampires: that they were walking corpses, smelling of putrefaction and incapable of any human emotion or thought save the needs to copulate and to survive by drinking blood – Western equivalents of Zombies, the Undead in Voodoo myth.

⋙→ demons, Flying Head, Namorodo

VANIR
Europe (North)

The Vanir ('beautiful ones'), in Nordic myth, were a family of **fertility**-gods led by **Njörd** (the Old Man of the **Sea**) and his twin children **Frey** and **Freyja**. They guarded the fruitfulness of Sea and Earth, and the mating of every living creature in existence. They were gentle and creative, and distrusted the other family of gods who shared the universe, the **Aesir**.

One of the Vanir – some say it was Gullveig, others Freyja herself disguised as Gullveig – visited **Asgard**, the citadel of the Aesir. She never stopped talking of gold, the warmth and glow of gold, and the Aesir, irritated, burned her three times in fire, only to see her reborn each time. When the Vanir heard of it, they declared war on the Aesir, who eagerly snatched the chance of eliminating their rivals for supreme authority in the universe. The war raged for centuries of mortal time. The Aesir laid waste Vanaheim, home of the Vanir; the Vanir reduced Asgard, home of the Aesir, to a heap of rubble. In the end, since neither side was winning, the Aesir and Vanir made an uneasy truce, and agreed to exchange hostages to ensure its survival. Njörd and Frey went to live for part of each year among the Aesir, and **Honir** and **Mimir** went from Asgard to live with the Vanir.

Although this settlement brought peace, it failed to reconcile the gods. Ever afterwards, the Aesir and Vanir regarded each other with suspicion. The Vanir thought that in some way the Aesir had tricked them, that Honir and Mimir were living with them not as friends but as spies. They hacked off Mimir's head and sent it back to Asgard. This move was disastrous for the Vanir. Mimir's head carried all the wisdom of the gods, and Odin rubbed it with herbs of **immortality** and kept it to speak and advise the Aesir. So the Aesir had all-knowledge, and they also had all-power (in the shape of **Thor** and his thunderbolts) and, in Njörd, Frey and Freyja, the regenerative power once controlled by the Vanir. As for the Vanir, they rebuilt Vanaheim and lived on, but without power or authority, an ever-fading memory of what they once had been.

*Later scholars explained this myth as an allegory of the conflict in the universe, and in human nature, between the opposing forces of generation and destruction. In such a view, the Vanir came to symbolize a kind of lost Golden Age, and the Aesir stood for the hard-faced cruelty of present existence. Some writers said that so long as the Vanir continued to exist, even as shadows of their former selves, there was still hope of a return to Golden Age peace and prosperity, before the final battle of **Ragnarök** when all **creation** would be destroyed. Others used the current stalemate between the two families of gods as a springboard for preaching the new religion which swept Northern Europe in the tenth-fourteenth centuries CE: redemptive Christianity.*

VARAHA
India

Varaha in Vedic myth. Varaha ('boar'), in the Vedic **creation**-myths of the Aryan people who invaded India in the seventeenth century BCE, was a form taken by **Brahma** to bring the world from the depths of the primordial ocean to the surface. When no land, no sky, no middle air existed, Brahma noticed a lotus growing on the surface, and swam down to see what was anchoring its stem. He discovered the Earth, deep in the ocean depths, formed himself into a gigantic boar and heaved it to the surface with his tusks. In some versions the Earth was as we know it: mountains, forests, plains. In others it was a beautiful goddess, **Privithi** Mother of All, riding serenely on Varaha's forehead.

Varaha in Hindu myth. In a Hindu version of the same **creation**-myth, Varaha was the third avatar of **Vishnu**. The Earth had already been created and stocked with plants, animals, people – and **demons**. One demon, **Hiranyaksha**, by sacrifice and prayers, had persuaded the gods to make him invulnerable, and had listed everything on Earth against which he wanted protection – except one, the boar. Once the gift was granted, he terrorized all creation, and finally pulled the Earth deep under the primordial ocean and held it there to drown everything on it. Vishnu changed himself into a boar: his size was a mountain's, his roar was **thunder**, his hide radiated heat-arrows like those of the **Sun** and his eyes flashed **lightning**. He dived into the ocean, killed Hiranyaksha and tossed the Earth safely to the surface with his tusks before a single insect, animal, plant or human drowned.

≫→ animal-gods

VARPULIS
Europe (East)

Varpulis, in Southern Czech myth, was a wind-god who ran beside **Pyerun**'s chariot as it galloped across the sky. His panting was the grumble and mutter of thunderstorms.

VARUNA
India

Varuna ('encompasser'), in the Vedic myths of the Aryans who invaded India in the seventeenth century BCE, was the god of the **sky**. He was known as Aditya ('**Aditi**'s son', that is 'light of **Heaven**'), and his other names included Pasabhrit ('noose-carrier'), Pasi ('judge') and Prasetas ('all-wise'). After something like 1000 years his power and functions changed. He became the god of **water**, and his honorary second names included Kesa ('liquid-lord'), Variloma ('water-hair') and Yadhapati ('ruler of water-creatures').

Varuna the Creator. Varuna oversaw, and indeed embodied, *rita* ('world-order'): the truth, the ultimate reality against which all other realities were matched. One of the earliest **creation**-myths says that he stood in emptiness and made three worlds simply by exercise of will: **Heaven**, Middle Air and Earth. He then continued to create, or sustain, the universe by unceasing effort of will – and if that effort ever slackens, the universe will end. In some accounts he physically supported the sky, surveying it sternly, unceasingly, with his eye the **Sun**. In others he lived in a sky-palace with a thousand doors, and his agent the Sun travelled about the firmament and returned to him each evening to report on the doings of gods and mortals.

Varuna the Encompasser. In later Aryan myth, Varuna shared his power with his brothers Mithra and Aryaman. Aryaman's powers are hardly remembered – he was some kind of sky-god. But with Mithra, Varuna the Encompasser formed a duality. He was sternness, Mithra was compassion; he was rigidity, Mithra was flexibility; he was night, Mithra was day. Varuna lived in the middle of the sky, in void – and he was that void. He was the god of the Moon, and protected *soma*, the **nectar** of the gods. Because of his impartial judgement, he conferred, or removed, **immortality**. On Earth, he oversaw good government, the rule of law, the hierarchies of society and families – and above all, the correct forms and rituals for sacrifice. He himself accepted offerings of horses, symbolizing the life-force. When he was angry, he sent disease and earthquakes; when he was pleased, he sent healing and peace.

Varuna Lord of Water. In early Aryan myth, **Heaven** was imagined as a celestial **sea**, and it was this which Varuna ruled. At first his power was all-encompassing. But there was a cataclysmic war between gods and **demons**, and when it was over the gods reorganized their powers. Varuna's influence declined, and he ruled only the Western quadrant of the sky, above the Indian Ocean on Earth. He was, however, made supreme lord of Earthly oceans, and therefore supervisor of the demons who lived in them. His palace was built on an underwater mountain, Pushpagiri, and from it he rode out on his sea-charger Makara, a fish with a deer's head and antelope's legs. His retinue of river-warriors and waves streamed after him, as he galloped across the sea, noose in hand, to catch and punish demons who challenged the gods.

Varuna the Regulator. As water-lord, Varuna kept a few of his former powers. He scooped out river-beds on Earth, and gathered rain-clouds to fill them. He controlled the tides, using them to regulate the depth of the oceans. He was a god of fishers and sailors, and took special care of drowned people, welcoming them to his underwater kingdom. If mortals offended him, he filled their joints and limbs with liquid, in a particularly painful form of dropsy.

As 'encompasser', Varuna had no shape. He was the personification of the night sky; the wind was his breath, his eyes were stars. He was rarely depicted in art, and then usually as a prince dressed in a cloud-cloak, riding a tortoise and carrying a noosed rope (symbol of his status as binder, knot-master). As 'water-lord', he was depicted either as a prince with foam-white skin, riding his sea-charger, or as a creature, part crocodile, part dolphin, part shark.

≫→ **justice and universal order**

VARUNI
India

Varuni (also known as Mara, 'destroyer'; 'intoxication' – not the same person as **Mara**, mother of **Buddha**), in Hindu myth, was the goddess of wine. She was either the daughter of **Varuna**, or was born from the churning of the Sea of Milk (see *amrita*). She had big, rolling eyes, and whoever once enjoyed her favours, whether god, **demon** or mortal, could never resist her afterwards.

VASHISHTRA
India

Vashishtra, in Hindu myth, was one of the **Seven Seers**. He was priest of King **Dasaratha**, **Rama**'s mortal father, and owned Nandini the cow of plenty. He is chiefly remembered, however, as the Seer who opposed the promotion of **Vishvamitra** and suffered for it.

VASUDEVA
India

Vasudeva ('good god'), in Hindu myth, began as an honorific name for **Krishna**, and then became used for the mortal prince whose wife, **Devaki**, gave birth to Krishna and his brother **Balarama**. In the myth, when Krishna later died and returned to **Heaven**, Vasudeva threw himself on the god's funeral pyre and ascended with him.

In Jain myth, each cycle of the universe is led by 24 Saviours, 12 Emperors and nine triads of heroes. One third of each triad is a 'Vasudeva', and there are therefore nine of them in each universal cycle.
≫→ **Vasus**

VASUKI
India

Vasuki, in Hindu myth, was the son of the world-**snake Shesha**. When the gods churned the Sea of Milk to produce *amrita*, they used a mountain as a churning-pole and Vasuki as a rope. Vasuki tried to poison the *amrita* by spitting venom into it, but **Shiva** caught the venom in his mouth and so stopped the gods' **immortality** from being forever tainted. Vasuki was punished by being made to support the entire weight of the Earth on his many heads. Whenever he stirs, he causes an **earthquake**.

VASUS
India

Vasus ('good ones'), in Hindu myth, were eight minor deities who bustled about the universe doing good. Their names were Anala ('fire'), Anila ('air'), Apa ('water'), Dhara ('contemplation'), Dhruva ('sacrificial ladle'), Prabhasa ('radiance'), Pratyusa ('holder of the sacrificial dish') and **Soma**. They had no special functions, but listened to prayers and did their best to help them come true. In one account they took pieces of the **Sun** and moulded them into a golden horse which pulled **Indra**'s storm-chariot; in another, unable to get hold of the Sun, they made themselves into a team of horses instead and presented themselves to Indra.

VAYU
Asia (West); India

Vayu in Iranian myth. Vayu ('breath') was originally one of the grandest of Iranian gods. He ruled – and indeed was – the middle air, and was equal in rank to **Ahura Mazda** and **Ahriman**. But when Ahura Mazda became supreme ruler of the universe, Vayu was demoted to being wind-lord and god of storms.

Vayu in Vedic Indian myth. Vayu came to India from Iran with the Aryan invasions of the seventeenth century BCE. With **Agni**, god of **fire**, and **Surya** the **Sun**-god, he formed a triad which ruled the universe. But new gods came into being, there was a power-struggle, and Vayu once again lost status, taking the position of charioteer to **Indra** god of storms. He was barred from the **sky**-palace on the summit of Mount **Meru**, and lived in its foothills among the **Gandharvas**. He made war on the sky-citadel, trying to blow down its defences. But **Garuda**, king of the birds, protected it with outspread wings, and it was a year before Vayu was able to rip off the mountain-tip and hurl it into the sea. It became the island of Sri Lanka, home of Vayu's son the monkey-god **Hanuman**.

Vayu in Hindu myth. In later myth, Vayu lost even more status. In some accounts he remained an uncontrolled buccaneer among the gods, blustering round the sky, fathering illegitimate offspring and attacking anything in his path. In others he was a servant of **Vishnu** and **Lakshmi**, sometimes raging but often gentle and balmy, breathing perfumes across the world. In his most undignified manifestation of all, he is wind trapped in the human gut, and we fart him out.

VE
Europe (North)

Ve and his brothers **Odin** and **Vili**, in Nordic myth, were sons of **Bor**, father of the gods. They fought the frost-**giants** and then dismembered **Ymir** to create the universe. After this Odin went on to rule the gods, and Ve and Vili retired from myth.
≫→ creation

VECHERNYAYA ZVEZDA AND ZVEZDA DENNITSA
Europe (East)

Vechernyaya Zvezda ('evening star') and Zvezda Dennitsa ('morning star'), in Slavic myth, were the daughters of **Dahzbog** the **Sun**, and in some myths one or the other, or both, married **Meness** the **Moon**. They supervised the Sun's chariot-horses, keeping them overnight in the Moon's stables and harnessing them for their father each morning.

VENUS: *see* Aphrodite

VERTUMNUS: *see* Pomona and Vertumnus

VESTA
Europe (South)

Vesta ('hearth'), in Roman myth, was one of the four **Hesperides** who tended the Golden Apples of **Immortality**. She also tended immortality in the form of fire, in a wheel of **fire** or in an undying flame constantly tended in an open hearth. The Romans thought that the immortality of their state depended on such an eternally-burning fire, built a temple to her in Rome and founded a sisterhood of high-born priestesses, the Vestal Virgins, to tend it.

Vesta is identified with the Greek goddess Hestia, though parts of her story (for example her parentage) are quite different.

VIBISHANA
India

Vibishana ('terrifying'), in Hindu myth, was the good brother of the **demons Ravana** and **Kumbhakarna**. He won **Brahma**'s favour with sacrifice, then asked him to ensure that he (Vibishana) never did 'anything unworthy'. He tried to persuade Ravana not to kidnap **Rama**'s wife **Sita**, and when Ravana refused, he soared across the sea from Sri Lanka and joined Rama's army. After Rama killed Ravana, the gods rewarded Vibishana by making him king of Sri Lanka and granting him **immortality**.

VICTORIA: *see* Nike

VIDAR
Europe (North)

Vidar, in Nordic myth, was the son of **Odin** and the metal-working sorceress **Grid**. His mother equipped him with iron weapons made invincible by magic, including an enormous shoe with which he could trample any created thing to death. Armed with these, Vidar will kill the wolf Fenrir at **Ragnarök**. He will be one of the few survivors of the end of this cycle of the universe, and one of the rulers of the next.

VILI
Europe (North)

Vili and his brothers **Odin** and **Ve**, in Nordic myth, were sons of **Bor**, father of the gods. They fought the frost-**giants** and then dismembered **Ymir** to create the universe. After this Odin went on to rule the gods, and Vili and Ve retired from myth.

⋙→ creation

VINATA
India

Vinata, in Hindu myth, was the second wife of **Kasyapa**. Kasyapa's senior wife was the **snake**-queen **Kadru**, and Vinata was jealous. Kasyapa, a powerful sage, offered each of them as many children as they wanted, and when Kadru asked for a thousand, Vinata asked for two sons only, but specified that they should outrank all of Kadru's children. In due course the children were born: a thousand snakes to Kadru, and to Vinata the **Sun**-charioteer **Varuna** and the eagle-king **Garuda**.

Kadru, furious, used her serpent's cunning to hypnotize Vinata, and persuaded her to agree to become her slave. She made Vinata's existence a misery, and refused to set her free unless one of her children stole some **amrita**, **immortality**, from **Heaven**. With enormous difficulty, Garuda did this, and Kadru drank it and freed Vinata. At once Vinata's children declared war on all Kadru's descendants, and eagles and the Sun have been enemies of snakes from that day on.

VIRACOCHA
Americas (South)

Viracocha ('lake of creation'), in the myths of the pre-Inca peoples of Peru and then in Inca myth, was the god of the **Sun**, storms and **creation**. His other names included Illa ('light') and Tici ('birth'). He rose from Lake Titicaca at the dawn of the universe, and made the Earth, Sky, **Sun**, **Moon** and stars. He peopled the Earth with creatures, and then set about making human beings by breathing life into stones. The first people were brainless giants, and he swept them away in a **flood** and made a second human race, this time from pebbles. He scattered them all over the Earth. Ever afterwards, to give them knowledge and goodness above that of wild beasts, he regularly disguised himself as a beggar and wandered the world to teach and work miracles. Because so many of his humans refused to listen to this teaching, preferring crime and war, Viracocha always returned from these trips in tears – and if we ever become all-wicked, those tears will turn into a second flood and drown us as the giants were drowned.

*In another account, Viracocha was one of three sons of **Inti** the sun god, and brother of Manco Capac and **Pachacamac**. In others, he and his brothers were not separate entities at all, but three different aspects of the sun-god. At the height of Inca* *civilization, at his temple in the heart of Cuzco, he was worshipped in a huge, gold-covered statue of a king in splendour, crowned with the Sun, carrying thunder-bolt-spears and weeping rivers of golden tears. After the Spanish conquest many surviving Incas believed that he put on his beggar's disguise and disappeared into the West, walking over the sea as if it were dry land – and that he will come back one day, either to redeem the human race or drown us.*

⟫→ civilization, Deucalion and Pyr-rha

VIRAJ
India

Viraj ('femaleness'), in one **creation**-myth of the Aryans who invaded India in the seventeenth century BCE, was the second being in the universe. She came into being when **Purusha**, the first being, divided himself in two, and she then mated with him to produce every-thing in existence.

VISHNU
India

Vishnu in Vedic myth. Vishnu ('all-pervader' or 'many-shaped'), in the myths of the Aryan people who in-vaded India in the seventeenth century BCE, was the power of light, the first force in the universe. His beams danced in the ripples of the primordial ocean, or he rested on the surface, floating on the thousand-headed cosmic **snake Shesha**, until **Brahma** was born from a lotus which grew in his navel. His names included Ananta ('infinite'), Ke-sava ('hairy', because light-beams

streamed from his head like hair) and Mukunda ('liberator'). When gods and **demons** argued about who should rule the universe, Vishnu changed into a dwarf and proposed that the gods should rule as much territory as he could cover in three strides, and the demons should take the rest. When the demons agreed, he took three steps which covered, in turn, Earth, Middle Air and **Heaven**.

Vishnu in Hindu myth. In Hindu myth, Vishnu is one of a triad of gods who oversee and maintain **justice and universal order**. He is the preserver, the force which radiates from a still centre; **Shiva** is the destroyer, the force which sucks everything inwards like a whirl-pool; Brahma is the equilibrium be-tween them. As Preserver, Vishnu personifies sacrifice. His existence, and the continuance of ritual offerings for which he stands, guarantee universal stability. He and his wife **Lakshmi** live in a Heaven, Vaikuntha, made entirely of gold and jewels, and with a garden centred on five lotus-filled, world-span-ning pools; they sit enthroned on white lotuses, while the Ganges flows from Vishnu's right foot.

Vishnu's avatars. Vishnu's concern for creation leads him to leave Vai-kuntha at moments of extreme tension in the universe, when the equilibrium between light and dark seems about to tip towards dark. On each of these occasions he makes a descent (*avatar*) into the world, taking the form either of a hero or a creature or object filled with his own power and radiance. There have been innumerable such avatars, too many even for gods to count. But ten are of particular significance for mortals. In order, they are: **Matsya** the fish, **Kurma** the tortoise, **Varaha** the boar, **Narasimha** the man-lion, **Vamana** the dwarf, **Parashurama** the axe-wielder, **Rama**, **Krishna**, the **Buddha** and **Kalki** the destroyer. (The last is still to come.)

*Vishnu is a favourite subject for paintings and sculptures of all kinds. He is often shown asleep on Shesha, in the peace before **creation**, or sitting enthroned on a white lotus, his head haloed with Sun-radiance and his four hands holding sacred objects: a conch-shell (symbolizing the origin of existence), a wheel (symbolizing the Universal Mind and the cycle from creation to destruction), a club (symbolizing power, both physical and intellectual) and a lotus (symbolizing purity). Sometimes his wife Lakshmi is beside him, in earlier art one quarter his size, in later art of equal stature. Other favourite subjects are panels or discs showing Vishnu and his avatars, or Vishnu (sometimes with Lakshmi) riding **Garuda**, king of birds and with his outrider **Hanuman** the monkey-king. In most such pictures he is a smiling prince, with blue skin and robes of golden yellow.*

⧛⧛→ **light and dark, supreme deity**

VISHVAKARMAN
India

Vishvakarman or Visvakarma ('all-creator'), in the earliest Vedic myths of the Aryans who invaded India in the seventeenth century BCE, created the universe and everything in it. He was a totality, all things in one, and made the world by dismembering himself and scattering the pieces. By the time of the Aryan invasions, this myth had been super-seded by those of **Brahma**, the universal principle, and **Tvashtri**, in whom all seeds or embryos resided.

In later, Hindu, myth, Vishvakarman was reduced in status to the architect of the gods. His daughter Sanjna married the Sun-god **Surya**, and Vishvakarman turned the Sun on his lathe to reduce his dazzle, forging the shavings into weapons for the gods. (In earlier myth this feat was attributed to Tvashtri.) He built chariots and palaces for the gods, and also constructed a bridge across the sea to Lanka, which was ruled by his son Nala. The Lankans gave Nala the credit for this, calling the bridge Nala's Bridge and claiming that he had the power to make stones float on water.

⧛⧛→ **crafts; creation; smiths**

VISHVAMITRA
India

Vishvamitra, in Hindu myth, was one of the **Seven Seers**. He was born a mortal king, but prayed and sacrificed so diligently that he persuaded **Brahma** to grant him magical powers. Five of the other Seers welcomed him to their number, but the sixth, **Vashishtra**, refused and the two became enemies. The *Mahabharata*, parts of which Vishvamitra is said to have written, tells of the Seers' battles on behalf of gods and mortal **heroes** against the **demons** – but it also, endearingly, keeps breaking off to tell anecdotes of the feud between Vashishtra and Vishvamitra – who on one typical occasion fed his rival's hundred sons to a hungry demon, so causing them to lose caste for 700 future births.

VIVASVAT
India

Vivasvat ('dazzle'), in the Vedic myths of the Aryans who invaded India in the seventeenth century BCE, was god of the rising **Sun**, father of the healing-**twins** the **Ashvins** and of **Yama** and Yami, the first human beings. Despite such splendour, he features in myth as one of **Heaven**'s unfortunates. Under his original name, Marttanda ('born from an unfertilized egg'), he was the eighth son of **Aditi**. He was born as a lump of shapeless matter, and his horrified mother threw him out of Heaven. **Tvashtri**, smith of the gods, rescued him and moulded him into a god (throwing away unwanted scraps which fell to Earth and were regenerated as elephants). The gods honoured Marttanda's new identity by giving him a new name, Vivasvat, and the job of a Sun-god, and marrying him to Tvashtri's daughter **Saranyu**. But the bride disappeared just after the wedding-feast, and Tvashtri hastily created an exact double, who went on to be the mother of Vivasvat's children. In later myth, Vivasvat surrendered his status as Sun-god to his brother **Surya**, and became his charioteer.

VODYANOI
Europe (East)

The Vodyanoi (from *voda*, 'water'), or Vodnik, in Slavic myth, were **water**-spirits and **shape-changers**. They appeared sometimes as beautiful girls, sometimes as floating logs, sometimes as themselves – green-skinned, weed-slimed and covered with bumps and warts. They prowled lake-sides and river-banks at nights, particularly favouring mill-races, and dragged unwary humans underwater to be their slaves.

VOLKH
Europe (East)

Volkh, in Slavic myth, was a **shape-changer**, one of the *bogatiri*. He used his powers in a huge battle to save the churches of Kiev from invading infidels led by the Tsar of India. His name hedges its bets between paganism and Christianity: it means both 'priest' and 'sorcerer'.
≫→ **heroes**

VOLUND
Europe (North)

Volund (or Wieland or Wayland), in Nordic and Celtic myth, was a blacksmith-god, expert at forging weapons. (In some accounts, he made King **Arthur**'s **Excalibur**.) He was bent and lame, and the reason was that after living with the three daughters of the mortal king Nidud on a remote island for seven years, Nidud punished him by stealing his immortal weapons, hamstringing him and marooning him. Volund retaliated by turning the daughters into swans, killing their brothers (and sending their skulls to Nidud as fantastically bejewelled and gold-embossed drinking-goblets), and then soaring into **Heaven** on wings he had made himself. Ever afterwards the gods made him a laughing-stock for what he had let a mortal do to him.

In Denmark and England especially, Vo-lund/Wayland was regarded not so much as a god to be feared as a kindly, super-natural uncle who supervised the growing of crops, the building of houses and men's and women's fertility. He was said to have built all stone circles, barrows and other prehis-toric remains, and to have carved, for fun, all the giants, horses and other figures in the chalk downlands of Southern England.

VRITRA
India

Vritra ('holder-back' or 'choker'), in the Vedic myths of the Aryans who invaded India in the seventeenth century BCE, was a drought-**demon**, a gigantic **snake** which swallowed the clouds and stopped the **rain**, or (in some accounts) lay in coils which entirely filled the space between **Heaven** and Earth, so blocking out the rain. **Indra** killed him, water gushed from his corpse like horses galloping, and **fertility** was restored to Earth.

VULCAN: *see* Hephaestus

VYASA
India

Vyasa, in Hindu myth, was a sage, son of the **apsara** Satyavati and the holy man Parasara. He spent his life meditating in the forest, and never cut his hair, shaved or washed. His mother married King Santanu, and bore two sons who grew up and married but died before they could have children. According to the custom that a dead husband's near male relative could have **sex** with his wives and give them children which would count as his, Vyasa was summoned to bed with his nieces **Ambika** and **Amba-lika**. Their horrified reactions to his appearance affected the sons they con-ceived. Ambika shut her eyes, and her son **Dhritarashtra** was born blind; Am-balika turned pale, and her son **Pandu** was born an albino.

*Some myths say that Vyasa went on to compose the **Mahabharata**, the ac-count of the epic war fought for the king-dom of **Bharata** by the **Pandavas** (grandsons of Ambika and Ambalika) and their cousins the **Kauravas** – and that he dictated it to **Ganesh**, who wrote it down using one of his own elephant-tusks as a pen. But this may be simple confusion, since the Sanskrit word Vyasa simply means 'editor' or 'assembler'. Vya-sa narrates the Mahabharata, but need not also be one of its characters – unless we take the allusions to his uncouth ap-pearance to be self-mockery.*

WAHARI AND BUOKA
Americas (South)

Wahari and his brother Buoka, in the myths of the Piaroa people of Venezuela, shared the sexual favours of a large family of women. One day, the women were swinging on a liana across a ravine in the jungle, and while each one swung, Buoka wrapped the others, one at a time, in his long, **snake**-like penis, drew them down to the ravine floor and mated with them. Instead of exhausting Buoka, the **sex** excited him more and more – and when Wahari came along he wrapped his penis round him and tried to find an orifice to mate with him. Irritated, Wahari chopped Buoka's penis down to normal size – it was so long that he had to cut it into five sections – and Buoka hobbled back to the village and lay in his hammock, bleeding.

The women, who had seen none of this, asked Wahari where Buoka was. 'At home. It's that time of the month,' answered Wahari. The women didn't know what this meant, as periods were then unknown. But they soon found out. One by one, they crept into Buoka's hut and seduced him into making love with them. The blood from his penis entered their vaginas – and from that time onwards, both they and all other women bled every month, and each Piaroa women spent the first day of her period alone in her hammock in her hut. As for the chopped-off parts of Buoka's penis, they wriggled off into the ravine and hid there, lively as snakes, on the lookout for unwary females to mate with.

WAK
Africa

Wak, the Ethiopian creator-god, made

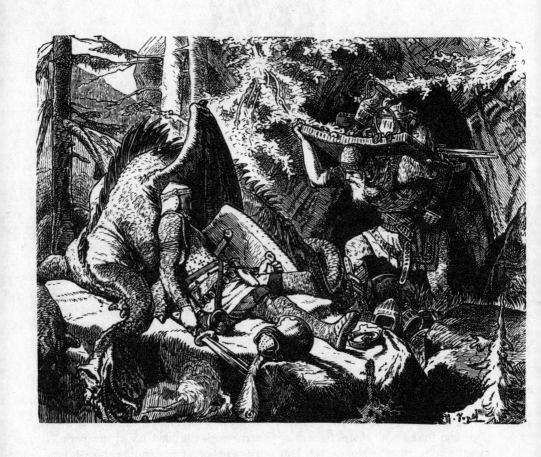

The death of Beowulf (*N. Vogel, 19th century*)

the sky by propping a bowl upside-down over the flat plate of the Earth, and studding it with stars. In a fit of absent-mindedness, he created the first human being before Earth was finished, and had to bury him in a coffin while he made mountains, seas and forests. (As a result of this incarceration, human beings have ever since spent half of their lives in the spirit-world, asleep, and the other half awake.) When First Man emerged from the coffin, Wak took a drop of his blood and made First Woman. He gave Man and Woman the gift of **sex**, and left them alone for a time to enjoy it – which they did so enthusiastically that thirty children were born. They heard Wak coming back, and, embarrassed at their own fecundity, hid fifteen of their offspring in holes in the ground. Wak blessed the other fifteen, who became ancestors of all the peoples of the world – and from the hidden fifteen he created the ancestors of every wild predator, poisonous **snake** and **demon** ever born.
≫→ **creation**

WAKAN TANKA
Americas (North)

Wakan Tanka ('great mystery'), in the myths of the Dakota people of the US Great Plains, existed alone in the void before existence. He was lonely, and made company for himself by dividing himself into four. He began by gathering his energy into a single enormous force: Inyan (Rock). From this he made Maka (Earth), and mated with her to produce Skan (Sky). Skan then mated with Inyan and Maka to make Wi (the **Sun**). After this, **creation** continued to

grow from Wakan Tanka as leaves, twigs and branches grow on trees. Inyan, Maka, Skan and Wi, the four High Ones, made four Companions to help them create and people the universe: **Moon**, Wind, Falling Star and the **Great Thunderbird**. The four Companions, in turn, made four Related Ones: Whirlwind, Four-Winds, Four-legs and Two-legs. After the four Related Ones came four Godlike Ones: Nagi (spirit of **death**), Nagila (shadow), Niya (breath-of-life) and Sicun (Thought). All sixteen of these beings were aspects of Wakan Tanka, who was in all of them and was composed of all of them – and between them they created and oversaw all that exists.

This is an elaborate version of a common **creation***-account, in which the Great Spirit, the original principle, makes the universe and everything in it by a process of organic self-division. These systems explain the presence in the world of such things as evil, suffering and death by saying that division was interrupted or diverted by some chance event, or that merging took place between two incompatible beings, such as fire and whirlwind – and the result was a* **trickster** *(Spider, in Dakota myth; Coyote, in many other Plains accounts) or a destructive power such as hail. But the point of all the stories is the same: that all creation, everything which exists, is part of a single organic and interdependent whole.*

WAKONDA
Americas (North)

Wakonda ('power above'), in the myths of the Sioux people of the US Great Plains, was the supreme authority in the universe, keeping it in balance and revealing its secrets only to a few favoured shamans. In Dakota myth he was incarnated as the Great Thunderbird who ruled the world of light and led his flocks of **thunderbirds** in endless battles with the **demon** water-**snakes** of darkness.

≫→ supreme deity

WAR: *see* Adad, Aesir, Ares, Athene, Bellona, Cihuacóatl, Durga, Eris, Hachiman, Huitzilopochtli, Ishtar, Jun Di, Kali, Karttikeya, Krishna, Mars, Min, Morrigan, Nike, Ninurta, Ogoun, Ogun, Qi Nu, Rugievit, Sekhmet, Teutatis, Thor, Tyr, Unkulunkulu

WARAMURUNGUNDJU AND WURAKA
Australia

Waramurungundju (or Imberombera, 'mother who made us all') and her consort Wuraka, in the myths of many coastal peoples of Arnhem Land in Northern Australia, walked out of the **sea** in the Dream Time. Waramurungundju was aching with **fertility**, but had no means of making herself pregnant or giving birth. For his part, Wuraka had a penis so long that he carried it in coils round his neck and it bent his back like an old man's. But when they reached the shore, the penis began to uncoil and stiffen. It searched out Waramurungundju's vagina and impregnated her. Instantly she began giving birth, filling land and sea with creatures which Wuraka then named and taught their various languages. When **creation** finished, the two spirits turned and walked back into the sea, never to be seen again.

WATER

From the primordial ocean to the smallest well or pool on Earth, water and its gods and creatures were treated, in most myth-traditions, as entirely separate from the rest of **creation**. Sometimes they were at war with the rest of us, sometimes friendly and life-giving, sometimes aloof. Each river or lake had its own inhabitants (often imagined as **snakes** or hybrids of gods and snakes), and the **sea** was a realm as vast and varied as **Sky** or Earth themselves. Water-snakes in many traditions made the landscape of **Mother Earth**, and clothed her with vegetation; water-creatures were full of generative power, endlessly lustful and hopeful for mates – something which made them particularly dangerous to mortals, since they never understood why we drowned in their embraces or died in their underwater dens. They were also susceptible to flattery – more so than any other supernatural beings – and could be persuaded, with the right offerings and ceremonies, to help human beings instead of harming them.

≫→ (Americas): Agwe, Temazcalteci; (China): Gong Gong, Long Wang, Yao; (Egypt): Hapi, Nun and Naunet; (Greece): Achelous, Acheron, Arethusa, Ocean, Scamander; (India): Ganga, Indra, *nagas* and *naginis*, Sarasvati, Varuna; (Mesopotamia): Leviathan, Tiamat; (Rome): Tiber; (Slavic): *Bannik*, Russalki, Vodyanoi; (general): floods, rain

WAYLAND: *see* Volund

WELE
Africa

Wele ('high one'), also known as Isaiwa ('honoured in ritual') and Khakaba ('distributor'), creator-god in the myths of the Abaluia people of Kenya, built himself a house on stilts (**Heaven**), and then created **Sun** and **Moon**. Sun and Moon were originally **twins**, with equal radiance, but they fought and Sun spattered Moon with mud to reduce his brightness. Wele gave Sun the day to rule and Moon the night. He then made stars, clouds, lightning (in the form of a crowing cock), rain (and rainbows to control it), frost, the Earth and finally plants, animals and the first human beings **Mwambu and Sela**, whom he settled in a stilt-house of their own on Earth. All this activity took six days, and on the seventh day Wele rested, beginning a sabbatical from the affairs of Earth which has lasted ever since.
≫→ creation

WEN JANG
Asia (East)

Wen Jang ('god of literature'), in Chinese myth, was the deification of a scholar and administrator of the eighth century CE who disappeared without trace during a battle and was assumed to have been taken into **Heaven**. He was worshipped as a dwarf with a demon's face – perhaps because of his association with **Kui**, the phenomenally ugly god of success in examinations – and supervised everyone involved with literature, especially writers, students and stationers. He gave his secrets generously to honest worshippers, but there was no hope for cheats trying to winkle them out of his attendants, since one (Tien Long) was deaf and therefore never heard the prayers and the other (Ti Ya) was mute and never answered them.

WEREWOLVES
Europe (East; North)

Werewolves (Vlkodlaks or Vookodlaks, 'wolf-hairs'; the English name comes from the Saxon *wer*, 'man' and *wulf*, 'wolf') were widely feared throughout Northern and Eastern Europe. They were born to human mothers but out of human time, and harked back to an age when shape-changing animals (in this case, wolves) roamed the world. Werewolf-children were particularly hairy at birth, or had extra cauls of skin on their heads. They sometimes had wolf-claws and fangs, biting their mothers as they suckled. Often, they were often **twins** (as in the cases of such mythic pairs as **Romulus and Remus**), and in human form, at least, they were sexually as attractive to women as they were voracious. They were associated with the **Moon** (in ancient myth, the Moon-goddess' hunting dogs were often humans miraculously turned into wolves), and changed into wolves each full Moon. Some were invulnerable to mortal weapons; others could be hurt by silver arrows (or later, silver bullets); others again could be wounded in the ordinary way, but slunk to their human homes and resumed their human shapes to die – after which their immortal selves were reborn to another human mother.

*Although belief in werewolves is recorded as far back as the first millennium BCE, and in all Northern regions of the world including Canada and the Siberian Arctic, their greatest upsurge was in late medieval and Renaissance Europe. Here, they were ranked with witches and **demons**, emissaries of **Satan**, and anyone suspected of lycanthropy – all werewolves were male, and the signs were hairiness, the port-wine birthmark known as the 'mark of **Cain'**, stubby fingers with sharp nails, threatening sexuality and in extreme cases cannibalism – was persecuted. In France alone between 1520 and 1630, over 30,000 suspected werewolves (all in human form) are known to have been executed. The werewolf, or 'Big Bad Wolf', of fairy-tale has been their enduring legacy, though they had a resurgence in the 1920s, in adult horror stories such as those of E.W. Hornung, and in Hollywood.*

*Fearsome human-animal hybrids were common in other cultures. Those which shared all the characteristics of werewolves include werebears (North America), wereboars (Greece – the **Erymanthian Boar** is now best-known), werecrocodiles (Africa and Australia), werepanthers (South America), weresnakes (China) and weretigers (India).*
≫→ **monsters and dragons**

WHEEMEMEOWAH
Americas

Wheememeowah ('great high chief'), in the myths of the Yakima people of the US Plateau region, lived alone in the Sky at the start of **creation**. Nothing existed but him, Sky and the primordial ocean. Bored, he went down to the shallowest part of the ocean and began playing in the mud. He tossed it up in handfuls – and it stuck to Sky or floated, making continents and islands. He shaped the surface, moulding river-beds and mountains. Finally, he breathed life into mud-droplets to make plants, animals and our ancestors, First Man and First Woman.

A somewhat preachy pendant to this myth, added after the European conquest, says that human beings were no sooner made than they began to quarrel, and the time will come when Wheememeowah grows tired of them and returns them to primordial mud. He has sent floods and earthquakes as warnings, and we have taken no notice. Already the spirits are leaving the world, and unless we change our ways and woo them back, our destruction is assured.

WHITE SHE-BUFFALO
Americas (North)

White She-Buffalo (also known as White Buffalo Calf-Woman), in the myths of the Lakota people of the US plains, taught the people how to plant and farm corn. Hunters on the plain one day saw a beautiful stranger, and went closer, hoping that she would agree to **sex**. But she told them that she was not their plaything; they should go home and prepare to welcome her as a queen deserved. They hurried to build a lodge for her in the village – and when it was ready she appeared. She gave them a ceremonial tobacco-pipe, and a package which she said contained four drops of her milk. The drops, if planted, would grow into corn-stalks, and feed the people. (Corn grains are milky to this day.) She went on to teach them **mysteries**: the winds' secrets and seven life-prolonging rituals. These were all associated with the pipe, her first gift to them. When she'd finished her teaching she changed into a buffalo and disappeared.

≫→ **farming**

WIDJINGARA
Australia

Widjingara, in the myths of the Worora people of the Kimberleys in Northern Australia, was the first human being ever to die. In the Dream Time, he protected a woman against the **Wondjina**, who retaliated by killing him. His wife wrapped his body in bark, shaved her head, smeared her face with ashes and mourned for him. This was the first time anyone on Earth had ever mourned, and when Widjingara came back from the Dead after three days (as custom was) he was so angry at his wife's changed appearance that he went straight back again – and **death** and mourning have ever since been part of the human condition.

WIND: *see* Aeolus, Boreas, Dajoji, Ehecatl, Enki, Fei Lian, Futen, Ga-oh, Gucumatz, Hraesvelg, Hurukan, Ilma, Kukulkan, Michabo, Quetzalcóatl, Stribog, Varpulis, Vayu, Zephyrus

WISDOM: *see* Agastya, Athene, Atri, Bhagiratha, Bhisma, Brighu, Chiron, Chyavana, Drona, mysteries, Prometheus, prophecy, Rishis, Thoth, Vashishtra, Vishvamitra, Vyasa, writing

WISHPOOSH
Americas (North)

Wishpoosh, in the myths of the Nez Perce people of the Northwestern US, was a monstrous beaver which ruled the primeval lake and refused access to any other creatures. **Coyote** the **trickster** went to the lakeside to fish, and Wishpoosh attacked him. They fought, and as they rolled and wrestled among the mountains they gouged out canyons and river-gorges. Wishpoosh swam into the sea and began gulping down whales to give himself strength. Coyote turned into a fir-branch and floated, resting – until Wishpoosh realized who he was and swallowed him. Inside the monster, Coyote swam up Wishpoosh's veins and arteries and stabbed his heart. He floated the huge carcass to shore, hacked it to pieces, and used the fragments to make the first human beings.

≫→ **animal-gods**

WONDJINA, THE
Australia

The Wondjina, in the myths of the Worora and Ungarinjin people of the Kimberleys in Northwestern Australia, were **rain**-spirits of the Dream Time who helped to shape the world and everything in it. They were **shape-changers**, taking the forms of giant owls, pigeons and hawks, or of humans. They were so disgusted with the lawlessness and lust of the first human beings that they opened their mouths and vomited huge **floods** which drowned them all. The Wondjina then remade the human race and taught them civilized behaviour. They used to fly round their creation, enjoying its praise, or bask on the rocks in human shape. They kept their mouths shut to prevent any further floods, and in due course the mouths disappeared altogether. (Fortunately the Wondjina, like all supernatural creatures, had no need to eat or drink.) When in due course the Wondjina abandoned visible shape, their spirits went to live in water-holes and creeks and the image of their bodies remained as paintings on the rocks where they used to sunbathe. Every year those paintings were refurbished at the end of the dry season, and the Wondjina responded by sending rain.

≫→ animal-gods, civilization, creation

WONOMI
Americas (North)

Wonomi ('no **death**'), in the myths of the Southwestern and Western US, created the universe and everything in it, and gave them their names. He ruled serenely and peacefully until **Coyote** the **trickster** came and started renaming everything. Giving new identities brought Coyote all-power, and he even persuaded human beings to give up their **immortality** for the pleasures of the world. From then on, Coyote ruled our mortal bodies on Earth, but Wonomi took our souls to his sky-kingdom after death, restored their immortality and ruled them.

≫→ creation

WOODEN HORSE, THE
Europe (South)

The Wooden Horse, in Greek myth, was a trick devised by **Athene** to get Greeks inside the walls of Troy and end the **Trojan War**. She told the trick to **Odysseus**, and he proposed it to a council of the Greek commanders. They should build a huge pinewood horse, with a hollow belly large enough to hide twenty-four armed men, and trick the Trojans into dragging it into the city. Then, at night, the men inside should open the city gates and let in the rest of the army.

To build the Horse, the Greeks chose Epeus the shipwright. He was as cowardly as he was skilful, and agreed to build the Horse only if no one made him ride in it. He made it of pine-planks, pegged like ship's timbers; it rode on solid wooden wheels, and on its side he carved 'Offered to Athene, to grant the Greeks safe voyage home'. In one flank he made a trapdoor, carefully concealed – and he was so carried away with his own craftsmanship that he made a fastening which no one but himself could work. Unfortunately for him, this meant that the Greeks had to take him with them after all, and he sat, whimpering, with the twenty-three **heroes** in the Horse's belly while the next part of the trick was played.

As soon as the heroes were in place and the trapdoor was shut, the rest of the Greeks made a bonfire of all their tents, animal-pens and the other paraphernalia of a ten-year siege, and, taking nothing but their weapons, launched their ships and sailed away – not to Greece, as the Trojans immediately assumed, but to the far side of the island of Tenedos, out of sight of Troy. There was nothing left on the plain but the smouldering bonfire, scattered debris, and the Wooden Horse pregnant with armed men.

Convinced that the Greeks had gone, the Trojans poured out of the city to inspect the Horse. The Trojan leaders immediately began arguing about what to do with it. **Priam** and his warrior-sons thought it harmless, and wanted to drag it into the city and offer it to Athene to whom it was dedicated. Others, including Priam's prophet-children, said that if it entered the city Troy would fall, and wanted to drag it down to the shore and burn it in honour of **Poseidon**. Priam's son **Laocoön** led this second group, and nearly convinced the Trojans, hurling a spear which jarred into the Horse (its point narrowly missed **Neoptolemus**' head, inside) and made the hollow belly boom and roar. But the gods sent a portent – sea-serpents which ate Laocoön and his sons alive – and the Greek **trickster** Sinon, who had been hiding for this very purpose in the marshes, persuaded the Trojans that if the Horse were dragged into Athene's temple, the Greeks would never get home alive.

Convinced, the Trojans knocked down part of the city walls and dragged the Horse into Troy. As they did so, **Cassandra** ran wildly round them, screaming that the Horse was full of armed men and would eat the city – and, as always, no one believed her. The gods put it into **Helen**'s mind to walk round the Horse with her young husband **Deiphobus**, telling him about each of the great Greek heroes (the ones inside the Horse) and their wives, imitating their voices and the way they talked. Several of the heroes inside the Horse thought that their wives were actually there, and groaned and sweated to think that they were prisoners in Troy. One man, Antielus, was even about to call out when Odysseus grabbed him by the throat to silence him (some say so fiercely that he broke his neck).

The Trojans placed the Horse in the courtyard of Athene's temple, decorated it with flowers, and spent the day in an orgy of celebration for the end of the war. That night, no guards were posted – there was no need, now that the war was done – and while the Trojans slept, Epeus opened the secret trapdoor and let his companions down on ropes. They took possession of the gates and guard-posts, Helen lit a beacon to summon back the Greeks waiting at Tenedos, and the Trojans awoke to find their city swarming with armed men.

WOTAN: *see* Odin

WOYENGI
Africa

Woyengi the creator, in the myths of the Ijaw people of Nigeria, stepped down from **Heaven** to Earth in a lightning-storm. Nothing existed there except a chair, a table and a flat creation-stone. Woyengi scooped up handfuls of mud and put them on the table. Then she sat on the chair, rested her feet on the creation-stone, and shaped the mud into dolls. As she finished each one she picked it up, gently opened its eyes, gave it the breath of life. She asked them, 'What would you like to be, man or woman' – and gave them sexual organs according to their answers.

When all the dolls were finished, and the table-top was covered with them, she told them, 'Your first gift was life and your second was gender. Now choose a profession to keep throughout your lives.' The dolls made a thousand choices, everything from baker to warrior, from farmer to poet, and when they'd finished Woyengi gathered them in handfuls and put them on the ground. There were two streams leading to the horizon, and she said, 'One leads to luxury, the other to ordinariness. You've chosen the life you want to lead; now let the correct stream carry you to where you chose to be.' The people who'd chosen high-ranking lives stepped into the first stream, and found it fast-flowing and full of rapids. The people who'd chosen the second stream found it clean and clear but shallow. Each group shouted its discoveries back to those still on the bank, and some drew back and asked Woyengi if they could change their minds. But she refused: they'd made their choices, and those choices were irrevocable. So the dolls all waded into the water, and the streams carried them away, irrigating the world with the human race.

>>→ Chinigchinich, creation, Enki, Esaugetuh Emissee, Humanmaker, Hurukan, Na'pi, Prometheus, Tagaro

WRITING: *see* Bragi, Fu Xi, Ganesh, Guan Di, Nabu, Ogmios, Sarasvati, Seshat, Thoth, Wen Jang

WURAKA: *see* Waramurungundju and Wuraka

WYRD
Europe (North)

Wyrd ('fate'), in Nordic myth, was in some accounts mother of the three **Norns**. In others, she was the same person as the Norn Urd, and in others again she was all three Norns, merged into an unknowable, unconquerable, trinity-in-unity.

One of the best-known literary appearances of Wyrd is as the 'three weird sisters', the Witches in Shakespeare's Macbeth who tell him his destiny.

XI HE AND HENG XI
Asia (East)

Xi He and Heng Xi, in Chinese myth, were the wives of **Di Jun**, Emperor of the Eastern sky. Each bore him ten children. Xi He's children, born in the morning, were the ten **Suns**, and she bathed them before dawn each day in a pool at the foot of the 150km-high mulberry tree in the far East of the universe, before taking one of them in turn each day in her chariot to ride the sky. Heng Xi's children, born in the evening, were the ten **Moons**, and she bathed them each evening in a pool at the foot of the *ruo* tree in the far West of the universe, before taking one of them in turn in her chariot to ride the sky each night.

In some accounts, Heng Xi is identified with the moon-goddess **Heng O**.

XIPETOTEC
Americas (Central)

Xipetotec ('flayed lord'), in Aztec myth, was the god of spring **fertility**. When human beings were starving, he skinned himself alive to show how the seed bursts from the bud.

*Scholars think that the Xipetotec spring ritual, which involved shooting victims with arrows, letting their blood drip into the ground like **rain**, then skinning them, began as simple re-enactment of the myth, designed to coax fertility back to the soil. (The victims, had anyone ever bothered to ask them, might have said that their suffering was a form of exaltation, a means of escape from the agony of this world into the peace of **Mictlan**.) Later, however, the cult developed a dark psychological rationale: that no blessing came without suffering, and therefore the greater the suffering,*

Thor (*17th-century engraving*)

the more the blessing. Xipetotec's devotees wore the flayed skins of his victims to give themselves strength in battle, or to cure the huge range of skin ailments, from warts to leprosy, from smallpox to plague, which he was thought to send mortals who offended him. He was also the patron god of gold-smiths – some scholars say because he was originally a **Sun**-god, others (with, one hopes, more imagination than experience) because of the golden-yellow colour of freshly-flayed skin.

»+ civilization, crafts, disease and healing

XIUTECUHTLI
Americas (Central)

Xiutecuhtli ('**fire**-lord'), or Huehuetéotl ('old god'), in Aztec myth, was the fire-god who sustained the entire universe. His origin was in a hearth in **Mictlan**, the spirit-world, and he soared up from there in a pillar of flame which passed through Earth and **Heaven**, keeping them permanently in place. If ever he died, the entire universe would collapse in ruins. He was also the guide of souls between one plane of existence and another: when sacrificial victims were cremated, he took them from this world to their final homes.

The Aztec cycle of time renewed itself every fifty-four years, and people believed that it was essential, at each turn of this all-but 'century', to renew the compact between gods and mortals. Xiutecuhtli was the centre of this ritual. Every fire in the kingdom was put out, his priests ceremonially lit new fire and distributed it to the people, and the world was safe again.

XOCHIPILI
Americas (Central)

Xochipili ('flower lord'), in Aztec myth, was the god of flowers, **music** and dancing, the male equivalent of **Xochiquetzal**. In particular, he guarded the humming-bird souls of dead warriors. He was spirit personified, and was shown in portraits as red and skinless – his flayed condition symbolizing his indifference to things of the flesh.

One of the oldest of all Aztec gods, Xochipili was later – and somewhat surprisingly – subsumed into the cult of the war-god **Huitzilopochtli**.

»+ farming

XOCHIQUETZAL
Americas (Central)

Xochiquetzal ('flower feather'), in Aztec myth, was the goddess of flowers, fruit and **music**, the female equivalent of **Xochipili**. Just as he represented pure spirit, so she represented pure body, and was shown as a buxom, beautiful and serene young woman, mother of all. She was, however, also a war-goddess, and ruled a paradise reserved for soldiers dead in battle and women who died giving birth to boys (that is, sacrificed their own lives to provide future warriors).

»+ beauty, farming, Idun

XÓLOTL
Americas (Central)

Xólotl ('animal'), in Aztec myth, was a deformed dog: his face pointed forwards but his feet ran backwards. He was the Evening Star, and every night he snatched the **Sun** and dragged it to the world of darkness. In some accounts, he created the human race by bringing our ancestors up from the spirit-world and giving them **fire**. But his contradictory nature (symbolized by his shape) meant that he hated his own **creation**, and spent his life bringing us bad luck. Praying to him was problematical, since the way he heard and reacted to each prayer depended on which way his ears were pointing – and until the prayer was finished and its effects were known, who knew?

⫸ **animal-gods**

YACATECUHTLI
Americas (Central)

Yacatecuhtli ('lord nose'), in Aztec myth, was the god of merchants. His power resided in a bundle of twigs which he carried everywhere, and this was also the symbol of the secret society of his worshippers. He was the hub of a mystery-cult, a mercantile freemasonry about whose practices and influence no information – including the reason for Yacatecuhtli's name – now survives.
≫→ **mysteries**

YAHWEH
Asia (West)

Yahweh, in Judaic belief, is the secret name of God, represented by the four letters YHVH and spoken only by the High Priest once a year in the Holy of Holies in the Temple at Jerusalem. Some scholars associate the name with an ancient volcano-god (Jahu), others with the Hebrew verb to be (so that it means 'Is'). It appears in short form as Yah (for example in the phrase Halle-lujah, 'Praise be to Yah'), and its non-Hebrew, perverted form Jehovah led some medieval churchmen to link it, quite wrongly, with Jove (that is **Jupiter** or **Zeus**).

Yahweh, as he survives, belongs entirely to the religions of Judaism and Christianity, and has no place in myth. But the Bible offers glimpses of possible mythic derivations or parallels. He is creative energy; he is protective of his **immortality** and refuses to share it with mortals. He is light, enemy of darkness. He sends a **flood** to wipe human evil from the world. As ultimate arbiter of good and evil, he will judge the universe at the end of time.
≫→ **supreme deity**

Faust tormented with doubts (*19th-century engraving*)

YAKSHAS: see Rakshasas and Yakshas

YALUNGUR
Australia

Yalungur ('eagle-hawk'), in the myths of the Wumunkan people of Cape York Peninsula in North Eastern Australia, was one of the supernatural beings who made the world during the Dream Time. His particular distinction was that he originated the female sex and **childbirth**. Another being, Gidja, lusted after him. To make intercourse easier, Gidja cut off Yalungur's penis, and to make Yalungur pregnant he made a wooden doll and stuffed it inside the wound. Yalungur quickened the doll to life and expelled it from the wound – and so the vagina, and childbirth, were created. As for Gidja, the other Dream Time beings were so disgusted with his behaviour that they tried to kill him; he escaped into the sky and became the **Moon**.

YAMA
India

Yama ('restrainer'), in the Vedic myths of the Aryans who invaded India in the seventeenth century BCE, was the son of **Vivasvat** and **Saranyu**. His **twin**, their daughter, was Yami, and she and Yama were the first beings in the world to experience mortality. When Yama died, he was granted dominion over the **Underworld**, made judge of the Dead and given the task of snatching the souls of the dead from their bodies and dragging them to the Underworld.

Yama is often shown as a black buffalo, or as a crowned king riding a black buffalo. He carries a noose to gather human souls, and a mace to subdue any who resist.

YAMASACHI
Asia (East)

Yamasachi, or Hikohohodemi, son of **Ninigi** and Konohana in Japanese myth, was a hunter-god who used magic arrows to kill his prey. His brother, the fisherman Umisachi, or Hosuseri, used a magic hook. Curious to see what fishing was like, Yamasachi asked Umisachi to exchange weapons – and as soon as he tried fishing, he lost his brother's hook. He offered him a thousand more, made from his own sword, but Umisachi refused. Yamasachi went to ask the sea god Owatatsumi for advice, and the hook was found at last in an enormous fish. But during the three mortal years it took to find it, Yamasachi fell in love with Owatatsumi's daughter Toyotama, and when he returned to land he took her with him. She said that she was pregnant, that she would have to return to her original form to bear her child, and that Yamasachi was not to watch. As he had done earlier, when he wanted to try his brother's fishing magic, he let curiosity overrule common sense, and was horrified to see Toyotama change into a monstrous crocodile to bear her child. He shouted in alarm, and she was so embarrassed that she slithered back into the sea and disappeared. Yamasachi brought up the boy, half god, half **sea-monster**, and when the young man was old enough he married

Tamayori, his mother's sister. The eldest of their four children was Jimmu, founder of the Japanese Imperial dynasty.

≫→ archers

YAMBE–AKKA
Europe (North)

Yambe-akka ('old woman of the dead'), in Lapp myth, was the goddess of the **Underworld**. Her kingdom was a vast ice-realm under the mortal world, and its entrances were where rivers flowed into the frozen Arctic Ocean. In some accounts Yambe-akka supported the mortal world on her own upheld hands, and **earthquakes** happened when old age made her arms tremble.

YANAULUHA
Americas (North)

Yanauluha, in the myths of the Zuñi people of the Southwestern US pueblos, led human beings from the darkness of the **Underworld** to the surface of the Earth. They were misshapen creatures, part termite, part snake, part owl, part frog, and he improved their appearance and their skills (by teaching them **farming**, weaving, dancing and the other skills of **civilization**) until they became tall, elegant and confident, replicas of gods.

YAO
Asia (East)

Yao, or Di Yao ('Emperor Yao') or Dao Dung Shi ('lord of Dao and Dung'), was the fourth of the **Five Emperors** under whose rule the world moved from barbarism to **civilization**. When he inherited the throne the Imperial family lived in a grass-roofed hut and fed on porridge, a tradition of austerity begun by Yao's ancestor **Huang Di**, and Yao continued it throughout his long reign of seventy years. His time on the throne was marked by a series of quarrels with storm-gods and **water-monsters**: **Fei Lian** the storm-demon (formerly Huang Di's own son), Ho Po the river-lord and **Gong Gong** spirit of water. Yao employed the famous archer **Yi** to deal with the first two, but was unable to end the **flood** brought by Gong Gong – a job finished long after his reign by **Yu** son of Kun.

Yao ruled for seventy years, and during that time corruption grew so bad that he could trust no one, not even his own sons. Since one of high rank could be trusted to succeed him, Yao searched the kingdom for the most honest and dutiful man he could find. That man was **Shun**, the most upright individual who ever lived, and Yao married him to his daughter, made him his heir and abdicated in his favour, living on in retirement for another dozen years.

The mythical Yao was transformed in later times into the 'first historical Emperor', and his dates were given as 2357-2255 BCE. Archaeologists have discovered enormous drainage-schemes and patterns of irrigation from this period: possibly the origin of the myths of his battles against water-gods. There also survives a text, Edicts of the Emperor Yao, which among other things claims that he set up the first astronomical observatory ever known, and invented the calendar.

YARILO
Europe (East)

Yarilo (derived from *yary*, 'passionate'), or Erilo, god of **sex** in Slavic myth, supervised not only lust in living creatures but also the ground's eagerness to split open and receive seed in spring. He was a handsome youth who rode a white horse. In many areas, Yarilo festivals were held well into modern times: at the spring festival a beautiful girl was crowned with wild flowers as his queen, and after the harvest his straw image was burned during an orgy of eating, drinking and sex, and the ashes were strewn on the fields to ensure next year's crops.

≫→ fertility, Kama, Soido

YASHODHARA
India

Yashodhara, in Buddhist myth and legend, was the wife of Prince **Siddhartha**, the future **Buddha**. There are two accounts of how he won her. In one, he won a contest against his childhood companion and enemy **Devadatta**, and she was the prize. In another, Siddhartha's father brought 500 princesses together, and Siddhartha gave each of them a jewel – until he reached the last, Yashodhara, and gave her his ring as a sign of betrothal.

Yashodhara lived happily as Siddhartha's wife for years, and bore him a son. But there was no place for her in Siddhartha's new life as Buddha, and when he renounced the world he also bade farewell to his beloved wife and son, slipping out of the palace while they slept. At first, when Yashodhara discovered what had happened, she was heart-broken. But then she shaved her head, entered a monastery, and served her husband with joy and devotion as a nun until the day she died.

YASODA
India

Yasoda, in Hindu myth, was the wife (or queen) of the cowherd (king) **Nanda**. When **Krishna** was in danger from the **demon**-king **Kansa**, he was smuggled out of Kansa's dungeon to Yasoda, who brought him up as her foster-son. Her own newborn baby was smuggled back to the dungeon in Krishna's place (see **Deva**).

YEN LO
Asia (East)

Yen Lo, in Chinese myth, was originally King of the Dead. His kingdom was divided into several smaller courts – some say four, some ten, some fourteen – each with its own ruler and its own allotted area of expertise in punishment. Yen Lo was the supreme judge, against whose decisions there was no appeal. But the other rulers grumbled that he was too lenient, and when he refused to punish Monkey for coming to Hell and stealing the Scroll of Past Judgements (an essential list of precedents), they rebelled against him and reduced his privileges. He retained jurisdiction only over those who in mortal life had been sexually promiscuous, butchers or cruel to animals.

≫→ Underworld

YGGDRASIL
Europe (North)

Yggdrasil ('ash-tree horse of Ygg'), in Nordic myth, was a giant ash-tree, the hub and support of the universe. It got its name when Ygg (**Odin**) hung himself for nine days and nights on it, 'riding' it in order to learn all the secrets of **creation**. Yggdrasil had three roots. The longest grew from the icy well of Hvergelmir in **Niflheim** home of the Dead, where it was perpetually gnawed by **Nidhogg** the dragon, trying to kill it. The second grew from **Midgard**, where it drew nourishment from the Well of **Mimir**, source of all wisdom. The third grew from the well of Urd in Asgard, where the three **Norns** watered it and plastered it with clay to heal the wounds made by Nidhogg far below.

On Yggdrasil's topmost branch sat Vithofnir, the rooster whose crowing was to announce the beginning of **Ragnarök**, the end of this cycle of the universe. An eagle nested in the tree, and spent its days trying to distract Nidhogg the dragon from its task of destroying the tree; the squirrel Ratatosk scurried endlessly up and down Yggdrasil's branches and trunk, carrying insults between the combatants. Every morning, Yggdrasil's trunk exuded dew which four deer licked and changed into golden mead for the warriors feasting in **Valhalla**. Inside the trunk were the seeds of two human beings. They were to lie dormant until Ragnarök, when Yggdrasil would survive and they would grow into the ancestors of a new race of mortals, ready to tenant the world and begin the human race anew.

YI
Asia (East)

Yi ('archer'), the Sun-god in Chinese myth, was originally a mortal soldier, a bowman so expert that he was nicknamed Shen Yi ('divine archer'). In some accounts, he visited the palace of Xi Wang Mu, goddess of the air, and she gave him one of the Peaches of **Immortality**. This was stolen from him by Heng-O, sister of the god of the Yellow River, who soared to the **sky** and hid from him in the **Moon**. Yi travelled the Earth looking for her, riding the wind and feeding on flowers; eventually he was carried back to Xi Wang Mu's palace, and her husband Dong Wang Gong, lord of destiny, took pity on him, granted him immortality and gave him the **Sun** (or rather Suns) to rule.

At first, Yi ruled ten separate Suns. But when the Emperor **Yao** chose **Shun** as his successor instead of his own children, the ten Suns were so outraged that they all tried to appear in the sky at the same moment, which would have destroyed the Earth and everything on it. Yi shot dead nine of the birds which lived in the Suns, and himself took up residence in the tenth: the Sun we know today. He forged its light into unerring arrows, and used them to benefit mortals. When the wind-lord **Fei Lian**, disgraced son of **Huang Di**, gusted in terrible storms across the world, Yi told mortals to make an enormous windbreak from cloth anchored with stones, and when the winds bounced off it he rode on their wings to Fei Lian's mountain-top castle, weakened Fei Lian first by shooting a hole in the sack which contained all the winds and then by hamstringing him with a second arrow, and forced him to surrender. When Ho Po, **Heng O**'s brother and lord of the Yellow River, rose from his bed in floods and storms, Yi shot him in the knee and sent him limping back to his underwater lair. In some accounts, he then married Ho Po's wife Fufei, goddess of the river Lo; in others, he settled his differences with Heng O and married her.

»+ **archers**

YIMA
Asia (West)

Yima, in ancient Iranian myth, was the first human being. To begin with, his reign on Earth was a Golden Age. Humans shared the gods' **immortality** and powers, and drove out **demons**, conquered darkness and ruled the storms. But Yima spoiled it by killing flesh, and offering the meat of sacrifice not only to **Ahura Mazda** but to other gods as well – and Ahura Mazda punished him by removing his and his descendants' **immortality**. To prove how fragile human life had become, he sent Winter to tear the world to pieces – and has renewed it every year since then. Before the first storm, he told Yima to build an underground shelter, store in it the finest male and female examples of each species of animal and plant on Earth, and wait with them until the time came to restock the world and restore the Golden Age. Somewhere, the myth ends, Yima is still waiting; our human time will come.

YMIR
Europe (North)

Ymir ('two-in-one'), in Nordic myth, was the **giant** formed at the beginning of **creation**, when glaciers from the ice-kingdom **Niflheim** spread out across the void and were thawed by flames from the fire-kingdom **Muspell**. As Ymir's name implies, it was neither male nor female but both at once, and had the power to generate life spontaneously. As Ymir slept, it sweated, and giants were born from the sweat: a male and a female from Ymir's left armpit, and another male where Ymir's thighs touched as it slept.

Ymir's offspring began to mate with one another, spawning a race of ice-giants. But in the meantime a rival race had been created from ice: first the cow **Audumla**, then **Buri**, the first human, then **Bor** his son and Bor's sons **Odin**, **Vili** and **Ve**. These last three attacked the sleeping Ymir, and killed it. Ymir's blood was ice-water: it gushed from the giant's wounds in a flood which drowned all the frost-giants but two (**Bergelmir** and his wife), and bubbled and swirled in the void like an icy ocean. Into the middle of this ocean Odin, Vili and Ve carried Ymir's corpse. They broke it up to make the world. Ymir's flesh made earth, its bones made mountains, its teeth made boulders and its hair made trees. Its skull made the heavens, its brains made clouds, and the brothers set sparks from Muspell in them to make **Sun**, **Moon** and stars.

The brothers gathered the ocean of Ymir's blood into a fathomless, boundless **sea**, girding their creation like a belt. They called their creation **Midgard**, ('middle land'): that is, the one between Muspell and Niflheim. They built themselves a huge citadel, Asgard, and fortified it with a hedge made from Ymir's eyebrows. And finally, seeing maggots swarming in the remaining fragments of the earth-giant's corpse, they made them into dwarfs, burying them deep in the caves and crevices of their giant parent.

*Local details notwithstanding, the story of Ymir being dismembered to create the world is almost exactly paralleled in the Indian myth of **Purusha** – so much so that some scholars think that they have a common source.*

≫→ Ask and Embla

YO: *see* In and Yo

YOMI
Asia (East)

Yomi (short for Yomitsukumi, 'heart of night' or 'gloom-land'), the **Underworld** in Japanese myth, was originally no more than a mirror-image of the world of light, without inhabitants or character. But when **Izanami**, scorched to death giving birth to the fire-god **Kagutsuchi**, went to hide in Yomi, her body rotted and the maggots formed into **demon**-hordes, which lived on in the Underworld to torment the Dead.

In Japanese Buddhist myth, Yomi was ruled by Emma-O (the Japanese form of **Yama**). He lived in a castle crafted from all the jewels and precious metals found underground, and judged the Dead.

Their souls were fetched by demons in fiery chariots, or transported once a year by ship across the Sea of Darkness. In the darkness of the Underworld, the last embers of their life-force from the world of light above made them glow like fireflies. Emma-O judged the men, and his sister judged the women. The innocent were dispatched to the Upper World in a new incarnation, and the wicked were punished before being allowed to return to life. The punishments, overseen by Emma-O's **demon**-army of eighteen generals and 80,000 green-skinned or red-skinned warriors, ranged from physical torment (for example being boiled in molten metal or used for target-practice by demons) to the psychological agony of loneliness, wandering Yomi's barren plains and tunnels until they had expiated their crimes. These punishments were ordained by **Buddha**, and could not be changed or evaded except by those blessed with the intercession of Kannon (Japanese version of **Guan Yin**), goddess of mercy.

Although Yomi was a land of darkness, artists used their licence to show it as a kind of Imperial palace, whose chambers, corridors and gardens teemed with the Dead. In the central judgement-room, Emma-O sat on his throne, his advisers on stools beside him and his ink-brushes and scrolls on a desk in front of him. The Dead were paraded with planks round their necks on which their crimes were written. Some pleaded their cases before lesser demons before being allowed to make their last appeals to Emma-O; others, less hopeful, *surrendered immediately to their demon-tormentors. Other paintings showed the tunnels, gardens and barren landscapes of Yomi, tenanted by demons and the Dead, and full of every kind of torment: hair-pulling and toenail-pulling for minor offenders, scourging with chains or **snakes** for middle-rank sinners, and mutilation or boiling for the guiltiest.*

YSEULT: *see* Tristram and Yseult

YU
Asia (East)

Yu, in Chinese myth, was the son of Lord Kun, the minister of the Emperor **Yao** who had spent nine years ineffectively trying to control **floods** which were devastating China. In some accounts Yu was born directly from his father's corpse, cut open three years after the old man's death – he soared out as a dragon. In others his mother saw a meteor, swallowed a pearl and in due course gave birth to Yu in the normal way.

Kun had been executed on the orders of **Huang Di**, for going to **Heaven** and trying to steal a handful of magic Swelling Earth (Huang Di's own possession) to soak up the floodwaters. In some accounts, Yu, ordered by Emperor **Shun** to finish his father's work, went himself to Heaven, asked Huang Di politely for some Swelling Earth and used it to make mountains and river-channels which controlled the water. In others, Huang Di (or even, in some versions, **Fu Xi**) was so impressed with Yu's good manners that he not only showed him the Nine-fold Plan which controlled the entire universe, but also

taught him how to modify it to reorganize the movement of water over land.

In the third version of Yu's control of the waters, he discovered something that his father had never known: namely, that floods were caused by malicious water-spirits, evil children of the water-god **Gong Gong**, and that the way to end them was to kill the **monsters**, one by one. Using his shape-changing powers, Yu travelled the length and breadth of the world, battling monsters, cutting water-channels, making islands and marshes for Gong Gong's water-creatures and plains, forests and arable land for animals and humans. To fight water-**snakes** he made himself into a dragon. To tunnel through mountains he made himself into a bear, gouging out rock with his forepaws. To climb the peaks he became an eagle. To clear the undergrowth he became a **fire**.

The work of controlling the water took thirteen years, and the continual shape-changing exhausted Yu's mortal body. When he left home to begin the work he was a virile young man, when he came back he was a dotard. After Shun's death he took the throne, but was so worn out that he ruled for only eight years before he died.

*Some scholars claim that this myth was invented to explain real water-engineering, huge works from the third millennium BCE, including a 350km canal-and-tunnel system through the Wu Shan **mountains** which still bears Yu's name. In later times Yu was claimed as a historical figure, founder of the Xia dynasty, and the dates of his reign were given as 2205-2197 BCE. In historical accounts of his reign, he was said to have invented not only **farming** and fishing –*

skills attributed to all early Emperors – but also the first-ever systems for distribution and marketing, which in turn necessitated inventing cities. Myth stories credit him with inventions of a more tangible kind, designed to ease his travels round the country subduing monsters: the first wheeled carriage, the first boat and a pair of magic crampons which helped him walk up vertical mountainsides.

≫→ civilization, crafts, shape-changers

YUDHISHTHIRA
India

Yudhishthira, in Hindu myth, was the son of the god **Dharma** and the mortal queen **Kunti**, wife of King **Pandu** of **Bharata**. As the eldest of five brothers, he expected in due course to succeed to his father's throne, but was robbed of it by his cousin **Duryodhana**, eldest of the **Kaurava** brothers, who first tried to kill Yudhishthira and his brothers, the **Pandavas**, by burning their palace, then won the kingdom from Yudhishthira by cheating in a game of dice.

The battle for Bharata. A huge war followed. Gods and other powers for good in the universe supported the Pandavas; **demons** and other powers for evil supported the Kauravas. There was heroism on both sides, but there was also deceit – as when Yudhishthira half-lied to persuade the Kaurava commander **Drona** that his beloved son was dead. Accordingly, although the Pandavas won and Yudhishthira was restored to his throne, he felt morally compromised. As the time approached for him to leave the mortal world, he led his

brothers and their wife **Draupadi** on pilgrimage to **Indra**'s **Heaven** on Mount **Meru**. All died on the journey except Yudhishthira – and when he reached Mount Meru he was horrified to find there the spirits not of his friends and relatives but of his dead enemies the Kauravas.

Yudhishthira in Hell and Heaven. The gods next carried Yudhishthira to the **Underworld**, where he picked his way through pools of blood and piles of severed limbs from evildoers paying for their crimes in mortal life. He saw the tortures and heard the screams – and suddenly recognized the voices of his brothers and their wife. He promised to stay and help them, and at once the scene vanished like smoke before his eyes. It had been a vision sent by the gods. In the Ganges, he washed his mortality away, and so was able at last to enter Indra's Heaven, where he found his brothers, their wife, his followers and all his former enemies at peace in the radiance of the gods.

≫→ Arjuna, Bhima, heroes, *Mahabharata*

YU HUANG
Asia (East)

Yu Huang or Yu Di, short for Yu Huang Shang Di ('supreme jade Emperor'), in Chinese myth, was the Daoist version of the older figure **Shang Di**, supreme ruler of the universe. As a baby, he was given by the gods to human foster-parents, the Emperor Jing Te and his queen Pao Yu, and grew up as a prince before renouncing the world's pomp and spending his time helping the poor and sick. When his time on Earth ended he became supreme Emperor of the Daoist **Heaven**.

Yu Huang was created and given a mythology in the eleventh century CE, when the Emperor Zhen Tsong began ceremonies in his honour and declared him head of the Daoist pantheon. In the twelfth century Tsong's descendant Hui built temples to Yu Huang throughout the empire, and merged his worship with that of the older Shang Di, so that Yu Di (as he became popularly known) became the only supreme being.
≫→ supreme deity

YUN TUN: *see* Yu Zu and Yun Tun

YURIWAKA
Asia (East)

Yuriwaka, a warrior-prince in Japanese myth, owned a quiverful of magic arrows and an iron bow which only he could draw. Two of his lieutenants, Jiro and Taro, were jealous of him, and one day when they were all sailing back from a successful conquest and Yuriwaka fell asleep, they marooned him on a desert island, stole his bow and arrows and sailed home to tell his wife that he was dead. Taro began pestering her to marry him, and she held him at bay only by prolonging the period of mourning for her lost husband. After several years of this stalemate, Yuriwaka was rescued from his island by passing sailors, hurried home and entered his palace, disguised as a servant, on the very day when the wedding between his wife and Taro was announced. Foolishly, Taro began the proceedings with an archery competition – and Yuriwaka, still disguised, asked to be allowed to try the iron bow and magic arrows, successfully strung the bow and shot Taro dead.

*This adaptation of the story of **Odysseus** reached Japan during one of the brief periods when Japan opened up to the West in the sixteenth century CE. Although a late entry to the canon of Japanese myth, it has remained one of the most popular, inspiring art (paintings, cartoons and comic strips), plays and puppet shows, in many of which Yuriwaka also fights **giants**, **monsters** and **demons** in true Odyssean style.*
≫→ archers, heroes

YU ZU AND YUN TUN
Asia (East)

Yu Zu and Yun Tun, in Chinese myth, were two of the most important of a large contingent of weather-gods. Yu Zu carried the **rain** in a pot and flicked it over the Earth with the end of his sword. Yun Tun, a small boy, piled clouds in the sky like a mortal child playing with snowballs.

Zeus (*19th-century engraving, after an ancient Greek vase painting*)

ZAMBA

Africa

Zamba, creator-god of the Yaunde people of the Cameroons, made the Earth
and all its creatures except human
beings. He left that job to his four
sons, Ngi (gorilla) the strong, N'Kokon
(mantis) the wise, Otukut (lizard) the
fool and Wo (chimpanzee) the curious
– and each made human beings in his
own image, which is why we are the
way we are.

≫→ **creation**

ZANAHARY

Africa

Zanahary, in Madagascan myth, was
two gods in one: Light-Zanahary
('him above') and his mirror-image
Dark-Zanahary ('him below'). Light-
Zanahary was content with his exis-

tence, but Dark-Zanahary grew bored
and amused himself by making dolls
from clay, perfect in every respect
except that they were lifeless. He offered to trade some of them with Light-
Zanahary in exchange for the light of
life. Light-Zanahary looked at the dolls,
and was filled with a new emotion: lust.
He asked for some of the females, and
Dark-Zanahary promised. Light-Zanahary sent down the light of life, a share
in his own brightness. But Dark-Zanahary cheated him, sending him first a
basket of fish (pretending they were
women) and then refusing to part with
any of the real females. The two gods
never spoke to each other again.
Light-Zanahary sat sulking in his
Sky-kingdom and Dark-Zanahary
pranced about on the Earth below,
mocking him and amusing himself
by sending illness, pain and death
to torment the living dolls.

*In another version of this myth, there was originally only one Zanahary, the creator Light. He made the Earth but left it desert. But when he returned to **Heaven** some of his brightness remained below, and it fertilized the ground until a being formed itself: Ratovoantany ('self-maker'). Ratovoantany made doll-creatures, in the shapes of humans and animals, but could not give them life. Zanahary offered to animate the creatures if he could take them all back to Heaven, but Ratovoantany refused and after some argument Zanahary agreed to lend the creatures life for a short time on Earth, if he could take it back to Heaven on the day they died. This is why our spirits leave our bodies on death: they are going to spend eternity with Zanahary, while our bodies return to the clay from which Ratovoantany first made them.*

≫→ light and dark

ZEPHYRUS
Europe (South)

Zephyrus (Zephyros; Latin Favonius) was the son of Astraeus and the Dawn-goddess **Eos**. He was the West Wind, and his brothers were **Boreas** the North Wind, Notus the South Wind and Apheliotes (Latin Eurus or Vulturnus) the East Wind. As a young wind, Zephyrus was as tempestuous and piratical as his brother Boreas. He snatched whatever he fancied, answering to no one. But after he fell in love with **Apollo**'s darling **Hyacinthus**, and his attempts to snatch a kiss ended in the boy's death, Zephyrus completely changed his character. He became soft and gentle, and devoted his time to filling ships' sails and caressing the earth with his warm breath, bringing **fertility**. He married

the **rainbow**-goddess **Iris** (or, some say, the harvest-goddess **Flora**), and had many children, including a family of cherubic windlets (the Zephyrs) and the harvest-spirit Carpus, whose task each year was to put the bloom on fruit as it ripened.

ZETHUS: *see* Amphion and Zethus

ZEUS
Europe (South)

Zeus and Cronus. Zeus ('shining **sky**'; Latin **Jupiter**), in Greek myth, was the youngest child of **Cronus** and **Rhea**. His father had eaten his five elder siblings (**Demeter**, **Hades**, **Hera**, Hestia and **Poseidon**) as soon as they were born, and to prevent this happening to Zeus, Rhea gave him to **mountain-nymphs** to bring up secretly in Crete, and handed Cronus a stone wrapped in baby-clothes. On Crete, Zeus grew up in the Dictean Cave, fostered by the mountain-spirit Amalthea (half goddess, half goat; mother of Zeus' foster-brother, the god **Pan**) and taught martial skills by the Curetes, a band of shaven-headed warrior-spirits.

As soon as Zeus was fully-grown, he went to serve as Cronus' cupbearer. He gave his father a drink of **nectar** mixed with emetic herbs, and Cronus vomited up Zeus' brothers and sisters, now full-grown gods. At once there was war in the universe, the gods (led by Zeus) battling the **Titans** (led by Cronus). It ended when the giant children of **Gaia** (**Mother Earth**), came to help the gods. The **Cyclopes** made invincible weapons – a helmet of invisibility for Hades, an earth-shaking trident for Poseidon, and for Zeus the most powerful of all, the thunderbolt – and the **Hundred-handed Giants** stormed the Titans' citadel on Mount Othrys.

The three kingdoms. As soon as the Titans were defeated and banished, Zeus and his siblings met to decide who should rule the universe. Two of them, Hestia and Demeter, were gentle and unambitious, and settled on Earth, content to accept whatever came their way. The three brothers cast lots for kingdoms, and Zeus won the sky, Poseidon the sea and Hades the Underworld; the Earth was common territory, to be enjoyed by all.

Zeus and Hera. This division left Hera unsatisfied. Lacking invincible weapons to match those of her brothers, she retreated to Mount Thornax, a mist-ridden wilderness where she sat and sulked. She saw no other living being, until one day she found in the rain a bedraggled cuckoo, took pity on it and warmed it in her bosom – whereupon it changed into Zeus and mated with her. Zeus persuaded Hera to become his consort, sharing rule of the sky-kingdom. They spent their wedding-night on the island of Samos – a single night to gods, three hundred years to mortals – and then set up court on Mount **Olympus**.

Zeus' children. Zeus and Hera had children: **Ares**, **Eris**, **Hebe**, **Hephaestus**, **Ilythia** and others. But Zeus was not satisfied with a single partner. He mated with Titans, birds, animals, nymphs, clouds and running water; when **Prometheus** created human beings, and persuaded Zeus to let them survive, he began mating with mortal women too. His offspring began to people the

universe. Some (**Apollo**, **Artemis**, **Hermes**) were admitted at once to full Olympian godhead; others (**Dionysus**, **Heracles**) had to wait until the other gods were prepared to accept them; others again (the **Muses**, the Seasons) remained on Earth.

Revolts against Zeus. Zeus' affairs, together with the memory of the trick he'd played on Mount Thornax, kept Hera furious with resentment. But Zeus alone knew how to wield thunderbolts, and they made him invincible. He made laws for the universe, fixed the stars' courses in the sky and the order of the seasons, and proclaimed the future in omens and oracles. The only times Hera could master him were when she borrowed **Aphrodite**'s girdle of desire (a belt that made the wearer irresistible) and charmed him into making love. In the end she, Apollo and Poseidon began plotting to overthrow him. In order to catch him before he had time to snatch up a thunderbolt, they crept up while he was sleeping, and tied him to his bed with ropes made from the hides of the cattle of the **Sun** and therefore unbreakable, even by an immortal god. They tied a hundred knots; Zeus was helpless.

Hera, Apollo and Poseidon began squabbling about how to divide his power. Earth and **Heaven** shook with the echoes of their rage. Terrified of another civil war, like the one which had raged between gods and Titans, the ocean-nymph **Thetis** crept down to the **Underworld** and freed the **Hundred-handed Giant Briareus**, who swarmed up to Olympus, untied the knots and set Zeus free. Zeus hung Hera from the roof

683

of the sky on golden chains, weighting her ankles with anvils. Then he took his thunderbolt and forced every god in Olympus to kneel before him and swear eternal allegiance. He punished Apollo and Poseidon by making them serve one year as slaves to a mortal (King **Laomedon** of Troy). He cut Hera down, forced her to grovel at his feet and to accept, ever afterwards, subordinate status, female giving way to the male.

Gaia took advantage of the trouble on Olympus to stir the **Earthborn Giants** to revolt against the gods. The giants built a stonepile and climbed up it to attack Olympus, and the gods had to abandon their squabbles and defend themselves. There was a pitched battle, and the giants were defeated by Zeus' half-mortal son **Heracles** – who was later rewarded with full **immortality** and godhead. Mother Earth then sent her last and most hideous offspring, **Typhon**, to attack the gods – and when Zeus defeated him at last (thanks to cunning rather than brute strength), the rest of the gods, and all other beings, accepted his royal authority at last.

Zeus as supreme ruler. Once Zeus' throne was secure, he retreated from active involvement in the affairs of the universe. He was the supreme authority, the first and last decider against whom there was no appeal, and he used thunderbolts only sparingly to warn or punish. He left the running of the universe to the enormous family of gods and goddesses (many of whom were his own offspring), and spent his time supervising their councils and adjudicating their frequent quarrels and arguments. To Hera's irritation, he never abandoned his taste for promiscuous **sex**, and his chief diversion was visiting the Earth, choosing a new partner and taking on some appropriate disguise to enjoy sex with her.

Although Zeus is omnipresent in ancient literature, he is sparsely represented in art. The most famous ancient sculpture to show him in majesty was a 13-metre-high statue at Olympia, one of the seven Wonders of the World, and it was widely available in small copies (some of which may have originated as souvenirs sold at the Olympic Games). His amours were more often shown, in paintings and carvings – but he is there a bull, swan or shower of gold rather than a god. Perhaps the problem was representing daylight as a living thing – a mirror-image of the tabu on showing Hades, darkness and invisibility made immanent. (The Romans had no such problem with Jupiter: he was a prince enthroned, dressed in the clothes and carrying the regalia of a Roman ruler, proud and unequivocal.) In Delphi, the holiest object in Apollo's shrine was a phallic, pillar-shaped stone, the omphalos or 'navel'. It was said to be the stone which Rhea gave Cronus to eat instead of baby Zeus; when the adult Zeus forced his father to regurgitate his swallowed children, he hurled the stone down to Earth and it landed in the exact centre of the world, in the shrine at Delphi. Apollo's priestess sat on this stone to prophesy, and Apollo came down from Heaven and entered her.

➤➤→ **justice and universal order, shape-changers, supreme deity**

ZHI NU: *see* Qian Niu and Zhi Nu

ZHUAN HU
Asia (East)

Zhuan Hu, second of the **Five Emperors** in Chinese myth, came to power after a seven-year interregnum when **Huang Di** left Earth for **Heaven**. When he took the throne, Heaven and Earth were still accessible to one another. Heaven was propped above Earth on nine pillars (or, some say, on the mountains formed from the body and bones of the primordial giant **Pan Gu**). In Huang Di's reign relations between gods and mortals had been good-mannered and harmonious, but during the interregnum his teachings about how mortals should address gods and vice versa had become perverted to the point where some of the more confused gods were even offering sacrifices to mortals. Zhuan Hu ended this. He gave one of his sons, Chong, the job of organizing the gods into a separate kingdom and a recognizable hierarchy, and told his other son, Li, to do the same for mortals. Chong ruled the South and Li the North, and ever afterwards relationships between the two worlds observed established rules of diplomatic and religious precedent.

In some accounts, Zhuan Hu is the same person as **Shun**, the fifth of the Five Emperors.

ZORYA
Europe (East)

Zorya, in Slavic myth, was originally three goddesses, sisters. Morning Zorya opened the gates of the **Sun**'s palace each day to let him ride out across the sky, Evening Zorya opened them in the evening to welcome him home, and Midnight Zorya oversaw the darkness of night. The sisters also had charge of the dog tied to the Little Bear (or in some accounts, the Great Bear): if it ever broke loose, it would create havoc in the universe. Of the three sisters, the most beautiful and important was Morning Zorya, wife of the war god **Pyerun**. When he rode out to battle she armed herself and went with him, letting her veil down to protect favoured human warriors. In the course of time her worship eclipsed that of her sisters, so that Zorya (originally 'light') came to mean just 'Dawn'.

ZOSIM
Europe (East)

Zosim, god of bees in Slavic myth, was named after their buzzing. He was also the god of mead, and when humans drank enough of it he entered their throats and taught them bawdy songs.
»→ **Aristaeus, farming**

ZURVAN AKARANA
Asia (West)

Zurvan Akarana ('infinite time'), in Iranian myth, was the primordial being which existed before existence. It was both male and female, and inseminated itself. **Twins** grew in its womb: **Ahriman**, lord of darkness, and **Ahura Mazda**, lord of light. In the endless eons of its pregnancy, Zurvan Akarana idly wondered which twin would be greatest, and murmured 'The firstborn' – whereupon Ahriman ripped open the womb and shouldered his way out ahead of Ahura Mazda. Hastily, Zurvan Akarana finished its thought – 'for a thousand thousand years, until he is destroyed' – and the world has been waiting for this moment, the final destruction of evil, ever since.

⟫→ creation

ZVEZDA DENNITSA: see Vechernyaya Zvezda and Zvezda Dennitsa

INDEX

Main entries are shown in bold type.

Eschenbach, Wolfram von 480
Eset 59
Eshu **183**
Esia 360
Estsanatlehi **184**, 623
Esus 595
Eteocles 47, 131, **184**, 441, 547
Ethlin 85, 363
Etna, Mt 135, 626, 627
Euippe 153
Eumaeus 439
Eumenides 203, 204 *see also* Furies
Euneus 274
Euphrates River 6, 7, 177, 375, 387
Euphrosyne 225
Euripides 5, 10, 18, 44, 50, 111, 155, 174,
    245, 249, 256, 294, 295, 383, 386, 440,
    442, 452, 479, 502, 507, 600
Europa **184**, 524
Eurotas River 351
Euryale 225 *see also* Gorgons
Euryalus (Argonaut) 53
Euryalus (son of Erippe) 440, 478
Euryalus (Trojan) 423
Eurydice 55, 452
Eurynome **185**, 251
Eurystheus 29, 71, 75, 114, **185**, 253,
    254, 272, 328, 343
Eurytion 217, 488
Eurytus 165, 255, 488
Euterpe 401 *see also* Muses
Evander **186**
Eve **7**, 233, 533, 573
Evening Star 296, 314, 668
Everus 611
evil 9, 37, 686
evil, deities of 22, 147
Evnissyen 98
examinations, god of 337
Excalibur **186**, 398, 653
eye of Horus 265
    of Ra 515, 544
eyes 150, 168, 348, 553

Fa 184
Fa'ahotu 66, 585
Fafnir **189**, 524, 561

Falkenberg, Willem 199
Falstaff 114
families, god of 549
famine 147, 338, 354
Fan Guei **189**
Fand 371
Farbauti 359
farming 55, 127, **190**, 215, 308, 373,
    376, 400, 450, 465, 471-2, 498, 511,
    552, 593, 611, 634, 636, 660
farming, deities of 78, 145, 200, 371-2,
    498, 522, 541, 574, 592
farting 488, 649
fate 190, 428
fate, deities of 26, 428
Fates 24, 167, **190**, 236, 260, 398, 597, 626
Father Sky 305, 456 *see also* Ouranos
Fathir 246
Faulkner, William 452
Faumea 588
fauns 541
Faunus **190**
Faust **191**, 199, 540
Faust Part I 191
Faust-Book 191
Faustulus 529
Favonius 682
Fawn 212
feasts 86
feathers 125, 164, 221, 275, 367, 379,
    408, 413, 578
Fefafa 327
Fei Lian **192**, 266, 510, 672, 674
Feng Bo 192
Fenrir 247, 311, 360, 516, 627, 650
Fensalier 202
Ferdiad 133
fern-roots 221
fertility 176, 190, **192**, 243, 291, 403,
    581, 654
fertility deities 8, 50, 59, 61, 62, 85, 114,
    115, 126, 141, 142, 164, 198, 201, 210,
    226-7, 231, 235, 238, 239, 286, 323,
    353, 377, 393, 395, 397, 421, 434, 469,
    498, 506, 526, 527, 532, 546, 555, 559,
    574, 576, 582, 614, 624, 630, 631, 639,
    644, 654, 665, 682 *see also* creators of life

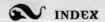

Mictlan **391**, 667
Midas **391**
Mide 408
Midgard 62, **392**, 674, 676
Midsummer Night's Dream, A 433
midwifery 421 *see also* childbirth
Mikula **392**
military bands, goddess of 69
milk 291, 334, 466, 498
Milky Way 29, 30, 52, 87, 93, 94, 253, 288, 419, 486, 489, 505, 587, 610, 636, 639
Miller, Henry 454
millet 400
Mimas 165
Mime 524
Mimi **393**
Mimir 15, 263, **393**, 645
Min **394**
Minawara **394**
Mindi 227
Minerva **68**, 69, 89, 314
Minos 131, 138, 235, 470, 598
Minotaur 54, 139, **394**, 470, 598
Mioya 203
Miralaldu **94**
Miraramuinar 313
mirrors 623
mischief, deities of 65, 489
Misery 247
Missouri River 608
mistletoe 83, 202, 261
Mithra 8, 19, **395**, 646
Mithras 218, **395**
Mitra 395
Mixcóatl 125, 279, **396**
Mjöllnir 560, 601
Mneme 401 *see also* Muses
Mnemosyne 612
Mockingbird 332
Modimo **396**
Modred 57, 348, **396**
Mohenjodaro 288
Mokosh **397**
Moloch 79
moly 122
Monkey 200, 238, 353, 617, 673
monkeys 46, 75, 102, 238, 400, 577, 579

monsters 23, 29, 88, 105, 114, 117, 131, 182, 191, 199, 203, 225, 226, 272, 299, 305, 337, 339, 347-8, 380, 383, 393, **397**, 399, 407, 415, 543, 564, 572, 576, 578, 580, 582, 587, 591, 616, 626, 631, 644, 659, 677
Monteverdi, Claudio 440, 454, 600
months 326
Moon 29, 34, 52, 141, 167, 211, 212, 226, 237, 242, 264, 316, 336, 341, 410, 451, 515, 603, 659, 665, 671
moon deities 44, 74, 95, 110, 115, 121, 127-8, 184, 242-3, 250, 279, 328, 329, 370, 386, 409, 460, 526, 545, 562, 574, 575, 615, 623, 634, 646
moonbeams 56
Moon-people 355
Moose 212
Mopsus 108, 109
Mordred 396
Morgan le Fay 213, 345, **398**, 433
Morgause 213, 396
Morholt 618
Morning Star 216, 489, 511, 512
Morongo 403
Morrigan 133, 140, 382, **398**
Morris, William 263
Mors **398**, 597
mortality 16, 17, 128, 214, 430, 448, 511, 661, 662, 671 *see also* immortality
Morte d'Arthur 58, 113, 263, 349
Morufonu 312
Moses 283, 443
Moshiriikkwechep **399**
Mot 6, 43, 606
Mother Earth 37, 125, 150, 152, 225, 280, 304, 312, 325, 377, **399**, 413, 418, 421, 444, 465, 498, 521, 536, 549, 566, 611, 631
see also Gaia; Great Goddess
mother-of-pearl 227
Mothir 246
Mountain (element) 204
Mountain Spirits **399**
Mountain-Lion 195
mountains 87, 197, 202, 291, 319, 336, 443, 449

wheels 200, 266, 298
Wheememeowah **660**
whetstones 601
whirlpools 23, 543
White Book, The 367
White She-Buffalo **660**
White, T.H. 58
whores 265
*Why There Are No More Bogatiri In Holy
    Russia* 96
Wi 657
Wichama 459
Widjingara **661**
Wieland 653
Wiglaf 90
Wild Boy 605
will-o'-the-wisps 156, 249
willow trees 88
Winabozho 408
Winchester 110
Wind (element) 204
Wind Breath 64, 236
wind deities 13-14, 96, 171, 177, 192,
    204, 231, 337, 390, 522, 556, 577,
    646, 648, 682
winds 141, 212, 265, 511, 552
    see also hurricanes; typhoons
Windsor Great Park 114
wine 113, 155, 287, 365, 414, 425, 562
wine, deities of 155, 647
winter 577 *see also* seasons
Winter 675
Winter Mother 195
Wisaaka 408
wisdom 59, 99, 120, 121, 652, 654
wisdom, goddess of 68
Wishpoosh 128, **661**
witches 202
witchetty-grubs 143
wizards 586
Wo 681
Woden 435
Woinunggur 227
Wolf 195, 610
Wollunkwa 227
wolves 365, 529, 563
women, supremacy of 115

women, goddess of 345
Women of Troy 44, 111, 245, 386
Wonambi 227
Wondjina 661
Wonomi **662**
Wood (element) 196
Wooden Horse 153, 248, 349, 416, **662**
woodpeckers 122, 191, 487
woodworms 384
Worlds, Nine **421**
Worombi 227
Wotan 435
Woyengi **663**
writing 97, 205, 267, 404, 444, 511, 540,
    603
Wu Cheng-en 617
Wu Shan 677
Wuraka **658**
Wyrd 112, **664**

Xanthus 543
Xi He **665**
Xi Wang Mu 674
Xipetotec 125, **665**
Xiutecuhtli **667**
Xochipili 268, **667**
Xochiquetzal **667**
Xólotl 511, **667**
Xuthus 294

Yacatecuhtli **669**
Yadhapati 646
Yadilyil 184
Yagami 446
Yahweh 87, 108, 173, 443, 540, **669**
Yakshas **518**
Yalu River 87
Yalungur 339, **671**
Yama 467, 539, 542, **671**, 676
Yama Kings, Ten **593**
Yamasachi **671**
Yambe-akka **672**
Yami 539, 671
yams 393, 450, 465, 533, 574
Yamuna 82, 322, 339
Yamuna River 539
Yanauluha **672**